11-21

THE WORKS OF ANNE FRANK

DRAWINGS BY PETER SPIER

THE WORKS OF
Anne Frank

INTRODUCTION BY ANN BIRSTEIN
AND ALFRED KAZIN

GREENWOOD PRESS, PUBLISHERS
WESTPORT, CONNECTICUT

Library of Congress Cataloging in Publication Data

Frank, Anne, 1929-1945.
  The works of Anne Frank.

    Reprint of the ed. published by Doubleday, Garden
City, N. Y.
  [PT5834.F78A25 1973]   940.53'1503'924 [B]
  ISBN 0-8371-7206-3   73-16643

Reprinted with the permission of Doubleday & Company, Inc.

Reprinted in 1974 by Greenwood Press
A division of Congressional Information Service, Inc.
88 Post Road West, Westport, Connecticut 06881

Printed in the United States of America

10 9 8 7 6 5 4

EDITOR'S NOTE:

The dates on the stories and essays are those that Anne herself
gave them when she wrote them in her notebook. In the case
of "Rita" and "Why?" there are no dates, because they were
not included in the notebook but were discovered on separate
scraps of paper.
The Diary of a Young Girl was translated from the Dutch by
B. M. Mooyaard-Doubleday; the Fables, Personal Reminiscences, and Short Stories were translated by Michel Mok.

Contents

8 CONTENTS

Introduction

BY ANN BIRSTEIN AND ALFRED KAZIN

In March 1945, a young girl died in Bergen-Belsen, unaware that she was leaving behind her a work that shed the first tiny human light on an episode in history that was unspeakably inhuman. She was a lovely girl, not quite sixteen when she died, with enormous dark gray eyes, a pretty little mouth, and a very brave heart. But like any awkward and self-conscious adolescent, she was weighed down by a sense of her shortcomings. She worried about her looks; she thought of herself as a coward, so often full of fear that she never realized how heroically she overcame it. Certainly, it would have been beyond her to imagine that the diary she kept for two years would have an impact on the entire world; how could it when the events of her lifetime were so enormous she could only seem puny by comparison? Her only real certainty was that she meant to be a writer anyway, and that her subject would have to be the world in which she found herself alive, no matter how terrible or even how unaccountably lovely her experiences in it might seem. For two years before her arrest she wrote all the time. She wrote while she was in hiding from the Nazis and could not take one step outdoors or in the daytime speak above a whisper. She wrote although the bombs came down so heavily at night that she fled for comfort into her father's bed. She wrote so steadily that by the time she was fifteen she had finished the equivalent of two books, one the *Diary*, the other a collection of short stories, essays, and reminiscences. As she said, with amazement at her own daring, she wrote because, "I want to go on living even after my death!" She has— reminding us that each of those millions who died in agony and despair, each of those victims whom the Nazis "exterminated" was, like Anne Frank, a separate and precious human spirit.

Of Anne Frank's actual life, as apart from her work, there is very little to tell; she did not live to see her sixteenth birthday. But because she had a great capacity for happiness, her life all in all was quite a happy one. She was born in Frankfurt, Germany on June 12, 1929, to fairly wealthy Jewish parents, and she was lucky in her family, for although no one in her lifetime considered her unusual or profound, she was always able to count on a great deal of love and mutual respect in her home. She had a grandmother whom she adored and whom she refers to both in her diary and her stories as a "guardian angel," and an older sister, Margot, who was by everyone's account both beautiful and kind. With her mother she got on less well, though her complaints are largely just the usual ones of any growing girl. Actually, her mother taught Anne a great deal, especially lessons in charity. "No one ever becomes poor from giving," Mrs. Frank used to say, and Anne herself repeats this in her little essay called "Give." But it was her father Anne loved best, and with reason. He was and is a cultured man of great personal nobility and quiet courage, exactly the kind of father an adolescent girl could always turn to. In 1933, when Hitler came to power, the Franks moved to Amsterdam, and though life soon closed in on them—the Franks, no longer wealthy, had to take in boarders; Holland was invaded and capitulated to Germany; the Nazis issued strict anti-Jewish decrees; Anne had to leave the Montessori School, which she had loved, and go to the Jewish Lyceum—Anne remained the same humorous child she had always been. Lies Goosens, an old school friend in Amsterdam, who later saw Anne in Belsen, remembers her being considered a "problem child, very talkative"; by Mr. Frank's own tender confession, she never in life seemed so "deep" as she appeared in her diary. She was a vivid girl, but definitely not a prodigy. Ironically enough, the very vividness and intensity of the adolescent self-confrontation that was to make the *Diary* famous perhaps made Anne seem more conventional than she really was. The headmistress of the Montessori School in Amsterdam (now the Anne Frank School) remembers that Anne did not show any early promise, and that many of her pupils wrote with more imagination and feeling than did Anne. When we read the accounts of those who had known Anne, we can see that although she had always been very distinct to them and often arresting, she had been seen only as a very young girl, and externally very much a girl of her own age. She had a passion for movie stars, whose pictures she collected, and for royalty—one of her main preoccupations was the difficulty of finding suitable husbands for Princess Elizabeth and Princess Margaret of Great Britain. She was a great talker, often an incessant one, as her family and teachers knew only too well, and her fondness for make-believe was such that she would bring a suitcase along even when she was just visiting for an hour next door. Anne giggled with her girl friends, was saucy and flirtatious with boys, played a lot of ping-pong, and consumed great quantities of ice cream afterward. She had a lovely thirteenth birthday with a party, home movies, flowers, and many presents, among them a small clothbound diary which Anne decided at once was "possibly the nicest of all." Then, a month after this birthday, life closed in on the Franks for good. On a hot July morning in 1942 they went into hiding, walking across Amsterdam in the pouring rain to a small group of rooms behind Mr. Frank's former offices. Here they and four others were to stay cooped up for more than two years, until the Dutch Green Police routed them out on August 4, 1944; and here Anne's diary, that nice present, was to grow and grow until, like all truly remarkable books, it finally outgrew its own author.

In a certain sense, however, it isn't fair to call *The Diary of a Young Girl* a diary at all, since from the very first it was more to her than a purely personal record of triumphs and defeats. Always she had toward her own experience the marvelous ambivalence of the born novelist, and immediately after claiming that "neither I—nor for that matter anyone else—will be interested in the unbosomings of a thirteen-year-old schoolgirl," on the very same page of her journal she has already chosen a literary form—the entries will be in the shape of letters to an imaginary girl named Kitty—and embarked on a concise sketch, not only of her own life, but of general conditions in Holland. This same uncanny sense of an unseen audience, actually of posterity, prevails throughout her work. Scared out of her wits as she must have been when she went into hiding, one of the first things she writes about it is a detailed description of the hiding place and the bits and pieces of furnishings that went into it. When new people arrive, first the Van Daans and then Dussel, the dentist, she has them down on paper practically the minute they are through the door. With a writer's eye for how much is implied in the ordinary events of an ordinary day, she describes a typical morning, afternoon, and evening in the annexe; how they went to the toilet; where they slept; what they talked about while they peeled potatoes and shelled peas and stuffed sausages. She fell in love with the boy upstairs, yearned desperately for her first kiss, and in the breathless moment before it finally came broke into tears—which she described meticulously: "I sat pressed closely against him and felt a wave of emotion come over me, tears sprang into my eyes, the left one trickled onto his dungarees, the right one ran down my nose and also fell onto his dungarees. Did he notice? He made no move or sign to show that he did. . . . At half past eight I stood up and went to the window, where we always say good-by. . . . He came toward me, I flung my arms around his neck and gave him a kiss on his left cheek, and was about to kiss the other cheek, when my lips met his and we pressed them together."

To everything that happened to her, to everything that she felt, Anne gave a kind of permanence by transcribing it, and day after day she went on adding still another segment to the world she was creating. In the stories, where she chose her subjects, this world is not so real. But in her diary, where her subject chose her, its vividness and poignance are overwhelming. We can see them all: Mrs. Frank, always a little in the shadows, defending the upbringing of her children, or discussing with Mrs. Van Daan the best way to address servants; Mrs. Van Daan taking time out for a little flirtation with Dussel, the pompous old dentist, or else picking a fight with Mr. Van Daan ("But Putti . . . Mr. Frank always answers his wife, doesn't he?"); young, shy Peter Van Daan lying listlessly in his cluttered boy's room upstairs; Margot, always composed and gentle; Mr. Frank putting aside his beloved Dickens to settle a quarrel and put things right again; their Dutch protectors coming upstairs with their thoughtful little presents and their tantalizing whiffs of the outside world; and Anne, working out her genealogical tables, pasting up her pictures of movie stars, talking so much that everyone has to tell her to shut up— and then transforming herself into the ninth member, the one who retired to the little table so hard won from Mr. Dussel to bring the others to life. What makes her achievement really amazing is how little, aside from her own natural gifts of observation and her sense of humor, she had to work with. Other people have countrysides and multitudes. For Anne, the one boy upstairs was love; a single chestnut tree seen from her window, nature; a patch of blue sky—heaven. No wonder that soon she began to think of her diary and some of her sketches as the basis for a book after the war. *Het Achterhuis* (The House Behind) she meant to call it—a perfect title for the first book of a young girl, suggesting mystery and suspense and excitement; she even had a list of pseudonyms for the people in it, pseudonyms which are used in this present edition.

But the duality of Anne's nature, that quality of mind that made her turn to her writing for solace and relief, that made of her diary her "only friend" and the first thing she packed when she went into hiding, was exactly what would not let her rest. Like all young growing things, Anne, forced into a premature ripeness by the terrible intensity of events, yearned and struggled for the light. It was not enough to take her own little part in the day's happenings, to chatter and laugh and cry with everyone else; the spectator in her kept pressing her to ask the meaning of it all, kept goading her into a search that could only take her deeper and deeper into the most painful realms of solitude. We tend to think of Anne now as pure innocence in captivity. But her mind and heart were never held captive by herself or anyone, and as for her innocence— it was the last thing she ever thought about. On the contrary, she wanted to take it all on her own shoulders, she considered herself responsible for everything, not only her own destiny— if she was permitted to live it out—but also the fate of everyone else who suffered. ". . . I believe," she said, "that God wants

to try me . . ." And this theme of being tested through con-
finement is repeated in her stories of Blurry, the Explorer, the
bear who goes out to see the world and is locked up instead,
and of Dora and Peldron, the two elves who are imprisoned
by a wise dwarf and emerge improved by their experience.
Somehow, Anne, too, would come out a better person, if only
she were good and strong enough. Of course it was hard, ago-
nizingly hard, to keep herself to such a strict moral account-
ing, especially when everything outside beckoned so sweetly:
"The sun is shining, the sky is a deep blue, there is a lovely
breeze and I'm longing—so longing—for everything. To talk, for
freedom, for friends, to be alone. And I do so long . . . to cry!
I feel as if I'm going to burst, and I know that it would get
better with crying; but I can't, I'm restless, I go from one room
to the other, breathe through the crack of a closed window,
feel my heart beating, as if it is saying, 'Can't you satisfy my
longings at last?' . . . I believe that it's spring within me, I
feel that spring is awakening. I feel it in my whole body and
soul." But still she kept at it, crying herself out when she
could, and then trying to unloose her own pity for herself into
a great stream of compassion for all suffering humanity. How
could she feel sorry for herself when just outside her door
children were running about half naked, begging food from
passers-by, and people did not dare leave their homes for fear
that when they came back no one would be left in them? It
was not enough to be glad of her own precarious safety; one
had to ask why even this was denied others. She dreamed of
her friend Lies Goosens, whom she imagined to have been sent
to a concentration camp, and woke in tears: "Oh, God, that I
should have all I could wish for and that she should be seized
by such a terrible fate. I am not more virtuous than she; she,
too, wanted what was right, why should I be chosen to live
and she probably to die?" And what about all Jews? What purpose was there in their common agony? "Who has inflicted
this upon us? What has made us different from other people?
Who has allowed us to suffer so terribly until now?"

Child or not, anyone who asks such questions can never find
an answer, only the strength of spirit to go on searching. Anne
found her strength in her love of the very world which was
denied her. Often in their "Secret Annexe" they talked of the
best cure for unhappiness, and Mrs. Frank's advice was to re-

member those who were even more unhappy. But to Anne, though no one listened to her, this could add only more misery to a cup already overflowing with it. "I simply can't build up my hopes on a foundation consisting of confusion, misery, and death. I see the world gradually being turned into a wilderness, I hear the ever approaching thunder, which will destroy us too, I can feel the sufferings of millions and yet, if I look up into the heavens, I think that this cruelty too will end, and that peace and tranquillity will return again." What she saw when she looked up was a reminder that despite all the ugliness inflicted on it, the world was still incredibly beautiful, and each time she could not get over the miracle of it. It was only from her very joy in being alive that she could draw her own sustenance, that and the sense of living things around her, first people—she was a city child and a gregarious one, and people were the nearest and dearest things to her heart—and then, like her lonely and exhausted flower girl and the terrified narrator of "Fear," from nature itself. Her own advice to those who suffered was: "Go outside, go to the fields, enjoy nature and the sunshine, go out and try to recapture happiness in yourself and in God." Unfortunately, she could not take her own advice literally, but she followed it as closely as she could. Peering through dirty net curtains and dusty windows, she marveled at the loveliness of the chestnut tree in the yard, thick with shiny green leaves, or on a cold winter morning climbed up to the attic where from her favorite spot on the floor she could catch a glimpse of the blue sky and of her beloved tree, now bare, "on whose branches little raindrops shine, appearing like silver, and at the seagulls and the other birds as they glide on the wind." Once, happening to be by an open window on a stormy evening, she was so spellbound by the beauty of the wind and rain that afterward she was willing to brave the dangers of a dark empty house—rats, burglars, raids—just to feel the night full on her face again. And these simple but piercing joys filled her with such gratitude and love that each night before she went to sleep, she prayed: "I thank you God, for all that is good and dear and beautiful."

Perhaps this was Anne's last prayer in hiding. Perhaps when she went to bed on the night of August 3, 1944, her last thought was of her own blessedness: her youth, her strength, her love for all the people and the growing things around her, her closeness to God, who had provided them. There is no way of knowing. On the next morning, the Dutch Nazi police suddenly stormed through the concealed doorway of the annexe with drawn revolvers and took all its inhabitants away. In a heap of papers and books which the police had dumped on the floor during their search for money and valuables, Miep and Elli later found the notebooks Anne had kept so carefully. They put them aside for the day when Anne would come back for them, a time which never came.

Only Mr. Frank came back—by way of Odessa and Marseilles. He had been saved at the last only because he had been in the hospital at Auschwitz, and so had been alive when the Russians liberated the camp. Mrs. Frank died on January 6, 1945. She had begun to lose her mind in the days preceding her death; given some bread, she would hide it under the blanket, explaining that she was saving it for her husband, because he needed it. Margot died at the end of February or the beginning of March. She had been gravely ill, in a coma for days. While unconscious, she had fallen out of bed and was dead when her friends tried to lift her back. Anne, who was already sick with typhus at the time, was not informed of her sister's death, but (as related by a witness to Ernst Schnabel for his beautiful little book on Anne Frank) "she sensed it, and soon afterward she died, peacefully, feeling that nothing bad was happening to her." Mr. Van Daan was gassed; Otto Frank himself saw him taken to the gas chambers. Mrs. Van Daan died; no one knows how. Young Peter Van Daan was marched away from Auschwitz by S.S. battalions fleeing into Germany from the Russians and was never seen again. Mr. Dussel died in Neuengamme Camp. Of those who had looked after them all in the Secret Annexe, and been taken to jail, all were eventually released, except Mr. Kraler; but he finally escaped and made his way back to Holland in time to see the liberation of the country from the Nazis.

Only the father returned—to learn that he alone was left and to be given his daughter's notebooks by Miep and Elli. The little books must have seemed pathetic enough to Otto Frank when, after his own slow recovery to health, he returned to Amsterdam to learn, after agonizing inquiries, that his wife and two children were dead. The diary was peculiarly heart-breaking, not only in its reminder of all that eight people had lived through and hoped for in more than two years of captivity, but in its revelation of Anne. Lies Goosens remembers Otto Frank's saying to her, when the *Diary* was first published: "Anne developed under our eyes in that room, but we went on treating her as though she still was a giddy little girl. All of us were too wrapped up in our own troubles to give her the understanding that she needed."

At first Mr. Frank had copies of the *Diary* privately circulated as a memorial to his family. It was a Dutch university professor who urged formal publication of the book, and with only very slight excisions by Mr. Frank, *Het Achterhuis* was published in Amsterdam by Contact Publishers, in June 1947. The book soon went through several editions. In 1950, it was published in Germany by the Heidleberg firm of Lambert Schneider. The first printing was 4500 copies, and many booksellers were actually afraid to show it in their windows; but the book caught on rapidly, and the sales of the pocket edition, published by S. Fischer Verlag, total more than half a million. In 1950 it was published in France; in 1952, in England and the United States. By now the book has been translated into twenty-two languages, has been published in twenty countries, and has sold more than two and a half million copies. In the United States it had an enormous success in the Pocket Book edition and later was circulated by the Teen Age Book Club, the Book Find Club, and republished in the Modern Library. The book was serialized by an American newspaper syndicate, with a calculated audience of ten million readers, and millions more read it when it was condensed in *Omnibook* and *Compact* magazines. A German translation of the book has been used in the United States as a school reader.

The book had a second life when it was dramatized by Frances Goodrich and Albert Hackett and became one of the most successful enterprises of the contemporary theater. In the United States the play won all the principal theater awards, and has since been produced in over twenty countries; it has now been made into a film, and soon the story of Anne Frank will have become perhaps the most celebrated document of a single human being's ordeal during World War II.

By now, in fact, Anne Frank has become a universal legend. Out of the millions who were gassed, burned, shot, hanged, starved, tortured, buried alive, the young girl who died so "peacefully" in Bergen-Belsen, almost in unconscious sympathy with her dead sister Margot, has become a prime symbol of the innocence of all those who died in the middle of the twentieth century at the hands of the most powerful state in western Europe. Perhaps more than any of the known dead, and certainly more than the now nameless ones who died scratching the ceilings of the gas chambers in the last agonized struggle against death, the girl born in Frankfurt of an upper-class Jewish family, whose father was a German officer in World War I, has become the personal example of the heartlessness, the bestiality, the still unbelievable cruelty of Germans in World War II. Upon her, at least, all agree; in her all peoples, in the uneasy peace since 1945 that is no peace, can find a moment's occasion for compassion and awareness. When *The Diary of Anne Frank* was produced on the Dutch stage, royalty wept; and by now, as everyone knows, Germans who had wept for no one but themselves, who had not allowed themselves to recognize the horror in their midst, who laughed in derision when they were made to see films of Auschwitz and Buchenwald, have wept in theaters over Anne Frank. In October 1956, when the play opened in seven German cities to silent audiences, there was by all accounts unexpected horror and dismay. Alfred Werner, in a study of "Germany's New Flagellants" (*The American Scholar*, Spring 1958), reports that not until 1956 was there a mass emotion of expiation in Germany, and that it started with the Hacketts' play. The play "broke through the tough shell that the German had grown around his soul. In what may be a natural drive for self-preservation, he had pushed all of the Nazi period into the remote corners of the subconscious mind. The victims who had lived through the Nazi era, or at least part of it, and visited Germany after 1945, knew all the time that this 'amnesia' of the Germans was only defense. But they also feared that this repression of a reality too painful to remember might eventually lead to an obliteration, to the myth that nothing had really happened between 1943 and 1945." Mr. Werner recalls Schiller's belief in the theater as a moral institution—"when a thousand burdens press upon our souls and the cares of our callings threaten to stifle our sensitivity, then, in such moods, the stage receives us: in this artificial world we dream the real one away . . ." but notes

that to the Germans of 1956, *Das Tagebuch der Anne Frank*
"meant something different . . . a much delayed rendezvous
with fate." The critic of the *Frankfurter Allegemeine Zeitung*
wrote:

> There is no drama in the old sense. It belongs to the Pas-
> sions of Christ, brought nearer to us step by step. Judging
> this play is beyond the capabilities of a German theater
> critic . . . Old wounds are broken open. The memory of
> shame and terror makes it almost impossible to subject this
> play to aesthetic rules of dramatic judgment, however broad
> they may be. . . . Those who feel guilty should feel it here
> most of all.

The German audiences who at the première of the play sat
through it in perfect silence—"the packed auditoriums were
frozen in silence when the curtain came down"—launched a
mood of "repentance" and philo-Jewish enthusiasm which was
a typically extremist German phenomenon. The programs re-
quested "no applause," and night after night silent crowds filed
out of the theaters. Television, radio, and press documented
the fate of Anne Frank; teachers marched their classes to see
the play; for the next few months, the *Diary* was the leading
German best seller. The sympathy of German youth was such
that on March 17, 1957, two thousand young people from Ham-
burg marched in the rain to the site of the former concentration
camp at Bergen-Belsen where, in some unknown spot, Anne
Frank lies buried. People traveled in trains, buses, on bicycles
through the chilling rain to the low hilltop marked by a huge
obelisk, a few gravestones, and the burial mounds. There were
many speeches. One came from an ex-Nazi, Hans Hanoch
Nissen, who was converted to Judaism, settled in Israel, and
at the memorial meeting announced that "it was a great and
comforting experience for me to see here the new German generation. I am united with you in the belief in a better
future . . ."

The production of *Das Tagebuch der Anne Frank* coincided
with what in certain intellectual circles became a pro-Jewish
philosophy, a return to the abstraction of the "noble Jew" among
the German intellectuals of the Enlightenment. It is for this
reason that Anne Frank has symbolized so much—so peculiarly
much—in current German thought. A sixteen-year-old girl, par-

ticipant in the Belsen pilgrimage, wrote a letter published in newspapers all over the Bonn Republic: "I have sworn that we must do better! All must be made to realize that the highest and the most beautiful being is man—regardless of whether he is a Jew, a Dane, a Russian, an Englishman, a Frenchman, or a German. . . .

"Anne, you did not die in vain. We, today's youth, want to believe in what is good in man—as you did. . . . We shall never forget you and all those innocent people who had to die like you. We do not want to forget, and we must never forget."

This is the tone of many letters that have come to Otto Frank from Germans, the most significant of which are from young people. The typical mood is one of adolescent identification with Anne. A Berlin girl of sixteen: "I could not get along with my parents, which brought me almost to despair. Then I received the diary of your daughter Anne: 'I believe in the good which is in Men' is written there. This I had forgotten completely. . . ." Other letters suggest that to young people, German or non-German, the world just now can seem as frightening as it did to a Jew in hiding from the Nazis; at least they seem more vulnerable in these letters than their youth alone can explain. One girl began: "I am only 19 years of age." Another: "I am fifteen years old. This statement perhaps explains much to you. . . ." The naïveté of teen-agers sometimes becomes grotesque. A boy who read an article about the *Diary* in *Reader's Digest* asked: "Did your family ever see Hitler? If so, when? What were your impressions of Hitler and the Nazi way of life?" On the other hand, a sixteen-year-old Jewish girl affirmed: "I feel that God made Anne for a specific purpose. . . . She accomplished in death something that would have been practically impossible to do in life." For some Catholic girls, she has become a "saint." A girl from Boston wrote: "Anne's struggles for maturity have reminded me of mine, and yet she was so much more mature than I who am now sixteen."

So the flood of emotion, of repentance, of identification and commiseration streams in. The figure of universally accepted innocence, a young girl, is so perfect a subject that young people can identify with her; older people can pity her; the world can almost believe that it has made peace with itself over

the unknown grave of Anne Frank. During the height of the
German emotion over the play, reports Alfred Werner, a few
Germans protested that "the play might be letting the Germans
off too lightly, that it did not even begin to suggest how frightful were the German actions." Yet it is also a fact that it is
impossible to make artistic use of the worst horrors of the concentration camps. *The Diary Of Anne Frank* does not deal
with horror—at least not directly; yet this, though it makes it
too easy for all of us not to think of the horror at all, is also
what makes both book and play *possible*. It was not only Germans who laughed derisively when shown the first films of the
concentration camps; so did the English in Piccadilly newsreel
theaters. The fact is that certain events in our time, prime and
unforgettable images of human suffering and degradation, seem
incredible to us even when we remember them, and are ungraspable even when we face them.

Anne Frank herself felt this about many horrors in her young
life. She was in the Secret Annexe, looking wistfully through a
powerful pair of field glasses into the lighted rooms of the
houses at the back: ". . . I never knew before that our neighbors could be such interesting people. . . . I found one family
having a meal, one family was in the act of taking a home movie;
and the dentist opposite was just attending to an old lady,
who was awfully scared." The day the Frank family was taken
off to the German detention camp was a beautiful summer day.
Anne's father told Ernst Schnabel, "As we rode toward Westerbork . . . Anne would not move from the window. Outside,
it was summer. Meadows, stubble fields, and villages flew by.
The telephone wires along the right of way curvetted up and
down along the windows. It was like freedom." It must have
seemed incredible to look at beautiful summer days, the peaceful summer scene, when she was in hiding because she was
a Jew, or when she was in a train being led off to a concentration camp. It is this radical injustice, this unaccountability,
that characterizes for children their most painful experiences;
the anthropomorphic child in all of us can still feel the injustice of slipping out of life while someone else is yawning,
or drinking beer. In the world of totalitarianism, the victim
suffers from the illogic of his fate as well as the terror of death.
But this incredibility is now what we feel about so many experiences in our time that it is no wonder that the most sensitive

imaginations in Europe have committed themselves to a sense of the "absurd." It was "absurd" as well as unspeakable to put children into concentration camps; "absurd" as well as unforgivable to allow millions upon millions of innocent civilians, Jews and non-Jews, to die as they did. But absurd, out of focus, beyond the human scale, utterly illogical and often ungraspable as the death of an innocent fifteen-year-old girl at the hands of the Third Reich may be, it is a fact. It is a fact that never can be forgotten, that never will be forgotten. But it is also a fact that the reality of what certain people have had to endure in our time can be grasped humanly and politically only because of the modulation of a document like *The Diary of a Young Girl,* which permits us to see certain experiences in a frame, in a thoroughly human setting, so that we can bear them at all.

Anne Frank's Diary has rarely been subjected to criticism. The dramatic economy of the book has moved its readers just as much as the fate of its author has served as an occasion of emotion. Yet it has been suggested that Anne was unable to confront the hideousness of her experience, that her diary was an escape into the ideal. And in one sense this "evasion" of reality, if one may so call it, though improbable coming from people who have never had to face anything like Anne Frank's experience, is perfectly true. It may be that the "ideal" quality of the book accounts for the universal acceptance of the *Diary;* has made it possible for Germans to ease their souls sitting in a theater; for Jews to honor their dead; for the Dutch and the French to remember their suffering under the occupation; for adolescent children to take imaginative refuge from their problems. And yet it is a fact that Anne Frank's wholly domestic picture of life works toward the understanding of her true situation, rather than the other way around. For truthfully direct "war literature," naked shots of the ultimate horror, are hard for everyone to get down—this is as true for the victims' kin as it is for the Germans eager to evade responsibility; they stupefy instead of awakening us. The last shudder of death, the shriek of crucifixion—these really belong to death, not life. If we are still in danger of evading the full truth of Nazism, we are also in danger, when we think we are confronting the truth, of adding to the extreme abstractness and tension of the human spirit which represents Nazism, with its insatiable slogans and its monolithic sense of truth. The enemy of Nazism is its enemy because it is different from Nazism in kind, in intention, in the spirit with which it addresses itself to life. In the "ideal" world of Anne Frank's diary, in the preoccupation with potato peels, a young girl's discovery of puberty, there is the truth of life as human curiosity and sensitivity and fellowship—while outside, the green and gray German army lorries trundle past bearing their helpless Jewish victims to the slaughter heap.

The Diary of a Young Girl has survived its author and most of her family, as it has already survived so many books about the war, because the faithfulness with which it records an unusual experience reminds us—as opposition to Nazism on its own terms never can—of the sweetness and goodness that are possible in a world where a few souls still have good will. The *Diary* moves us because its author had the strength to see, to remember, to hope. There are scenes in the *Diary* of pure terror, and scenes that are sheer pantomimic farce out of a silent movie—Mrs. Van Daan being examined by the dentist, Mr. Dussel, writhes so miserably that his scraper gets caught in her mouth. "After much turning, kicking, screaming, and calling out, she got the instrument free at last and Mr. Dussel went on with his work as if nothing had happened!" There are scenes of wistful impressionism, "the blues." Anne, "sitting cozily" in the main office, looking out on the street through a slit in the curtain, writes to "Kitty": "It is dusk but still just light enough to write to you. It is a very queer sight, as I watch the people walking by; it looks just as if they are all in a terrible hurry and nearly trip over their own toes." She sees unattractive starved children in the neighborhood, "real slum kids with running noses . . ." and adds, "Other things to see—cars, boats, and rain. I like particularly the screech of the trams as they go by." She sees two Jews passing by. "I could hardly believe my eyes; it was a horrible feeling, just as if I'd betrayed them and was now watching them in their misery."

Yet the writer is inside, watching from her temporary nest, and the contrast with her daily experience and her future is in one sense frightful, in another her salvation. We can never fully know our own experience; the words that help us to bear them also separate us from the extremity of our living and our death. And since never as in our time have men had to bear so much, never have we felt so great a disproportion between words and reality. No wonder that we are so impatient with "art" when it claims some ultimate ordeal for its subject. But courage is always a single human being's courage, not the world's; it is the courage to face one's own experience and to remember the abyss that now lies on every hand. More than that cannot be asked of any human being. Anne Frank died of typhus in the hell of Bergen-Belsen. Yet when one weeps for her it is not out of pity. Pity is for the faceless and the weak. Events could only make Anne helpless. And though it is a miracle that her diary and her little stories and essays have survived at all, the real miracle is that in the young girl who wrote them life was so strong to begin with.

THE DIARY OF
A YOUNG GIRL

On Friday, June 12th, I woke up at six o'clock and no wonder; it was my birthday. But of course I was not allowed to get up at that hour, so I had to control my curiosity until a quarter to seven. Then I could bear it no longer, and went to the dining room, where I received a warm welcome from Moortje (the cat).

Soon after seven I went to Mummy and Daddy and then to the sitting room to undo my presents. The first to greet me was *you*, possibly the nicest of all. Then on the table there were a bunch of roses, a plant, and some peonies, and more arrived during the day.

I got masses of things from Mummy and Daddy, and was thoroughly spoiled by various friends. Among other things I was given *Camera Obscura*, a party game, lots of sweets, chocolates, a puzzle, a brooch, *Tales and Legends of the Netherlands* by Joseph Cohen, *Daisy's Mountain Holiday* (a terrific book), and some money. Now I can buy *The Myths of Greece and Rome*—grand!

Then Lies called for me and we went to school. During recess I treated everyone to sweet biscuits, and then we had to go back to our lessons.

Now I must stop. Bye-bye, we're going to be great pals!

I had my birthday party on Sunday afternoon. We showed a film *The Lighthouse Keeper* with Rin-Tin-Tin, which my school friends thoroughly enjoyed. We had a lovely time. There were lots of girls and boys. Mummy always wants to know whom I'm going to marry. Little does she guess that it's

Peter Wessel; one day I managed, without blushing or flickering an eyelid, to get that idea right out of her mind. For years Lies Goosens and Sanne Houtman have been my best friends. Since then, I've got to know Jopie de Waal at the Jewish Secondary School. We are together a lot and she is now my best girl friend. Lies is more friendly with another girl, and Sanne goes to a different school, where she has made new friends.

Saturday, 20 June, 1942

I haven't written for a few days, because I wanted first of all to think about my diary. It's an odd idea for someone like me to keep a diary; not only because I have never done so before, but because it seems to me that neither I—nor for that matter anyone else—will be interested in the unbosomings of a thirteen-year-old schoolgirl. Still, what does that matter? I want to write, but more than that, I want to bring out all kinds of things that lie buried deep in my heart.

There is a saying that "paper is more patient than man"; it came back to me on one of my slightly melancholy days, while I sat chin in hand, feeling too bored and limp even to make up my mind whether to go out or stay at home. Yes, there is no doubt that paper is patient and as I don't intend to show this cardboard-covered notebook, bearing the proud name of "diary," to anyone, unless I find a real friend, boy or girl, probably nobody cares. And now I come to the root of the matter, the reason for my starting a diary: it is that I have no such real friend.

Let me put it more clearly, since no one will believe that a girl of thirteen feels herself quite alone in the world, nor is it so. I have darling parents and a sister of sixteen. I know about thirty people whom one might call friends—I have strings of boy friends, anxious to catch a glimpse of me and who, failing that, peep at me through mirrors in class. I have relations, aunts and uncles, who are darlings too, a good home, no—I don't seem to lack anything. But it's the same with all my friends, just fun and joking, nothing more. I can never bring myself to talk of anything outside the common round. We don't seem to be able to get any closer, that is the root of the trouble. Perhaps I lack confidence, but anyway, there it is, a stubborn fact and I don't seem to be able to do anything about it.

Hence, this diary. In order to enhance in my mind's eye the picture of the friend for whom I have waited so long, I don't want to set down a series of bald facts in a diary like most people do, but I want this diary itself to be my friend, and I shall call my friend Kitty. No one will grasp what I'm talking about if I begin my letters to Kitty just out of the blue, so, albeit unwillingly, I will start by sketching in brief the story of my life.

My father was thirty-six when he married my mother, who was then twenty-five. My sister Margot was born in 1926 in Frankfort-on-Main, I followed on June 12, 1929, and, as we are Jewish, we emigrated to Holland in 1933, where my father was appointed Managing Director of Travies N.V. This firm is in close relationship with the firm of Kolen & Co. in the same building, of which my father is a partner.

The rest of our family, however, felt the full impact of Hitler's anti-Jewish laws, so life was filled with anxiety. In 1938 after the pogroms, my two uncles (my mother's brothers) escaped to the U.S.A. My old grandmother came to us, she was then seventy-three. After May 1940 good times rapidly fled: first the war, then the capitulation, followed by the arrival of the Germans, which is when the sufferings of us Jews really began. Anti-Jewish decrees followed each other in quick succession. Jews must wear a yellow star,[1] Jews must hand in their bicycles, Jews are banned from trams and are forbidden to drive. Jews are only allowed to do their shopping between three and five o'clock and then only in shops which bear the placard "Jewish shop." Jews must be indoors by eight o'clock and cannot even sit in their own gardens after that hour. Jews are foribdden to visit theaters, cinemas, and other places of entertainment. Jews may not take part in public sports. Swimming baths, tennis courts, hockey fields, and other sports grounds are all prohibited to them. Jews may not visit Christians. Jews must go to Jewish schools, and many more restrictions of a similar kind.

So we could not do this and were forbidden to do that. But life went on in spite of it all. Jopie used to say to me, "You're

[1]To distinguish them from others, all Jews were forced by the Germans to wear, prominently displayed, a yellow six-pointed star.

scared to do anything, because it may be forbidden." Our freedom was strictly limited. Yet things were still bearable.

Granny died in January 1942; no one will ever know how much she is present in my thoughts and how much I love her still.

In 1934 I went to school at the Montessori Kindergarten and continued there. It was at the end of the school year, I was in form 6B, when I had to say good-by to Mrs. K. We both wept, it was very sad. In 1941 I went, with my sister Margot, to the Jewish Secondary School, she into the fourth form and I into the first.

So far everything is all right with the four of us and here I come to the present day.

Saturday, 20 June, 1942

Dear Kitty,

I'll start straight away. It is so peaceful at the moment, Mummy and Daddy are out and Margot has gone to play ping-pong with some friends.

I've been playing ping-pong a lot myself lately. We ping-pongers are very partial to an ice cream, especially in summer, when one gets warm at the game, so we usually finish up with a visit to the nearest ice-cream shop, Delphi or Oasis, where Jews are allowed. We've given up scrounging for extra pocket money. Oasis is usually full and among our large circle of friends we always manage to find some kindhearted gentleman or boy friend, who presents us with more ice cream than we could devour in a week.

I expect you will be rather surprised at the fact that I should talk of boy friends at my age. Alas, one simply can't seem to avoid it at our school. As soon as a boy asks if he may bicycle home with me and we get into conversation, nine out of ten times I can be sure that he will fall head over heels in love immediately and simply won't allow me out of his sight. After a while it cools down of course, especially as I take little notice of ardent looks and pedal blithely on.

If it gets so far that they begin about "asking Father" I swerve slightly on my bicycle, my satchel falls, the young man is bound to get off and hand it to me, by which time I have introduced a new topic of conversation.

These are the most innocent types; you get some who blow kisses or try to get hold of your arm, but then they are definitely knocking at the wrong door. I get off my bicycle and refuse to go furthur in their company, or I pretend to be insulted and tell them in no uncertain terms to clear off.

There, the foundation of our friendship is laid, till to-morrow!

Yours, Anne

Sunday, 21 June, 1942

Dear Kitty,

Our whole class B1 is trembling, the reason is that the teachers' meeting is to be held soon. There is much speculation as to who will move up and who will stay put. Miep de Jong and I are highly amused at Wim and Jacques, the two boys behind us. They won't have a florin left for the holidays, it will all be gone on betting "You'll move up," "Shan't," "Shall," from morning till night. Even Miep pleads for silence and my angry outbursts don't calm them.

According to me, a quarter of the class should stay where they are; there are some absolute cuckoos, but teachers are the greatest freaks on earth, so perhaps they will be freakish in the *right* way for once.

I'm not afraid about my girl friends and myself, we'll squeeze through somehow, though I'm not too certain about my math. Still we can but wait patiently. Till then, we cheer each other along.

I get along quite well with all my teachers, nine in all, seven masters and two mistresses. Mr. Keptor, the old math master, was very annoyed with me for a long time because I chatter so much. So I had to write a composition with "A Chatterbox" as the subject. A chatterbox! Whatever could one write? However, deciding I would puzzle that out later, I wrote it in my notebook, and tried to keep quiet.

That evening, when I'd finished my other homework, my eyes fell on the title in my notebook. I pondered, while chewing the end of my fountain pen, that anyone can scribble some nonsense in large letters with the words well spaced but the difficulty was to prove beyond doubt the necessity of talking. I thought and thought and then, suddenly having an idea, filled my three allotted sides and felt completely satisfied. My arguments were that talking is a feminine characteristic and that I would do my best to keep it under control, but I should never be cured, for my mother talked as much as I, probably more, and what can one do about inherited qualities? Mr. Keptor had to laugh at my arguments, but when I continued to hold forth in the next lesson, another composition followed. This time it was "Incurable Chatterbox," I handed this in and Keptor made no complaints for two whole lessons. But in the third lesson it was too much for him again. "Anne, as punishment for talking, will do a composition entitled 'Quack, quack, quack, says Mrs. Natterbeak.'" Shouts of laughter from the class. I had to laugh too, although I felt that my inventiveness on this subject was exhausted. I had to think of something else, something entirely original. I was in luck, as my friend Sanne writes good poetry and offered to help by doing the whole composition in verse. I jumped for joy. Keptor wanted to make a fool of me with this absurd theme, I would get my own back and make him the laughing-stock of the whole class. The poem was finished and was perfect. It was about a mother duck and a father swan who had three baby ducklings. The baby ducklings were bitten to death by Father because they chattered too much. Luckily Keptor saw the joke, he read the poem out loud to the class, with comments, and also to various other classes.

Since then I am allowed to talk, never get extra work, in fact Keptor always jokes about it.

Yours, Anne

Wednesday, 24 June, 1942

Dear Kitty,

It is boiling hot, we are all positively melting, and in this heat I have to walk everywhere. Now I can fully appreciate how nice a tram is; but that is a forbidden luxury for Jews—shank's mare is good enough for us. I had to visit the dentist in the Jan Luykenstraat in the lunch hour yesterday. It is a long way from our school in the Stadstimmertuinen; I nearly fell asleep in school that afternoon. Luckily, the dentist's assistant was very kind and gave me a drink—she's a good sort.

We are allowed on the ferry and that is about all. There is a little boat from the Josef Israelskade, the man there took us at once when we asked him. It is not the Dutch people's fault that we are having such a miserable time.

I do wish I didn't have to go to school, as my bicycle was stolen in the Easter holidays and Daddy has given Mummy's to a Christian family for safekeeping. But thank goodness, the holidays are nearly here, one more week and the agony is over. Something amusing happened yesterday, I was passing the bicycle sheds when someone called out to me. I looked around and there was the nice-looking boy I met on the previous evening, at my girl friend Eva's home. He came shyly towards me and introduced himself as Harry Goldberg. I was rather surprised and wondered what he wanted, but I didn't have to wait long. He asked if I would allow him to accompany me to school. "As you're going my way in any case, I will," I replied and so we went together. Harry is sixteen and can tell all kinds of amusing stories. He was waiting for me again this morning and I expect he will from now on.

Yours, Anne

Tuesday, 30 June, 1942

Dear Kitty,

I've not had a moment to write to you until today. I was with friends all day on Thursday. On Friday we had visitors, and so it went on until today. Harry and I have got to know each other well in a week, and he has told me a lot about his life; he came to Holland alone, and is living with his grandparents. His parents are in Belgium.

Harry had a girl friend called Fanny. I know her too, a very soft, dull creature. Now that he has met me, he realizes that he was just daydreaming in Fanny's presence. I seem to act as a stimulant to keep him awake. You see we all have our uses, and queer ones too at times!

Jopie slept here on Saturday night, but she went to Lies on Sunday and I was bored stiff. Harry was to have come in the evening, but he rang up at 6 P.M. I went to the telephone, he said, "Harry Goldberg here, please may I speak to Anne?" "Yes, Harry, Anne speaking."

"Hullo, Anne, how are you?"

"Very well, thank you."

"I'm terribly sorry I can't come this evening, but I would like to just speak to you; is it all right if I come in ten minutes?"

"Yes, that's fine, good-by!"

"Good-by, I'll be with you soon."

Receiver down.

I quickly changed into another frock and smartened up my hair a bit. Then I stood nervously at the window watching for him. At last I saw *him* coming. It was a wonder I didn't dash down at once; instead I waited patiently until he rang. Then I went down and he positively burst in when I opened the door. "Anne, my grandmother thinks you are too young to go out regularly with me, and that I should go to the Leurs, but perhaps you know that I am not going out with Fanny any more!"

"No, why is that, have you quarreled?"

"No, not at all. I told Fanny that we didn't get on well together, so it was better for us not to go out together any more, but she was always welcome in our home, and I hope I should be in hers. You see, I thought Fanny had been going out with another boy and treated her accordingly. But that was quite untrue. And now my uncle says I should apologize to Fanny, but of course I didn't want to do that so I finished the whole affair. That was just one of the many reasons. My grandmother would rather I went with Fanny than you, but I shan't; old people have such terribly old-fashioned ideas at times, but I just can't fall into line. I need my grandparents, but in a sense they need me too. From now on I shall be free on Wednesday evenings. Officially I go to wood-carving lessons to please my grandparents, in actual fact I go to a meeting of the Zionist Movement. I'm not supposed to, because my grandparents are very much against the Zionists. I'm by no means a fanatic, but I have a leaning that way and find it interesting. But lately it has become such a mess there that I'm going to quit, so next Wednesday will be my last time. Then I shall be able to see you on Wednesday evening, Saturday afternoon, Sunday afternoon, and perhaps more."

"But your grandparents are against it, you can't do it behind their backs!"

"Love finds a way."

Then we passed the bookshop on the corner, and there stood Peter Wessel with two other boys; he said "Hello"—it's the first time he has spoken to me for ages, I was really pleased.

Harry and I walked on and on and the end of it all was that I should meet him at five minutes to seven in the front of his house next evening.

Yours, Anne

Friday, 3 July, 1942

Dear Kitty,

Harry visited us yesterday to meet my parents. I had bought a cream cake, sweets, tea, and fancy biscuits, quite a spread, but neither Harry nor I felt like sitting stiffly side by side indefinitely, so we went for a walk, and it was already ten past eight when he brought me home. Daddy was very cross, and thought it was very wrong of me because it is dangerous for Jews to be out after eight o'clock, and I had to promise to be in by ten to eight in future.

Tomorrow I've been invited to his house. My girl friend Jopie teases me the whole time about Harry. I'm honestly not in love, oh, no, I can surely have boy friends—no one thinks anything of that—but one boy friend, or beau, as Mother calls him, seems to be quite different.

Harry went to see Eva one evening and she told me that she asked him, "Who do you like best, Fanny or Anne?" He said, "It's nothing to do with you!" But when he left (they hadn't chatted together any more the whole evening), "Now listen, it's Anne so long, and don't tell a soul." And like a flash he was gone.

It's easy to see that Harry is in love with me, rather fun for a change. Margot would say, "Harry is a decent lad." I agree, but he is more than that. Mummy is full of praise: a good-looking boy, a well-behaved, nice boy. I'm glad that the whole family approve of him. He likes them too, but he thinks my girl friends are very childish, and he's quite right.

Yours, Anne

Sunday morning, 5 July, 1942

Dear Kitty,

Our examination results were announced in the Jewish Theater last Friday. I couldn't have hoped for better. My report is not at all bad, I had one *vix satis,* a five for algebra, two sixes, and the rest were all sevens or eights. They were certainly pleased at home, although over the question of marks my parents are quite different from most. They don't care a bit whether my reports are good or bad as long as I'm well and happy, and not too cheeky: then the rest will come by itself. I am just the opposite. I don't want to be a bad pupil; I should really have stayed in the seventh form in the Montessori School, but was accepted for the Jewish Secondary. When all the Jewish children had to go to Jewish schools, the headmaster took Lies and me conditionally after a bit of persuasion. He relied on us to do our best and I don't want to let him down. My sister Margot has her report too, brilliant as usual. She would move up with *cum laude* if that existed at school, she is so brainy. Daddy has been at home a lot lately, as there is nothing for him to do at business; it must be rotten to feel so superfluous. Mr. Koophuis has taken over Travies and Mr. Kraler the firm Kolen & Co. When we walked across our little square together a few days ago, Daddy began to talk of us going into hiding. I asked him why on earth he was beginning to talk of that already. "Yes, Anne," he said, "you know that we have been taking food, clothes, furniture to other people for more than a year now. We don't want our belongings to be seized by the Germans, but we certainly don't want to fall into their clutches ourselves. So we shall disappear of our own accord and not wait until they come and fetch us."

"But, Daddy, when would it be?" He spoke so seriously that I grew very anxious.

"Don't you worry about it, we shall arrange everything. Make the most of your carefree young life while you can." That was all. Oh, may the fulfillment of these somber words remain far distant yet!

Yours, Anne

Wednesday, 8 July, 1942

Dear Kitty,

Years seem to have passed between Sunday and now. So much has happened, it is just as if the whole world had turned upside down. But I am still alive, Kitty, and that is the main thing, Daddy says.

Yes, I'm still alive, indeed, but don't ask where or how. You wouldn't understand a word, so I will begin by telling you what happened on Sunday afternoon.

At three o'clock (Harry had just gone, but was coming back later) someone rang the front doorbell. I was lying lazily reading a book on the veranda in the sunshine, so I didn't hear it. A bit later, Margot appeared at the kitchen door looking very excited. "The S.S. have sent a call-up notice for Daddy," she whispered. "Mummy has gone to see Mr. Van Daan already." (Van Daan is a friend who works with Daddy in the business.) It was a great shock to me, a call-up; everyone knows what that means. I picture concentration camps and lonely cells— should we allow him to be doomed to this? "Of course he won't go," declared Margot, while we waited together. "Mummy has gone to the Van Daans to discuss whether we should move into our hiding place tomorrow. The Van Daans are going with us, so we shall be seven in all." Silence. We couldn't talk any more, thinking about Daddy, who, little knowing what was going on, was visiting some old people in the Joodse Invalide; waiting for Mummy, the heat and suspense, all made us very overawed and silent.

Suddenly the bell rang again. "That is Harry," I said. "Don't open the door." Margot held me back, but it was not necessary as we heard Mummy and Mr. Van Daan downstairs, talking to Harry, then they came in and closed the door behind them. Each time the bell went, Margot or I had to creep softly down to see if it was Daddy, not opening the door to anyone else.

Margot and I were sent out of the room. Van Daan wanted to talk to Mummy alone. When we were alone together in our bedroom, Margot told me that the call-up was not for Daddy, but for her. I was more frightened than ever and began to cry. Margot is sixteen; would they really take girls of that age away alone? But thank goodness she won't go, Mummy said so her-

self; that must be what Daddy meant when he talked about
us going into hiding.

Into hiding—where would we go, in a town or the country,
in a house or a cottage, when, how, where . . . ?

These were questions I was not allowed to ask, but I couldn't
get them out of my mind. Margot and I began to pack some
of our most vital belongings into a school satchel. The first thing
I put in was this diary, then hair curlers, handkerchiefs, schoolbooks, a comb, old letters; I put in the craziest things with the
idea that we were going into hiding. But I'm not sorry, memories mean more to me than dresses.

At five o'clock Daddy finally arrived, and we phoned Mr.
Koophuis to ask if he could come around in the evening. Van
Daan went and fetched Miep. Miep has been in the business
with Daddy since 1933 and has become a close friend, likewise
her brand-new husband, Henk. Miep came and took some shoes,
dresses, coats, underwear, and stockings away in her bag, promising to return in the evening. Then silence fell on the house;
not one of us felt like eating anything, it was still hot and
everything was very strange. We let our large upstairs room
to a certain Mr. Goudsmit, a divorced man in his thirties, who
appeared to have nothing to do on this particular evening; we
simply could not get rid of him without being rude; he hung
about until ten o'clock. At eleven o'clock Miep and Henk Van
Santen arrived. Once again, shoes, stockings, books, and under-
clothes disappeared into Miep's bag and Henk's deep pockets,
and at eleven-thirty they too disappeared. I was dog-tired and
although I knew that it would be my last night in my own bed,
I fell asleep immediately and didn't wake up until Mummy
called me at five-thirty the next morning. Luckily it was not so
hot as Sunday; warm rain fell steadily all day. We put on heaps
of clothes as if we were going to the North Pole, the sole reason
being to take clothes with us. No Jew in our situation would
have dreamed of going out with a suitcase full of clothing. I
had on two vests, three pairs of pants, a dress, on top of that a
skirt, jacket, summer coat, two pairs of stockings, lace-up shoes,
woolly cap, scarf, and still more; I was nearly stifled before we
started, but no one inquired about that.

Margot filled her satchel with schoolbooks, fetched her bicycle, and rode off behind Miep into the unknown, as far as I was
concerned. You see I still didn't know where our secret hiding

place was to be. At seven-thirty the door closed behind us. Moortje, my little cat, was the only creature to whom I said farewell. She would have a good home with the neighbors. This was all written in a letter addressed to Mr. Goudsmit.

There was one pound of meat in the kitchen for the cat, breakfast things lying on the table, stripped beds, all giving the impression that we had left helter-skelter. But we didn't care about impressions, we only wanted to get away, only escape and arrive safely, nothing else. Continued tomorrow.

Yours, Anne

Thursday, 9 July, 1942

Dear Kitty,

So we walked in the pouring rain, Daddy, Mummy, and I, each with a school satchel and shopping bag filled to the brim with all kinds of things thrown together anyhow.

We got sympathetic looks from people on their way to work. You could see by their faces how sorry they were they couldn't offer us a lift; the gaudy yellow star spoke for itself.

Only when we were on the road did Mummy and Daddy begin to tell me bits and pieces about the plan. For months as many of our goods and chattels and necessities of life as possible had been sent away and they were sufficiently ready for us to have gone into hiding of our own accord on July 16. The plan had had to be speeded up ten days because of the call-up, so our quarters would not be so well organized, but we had to make the best of it. The hiding place itself would be in the building where Daddy has his office. It will be hard for outsiders to understand, but I shall explain that later on. Daddy didn't have many people working for him: Mr. Kraler, Koophuis, Miep, and Elli Vossen, a twenty-three-year-old typist who all knew of our arrival. Mr. Vossen, Elli's father, and two boys worked in the warehouse; they had not been told.

I will describe the building: there is a large warehouse on the ground floor which is used as a store. The front door to the house is next to the warehouse door, and inside the front door is a second doorway which leads to a staircase (A). There is another door at the top of the stairs, with a frosted glass window in it, which has "Office" written in black letters across it. That is the large main office, very big, very light, and very full. Elli, Miep, and Mr. Koophuis work there in the daytime. A small dark room containing the safe, a wardrobe, and a large cupboard leads to a small somewhat dark second office. Mr. Kraler and Mr. Van Daan used to sit here, now it is only Mr. Kraler. One can reach Kraler's office from the passage, but only via a glass door which can be opened from the inside, but not easily from the outside.

From Kraler's office a long passage goes past the coal store, up four steps and leads to the showroom of the whole building: the private office. Dark, dignified furniture, linoleum and carpets on the floor, radio, smart lamp, everything firstclass. Next door there is a roomy kitchen with a hot-water faucet and a gas stove. Next door the W.C. That is the first floor.

A wooden staircase leads from the downstairs passage to the next floor (B). There is a small landing at the top. There is a door at each end of the landing, the left one leading to a store-room at the front of the house and to the attics. One of those really steep Dutch staircases runs from the side to the other door opening on to the street (c).

The right-hand door leads to our "Secret Annexe." No one would ever guess that there would be so many rooms hidden behind that plain gray door. There's a little step in front of the door and then you are inside.

There is a steep staircase immediately opposite the entrance (E). On the left a tiny passage brings you into a room which was to become the Frank family's bed-sitting-room, next door a smaller room, study and bedroom for the two young ladies of the family. On the right a little room without windows contain-ing the washbasin and a small W.C. compartment, with an-other door leading to Margot's and my room. If you go up the next flight of stairs and open the door, you are simply amazed that there could be such a big light room in such an old house by the canal. There is a gas stove in this room (thanks to the fact that it was used as a laboratory) and a sink. This is now the kitchen for the Van Daan couple, besides being general living room, dining room, and scullery.

A tiny little corridor room will become Peter Van Daan's apartment. Then, just as on the lower landing, there is a large attic. So there you are, I've introduced you to the whole of our beautiful "Secret Annexe."

Yours, Anne

Friday, 10 July, 1942

Dear Kitty,

I expect I have thoroughly bored you with my long-winded descriptions of our dwelling. But still I think you should know where we've landed.

But to continue my story—you see, I've not finished yet—when we arrived at the Prinsengracht, Miep took us quickly upstairs and into the "Secret Annexe." She closed the door be-hind us and we were alone. Margot was already waiting for us, having come much faster on her bicycle. Our living room and all the other rooms were chock-full of rubbish, indescribably so.

All the cardboard boxes which had been sent to the office in the previous months lay piled on the floor and the beds. The little room was filled to the ceiling with bedclothes. We had to start clearing up immediately, if we wished to sleep in decent beds that night. Mummy and Margot were not in a fit state to take part; they were tired and lay down on their beds, they were miserable, and lots more besides. But the two "clearers-up" of the family—Daddy and myself—wanted to start at once.

The whole day long we unpacked boxes, filled cupboards, hammered and tidied, until we were dead beat. We sank into clean beds that night. We hadn't had a bit of anything warm the whole day, but we didn't care; Mummy and Margot were too tired and keyed up to eat, and Daddy and I were too busy.

On Tuesday morning we went on where we left off the day before. Elli and Miep collected our rations for us, Daddy improved the poor blackout, we scrubbed the kitchen floor, and were on the go the whole day long again. I hardly had time to think about the great change in my life until Wednesday. Then I had a chance, for the first time since our arrival, to tell you all about it, and at the same time to realize myself what had actually happened to me and what was still going to happen.

Yours, Anne

Saturday, 11 July, 1942

Dear Kitty,

Daddy, Mummy, and Margot can't get used to the sound of the Westertoren clock yet, which tells us the time every quarter of an hour. I can. I loved it from the start, and especially in the night it's like a faithful friend. I expect you will be interested to hear what it feels like to "disappear"; well, all I can say is that I don't know myself yet. I don't think I shall ever feel really at home in this house, but that does not mean that I loathe it here, it is more like being on vacation in a very peculiar boardinghouse. Rather a mad idea, perhaps, but that is how it strikes me. The "Secret Annexe" is an ideal hiding place. Although it leans to one side and is damp, you'd never find such a comfortable hiding place anywhere in Amsterdam, no, perhaps not even in the whole of Holland. Our little room looked very bare at first with nothing on the walls; but thanks to Daddy who had brought my film-star collection and picture postcards on beforehand, and with the aid of paste pot and brush, I have transformed the walls into one gigantic picture. This makes it look much more cheerful, and, when the Van Daans come, we'll get some wood from the attic, and make a few little cupboards for the walls and other odds and ends to make it look more lively.

Margot and Mummy are a little bit better now. Mummy felt well enough to cook some soup for the first time yesterday, but then forgot all about it, while she was downstairs talking, so the peas were burned to a cinder and utterly refused to leave the pan. Mr. Koophuis has brought me a book called *Young People's Annual*. The four of us went to the private office yesterday evening and turned on the radio. I was so terribly frightened that someone might hear it that I simply begged Daddy to come upstairs with me. Mummy understood how I felt and came too. We are very nervous in other ways, too, that the neighbors might hear us or see something going on. We made curtains straight away on the first day. Really one can hardly call them curtains, they are just light, loose strips of material, all different shapes, quality, and pattern, which Daddy and I sewed together in a most unprofessional way. These works of art are fixed in position with drawing pins, not to come down until we emerge from here.

There are some large business premises on the right of us, and on the left a furniture workshop; there is no one there after working hours but even so, sounds could travel through the walls. We have forbidden Margot to cough at night, although she has a bad cold, and make her swallow large doses of codeine. I am looking for Tuesday when the Van Daans arrive; it will be much more fun and not so quiet. It is the silence that frightens me so in the evenings and at night. I wish like anything that one of our protectors could sleep here at night. I can't tell you how oppressive it is *never* to be able to go outdoors, also I'm very afraid that we shall be discovered and be shot. That is not exactly a pleasant prospect. We have to whisper and tread lightly during the day, otherwise the people in the warehouse might hear us.

Someone is calling me.

Yours, Anne

Friday, 14 August, 1942

Dear Kitty,

I have deserted you for a whole month, but honestly, there is so little news here that I can't find amusing things to tell you every day. The Van Daans arrived on July 13. We thought they were coming on the fourteenth, but between the thirteenth and sixteenth of July the Germans called up people right and left which created more and more unrest, so they played for safety, better a day too early than a day too late. At nine-thirty in the morning (we were still having breakfast) Peter arrived, the Van Daans' son, not sixteen yet, a rather soft, shy, gawky youth; can't expect much from his company. He brought his cat (Mouschi) with him. Mr. and Mrs. Van Daan arrived half an hour later, and to our great amusement she had a large pottie in her hat box. "I don't feel at home anywhere without my chamber," she declared, so it was the first thing to find its permanent resting place under her divan. Mr. Van Daan did not bring his, but carried a folding tea table under his arm.

From the day they arrived we all had meals cozily together and after three days it was just as if we were one large family. Naturally the Van Daans were able to tell us a lot about the extra week they had spent in the inhabited world. Among other things we were very interested to hear what had happened to our house and to Mr. Goudsmit. Mr. Van Daan told us:

"Mr. Goudsmit phoned at nine o'clock on Monday morning and asked if I could come around. I went immediately and found G. in a state of great agitation. He let me read a letter that the Franks had left behind and wanted to take the cat to the neighbors as indicated in the letter, which pleased me. Mr. G. was afraid that the house would be searched so we went through all the rooms, tidied up a bit, and cleared away the breakfast things. Suddenly I discovered a writing pad on Mrs. Frank's desk with an address in Maastricht written on it. Although I knew that this was done on purpose, I pretended to be very surprised and shocked and urged Mr. G. to tear up this unfortunate little piece of paper without delay.

"I went on pretending that I knew nothing of your disappearance all the time, but after seeing the paper, I got a brain wave. 'Mr. Goudsmit'—I said—'it suddenly dawns on me what this address may refer to. Now it all comes back to me, a high-ranking officer was in the office about six months ago, he appeared to be very friendly with Mr. Frank and offered to help him, should the need arise. He was stationed in Maastricht. I think he must have kept his word and somehow or other managed to get them into Belgium and then on to Switzerland. I should tell this to any friends who may inquire. Don't, of course, mention Maastricht.'

"With these words I left the house. Most of your friends know already, because I've been told myself several times by different people."

We were highly amused at the story and, when Mr. Van Daan gave us further details, laughed still more at the way people can let their imagination run away with them. One family had seen the pair of us pass on bicycles very early in the morning and another lady knew quite definitely that we were fetched by a military car in the middle of the night.

Yours, Anne

Friday, 21 August, 1942

Dear Kitty,

The entrance to our hiding place has now been properly concealed. Mr. Kraler thought it would be better to put a cupboard in front of our door (because a lot of houses are being searched for hidden bicycles), but of course it had to be a movable cupboard that can open like a door.

Mr. Vossen made the whole thing. We had already let him into the secret and he can't do enough to help. If we want to go downstairs, we have to first bend down and then jump, because the step has gone. The first three days we were all going about with masses of lumps on our foreheads, because we all knocked ourselves against the low doorway. Now we have nailed a cloth filled with wood wool against the top of the door. Let's see if that helps!

I'm not working much at present; I'm giving myself holidays until September. Then Daddy is going to give me lessons; it's shocking how much I've forgotten already. There is little change in our life here. Mr. Van Daan and I usually manage to upset each other, it's just the opposite with Margot whom he likes very much. Mummy sometimes treats me just like a baby, which I can't bear. Otherwise things are going better. I still don't like Peter any more, he is so boring; he flops lazily on his bed half the time, does a bit of carpentry, and then goes back for another snooze. What a fool!

It is lovely weather and in spite of everything we make the most we can of it by lying on a camp bed in the attic, where the sun shines through an open window.

Yours, Anne

Wednesday, 2 September, 1942

Dear Kitty,

Mr. and Mrs. Van Daan have had a terrific quarrel, I've never seen anything quite like it before. Mummy and Daddy would never dream of shouting at each other. The cause was so trivial that the whole thing was a pure waste of breath. But, still, everyone to his own liking.

Naturally it is very unpleasant for Peter, who has to stand by. No one takes him seriously, he is so frightfully touchy and lazy. Yesterday he was badly upset because he found that his tongue was blue instead of red; this unusual phenomenon of nature disappeared just as quickly as it had come. Today he is going about with a scarf on, as he has a stiff neck; in addition "M'lord" complains of lumbago. Pains around the heart, kidneys, and lungs are not unusual either, he is a real hypochondria (that's the word for such people, isn't it?)! It is not all honey between Mummy and Mrs. Van Daan; there is plenty of cause for unpleasantness. To give a small example, I will tell you that Mrs. Van Daan has taken all three of her sheets out of the common linen cupboard. She takes it for granted that Mummy's sheets will do for all of us. It will be a nasty surprise for her when she finds that Mummy has followed her good example.

Also, she is thoroughly piqued that her dinner service and not ours is in use. She is always trying to find out where we have actually put our plates; they are closer than she thinks, they are in a cardboard box behind a lot of junk in the attic. Our plates are ungettatable at as long as we are here, and a good thing too. I always have bad luck; I smashed one of Mrs. Van Daan's soup plates into a thousand pieces yesterday. "Oh!" she cried angrily. "Couldn't you be careful for once—that's the last one I've got." Mr. Van Daan is all sugar to me nowadays.

Long may it last. Mummy gave me another frightful sermon this morning; I can't bear them. Our ideas are completely opposite. Daddy is a darling, although he can sometimes be angry with me for five minutes on end. Last week we had a little interruption in our monotonous life; it was over a book about women—and Peter. First I must tell you that Margot and Peter are allowed to read nearly all the books that Mr. Koophuis lends us, but the grownups held back this particular book on the subject of women. Peter's curiosity was aroused at once. What was it the two of them were not allowed to read in this book? He got hold of the book on the sly, while his mother was downstairs talking, and disappeared with his booty to the attic. All went well for a few days. His mother knew what he was doing, but didn't tell tales, until Father found out. He was very angry, took the book away, and thought that that would finish the whole business. However, he had not allowed for his son's curiosity, which waxed rather than waned because of his father's attitude. Peter, determined to finish it, thought of a way to get hold of this enthralling book. In the meantime, Mrs. Van Daan had asked Mummy what she thought about it all. Mummy thought this particular book was not suitable for Margot, but she saw no harm in letting her read most books.

"There is a great difference, Mrs. Van Daan," said Mummy, "between Margot and Peter. In the first place Margot is a girl and girls are always more grownup than boys, secondly, Margot has read quite a lot of serious books, and does not go in search of things that are forbidden her, and thirdly, Margot is far more developed and intelligent, shown by the fact of her being in the fourth form at school." Mrs. Van Daan agreed, but still thought it was wrong in principle to let children read books which were written for grownups.

In the meantime Peter had found a time of the day when no one bothered about him or the book: seven-thirty in the evening—then everyone was in the private office listening to the radio. That was when he took his treasure to the attic again. He should have been downstairs again by eight-thirty, but because the book was so thrilling he forgot the time and was just coming downstairs as his father came into the room. You can imagine the consequences! With a slap and a snatch, the book lay on the table and Peter was in the attic. That's how matters stood as we sat down to table. Peter stayed upstairs—

no one bothered about him, and he had to go to bed without any supper. We went on with the meal, chattering gaily, when suddenly we heard a piercing whistle; we all stopped eating and looked with pale changed faces from one to another. Then we heard Peter's voice, calling down the chimney, "I say, I'm not coming down anyway." Mr. Van Daan sprang to his feet, his napkin fell to the floor, and scarlet in the face he shouted, "I've had enough of this." Daddy took his arm, afraid of what might happen, and the two men went together to the attic. After a good deal of resistance and stamping, Peter landed up in his room with the door closed and we went on eating. Mrs. Van Daan wanted to save one slice of bread for the dear boy, but his father stood firm. "If he doesn't apolgoize soon, he will have to sleep in the attic." Loud protests from the rest of us, as we thought missing supper was quite enough punishment. Besides, Peter might catch cold and we couldn't call a doctor.

Peter did not apologize; he was already in the attic. Mr. Van Daan did nothing more about it, but I noticed the next morning that Peter's bed had been slept in. Peter was back in the attic at seven o'clock, but Daddy managed with a few friendly words to persuade him to come down again. Sour faces and obstinate silences for three days and then everything went smoothly once more.

Yours, Anne

Monday, 21 September, 1942

Dear Kitty,

Today I'm going to tell you our general news.

Mrs. Van Daan is unbearable. I get nothing but "blowups" from her for my continuous chatter. She is always pestering us in some way or other. This is the latest: she doesn't want to wash up the pans if there is a fragment left, instead of putting it into a glass dish, as we've always done until now, she leaves it in the pan to go bad.

After the next meal Margot sometimes has about seven pans to wash up and then Madame says: "Well, well, Margot, you have got a lot to do!"

I'm busy with Daddy working out his family tree: as we go along he tells me little bits about everyone—it's terribly interesting. Mr. Koophuis brings a few special books for me every

THE DIARY OF A YOUNG GIRL

other week. I'm thrilled with the *Joop ter Heul* series. I've enjoyed the whole of Cissy van Marxveldt very much. And I've read *Een Zomerzotheid* four times and I still laugh about some of the ludicrous situations that arise.

Term time has begun again, I'm working hard at my French and manage to pump in five irregular verbs per day. Peter sighs and groans over his English. A few schoolbooks have just arrived; we have a good stock of exercise books, pencils, rubbers, and labels, as I brought these with me. I sometimes listen to the Dutch news from London, heard Prince Bernhard recently. He said that Princess Juliana is expecting a baby about next January. I think it is lovely; it surprises the others that I should be so keen on the Royal Family.

I was being discussed and they decided that I'm not completely stupid after all, which had the effect of making me work extra hard the next day. I certainly don't want to still be in the first form when I'm fourteen or fifteen.

Also the fact that I'm hardly allowed to read any decent books was mentioned. Mummy is reading *Heeren, Vrouwen en Knechten* now, which I'm not allowed (Margot is). First I must be more developed, like my talented sister. Then we talk about my ignorance of philosophy and psychology, about which I know nothing. Perhaps by next year I shall be wiser! (I looked up these difficult words quickly in *Koenen*.)

I have just woken up to the disturbing fact that I have one long-sleeved dress and three cardigans for the winter. I've received permission from Daddy to knit a jumper of white sheep's wool; it's not very nice wool, but as long as it's warm that's all that matters. We have some clothes deposited with friends, but unfortunately we shall not see them until after the war, that is if they are still there then. I had just written something about Mrs. Van Daan when in she came. Slap! I closed the book. "Hey, Anne, can't I just have a look?"

"I'm afraid not."

"Just the last page then?"

"No, I'm sorry."

Naturally it gave me a frightful shock, because there was an unflattering description of her on this particular page.

Yours, Anne

Friday, 25 September, 1942

Dear Kitty,

Yesterday evening I went upstairs and "visited" the Van Daans. I do so occasionally to have a chat. Sometimes it can be quite fun. Then we have some moth biscuits (the biscuit tin is kept in the wardrobe which is full of moth balls) and drink lemonade. We talked about Peter. I told them how Peter often strokes my cheek and that I wished he wouldn't as I don't like being pawed by boys.

In a typical way parents have, they asked if I couldn't get fond of Peter, because he certainly liked me very much. I thought "Oh dear!" and said: "Oh, no!" Imagine it!

I did say that I thought Peter rather awkward, but that it was probably shyness, as many boys who haven't had much to do with girls are like that.

I must say that the Refuge Committee of the "Secret Annexe" (male section) is very ingenious. I'll tell you what they've done now to get news of us through to Mr. Van Dijk, Travies' chief representative and a friend who has surreptitiously hidden some of our things for us! They typed a letter to a chemist in South Zeeland, who does business with our firm, in such a way that he has to send the enclosed reply back in an addressed envelope. Daddy addressed the envelope to the office. When this envelope arrives from Zeeland, the enclosed letter is taken out, and is replaced by a message in Daddy's handwriting as a sign of life. Like this, Van Dijk won't become suspicious when he reads the note. They specially chose Zeeland because it is so close to Belgium and the letter could have easily been smuggled over the border, in addition no one is allowed into Zeeland without a special permit; so if they thought we were there, he couldn't try and look us up.

Yours, Anne

Sunday, 27 September, 1942

Dear Kitty,

Just had a big bust-up with Mummy for the umpteenth time; we simply don't get on together these days and Margot and I don't hit it off any too well either. As a rule we don't go in for such outbursts as this in our family. Still, it's by no means always pleasant for me. Margot's and Mummy's natures are completely strange to me. I can understand my friends better than my own mother—too bad!

We often discuss postwar problems, for example, how one ought to address servants.

Mrs. Van Daan had another tantrum. She is terribly moody. She keeps hiding more of her private belongings. Mummy ought to answer each Van Daan "disappearance" with a Frank "disappearance." How some people do adore bringing up other people's children in addition to their own. The Van Daans are that kind. Margot doesn't need it, she is a such a goody-goody, perfection itself, but I seem to have enough mischief in me for the two of us put together. You should hear us at mealtimes, with reprimands and cheeky answers flying to and fro. Mummy and Daddy always defend me stoutly. I'd have to give up if it weren't for them. Although they do tell me that I mustn't talk so much, that I must be more retiring and not poke my nose into everything, still I seem doomed to failure. If Daddy wasn't so patient, I'd be afraid I was going to turn out to be a terrific disappointment to my parents and they are pretty lenient with me.

If I take a small helping of some vegetable I detest and make up with potatoes, the Van Daans, and Mevrouw in particular, can't get over it, that any child should be so spoiled.

"Come along, Anne, have a few more vegetables," she says straight away.

"No, thank you, Mrs. Van Daan," I answer, "I have plenty of potatoes."

"Vegetables are good for you, your mother says so too. Have a few more," she says, pressing them on me until Daddy comes to my rescue.

Then we have from Mrs. Van Daan—"You ought to have been in our home, we were properly brought up. It's absurd that Anne's so frightfully spoiled. I wouldn't put up with it if Anne were my daughter."

These are always her first and last words "if Anne were my daughter." Thank heavens I'm not!

But to come back to this "upbringing" business. There was a deadly silence after Mrs. Van Daan had finished speaking yesterday. Then Daddy said, "I think Anne is extremely well brought up; she has learned one thing anyway, and that is to make no reply to your long sermons. As to the vegetables, look at your own plate." Mrs. Van Daan was beaten, well and truly beaten. She had taken a minute helping of vegetables herself. But *she* is not spoiled! Oh, no, too many vegetables in the evening make her constipated. Why on earth doesn't she keep her mouth shut about me, then she wouldn't need to make such feeble excuses. It's gorgeous the way Mrs. Van Daan blushes. I don't, and that is just what she hates.

Yours, Anne

Monday, 28 September, 1942

Dear Kitty,

I had to stop yesterday, long before I'd finished. I just must tell you about another quarrel, but before I start on that, something else.

Why do grownups quarrel so easily, so much, and over the most idiotic things? Up till now I thought that only children squabbled and that that wore off as you grew up. Of course, there is sometimes a real reason for a quarrel, but this is just plain bickering. I suppose I should get used to it. But I can't nor do I think I shall, as long as I am the subject of nearly every discussion (they use the word "discussion" instead of quarrel). Nothing, I repeat, nothing about me is right; my general appearance, my character, my manners are discussed from A to Z. I'm expected (by order) to simply swallow all the harsh words and shouts in silence and I am not used to this. In fact, I can't! I'm not going to take all these insults lying down, I'll show them that Anne Frank wasn't born yesterday. Then they'll be surprised and perhaps they'll keep their mouths shut when I let them see that I am going to start educating them. Shall I take up that attitude? Plain barbarism! I'm simply amazed again and again over their awful manners and especially . . . stupidity (Mrs. Van Daan's), but as soon as I get used to this— and it won't be long—then I'll give them some of their own back, and no half measures. Then they'll change their tune!

Am I really so bad-mannered, conceited, headstrong, pushing, stupid, lazy, etc., etc., as they all say? Oh, of course not. I have my faults, just like everyone else, I know that, but they thoroughly exaggerate everything.

Kitty, if only you knew how I sometimes boil under so many

gibes and jeers. And I don't know how long I shall be able to stifle my rage. I shall just blow up one day.

Still, no more of this, I've bored you long enough with all these quarrels. But I simply must tell you of one highly interesting discussion at table. Somehow or other, we got on to the subject of Pim's (Daddy's nickname) extreme modesty. Even the most stupid people have to admit this about Daddy. Suddenly Mrs. Van Daan says, "I too, have an unassuming nature, more so than my husband."

Did you ever! This sentence in itself shows quite clearly how thoroughly forward and pushing she is! Mr. Van Daan thought he ought to give an explanation regarding the reference to himself. "I don't wish to be modest—in my experience it does not pay." Then to me: "Take my advice, Anne, don't be too unassuming, it doesn't get you anywhere."

Mummy agreed with this too. But Mrs. Van Daan had to add, as always, her ideas on the subject. Her next remark was addressed to Mummy and Daddy. "You have a strange outlook on life. Fancy saying such a thing to Anne; it was very different when I was young. And I feel sure that it still is, except in your modern home." This was a direct hit at the way Mummy brings up her daughters.

Mrs. Van Daan was scarlet by this time. Mummy calm and cool as a cucumber. People who blush get so hot and excited, it is quite a handicap in such a situation. Mummy, still entirely unruffled, but anxious to close the conversation as soon as possible, thought for a second and then said: "I find, too, Mrs. Van Daan, that one gets on better in life if one is not over-modest. My husband, now, and Margot, and Peter are exceptionally modest, whereas your husband, Anne, you, and I, though not exactly the opposite, don't allow ourselves to be completely pushed to one side." Mrs. Van Daan: "But, Mrs. Frank, I don't understand you; I'm so very modest and retiring, how can you think of calling me anything else?" Mummy: "I did not say you were exactly forward, but no one could say you had a retiring disposition." Mrs. Van Daan: "Let us get this matter cleared up, once and for all. I'd like to know in what way I am pushing? I know one thing, if I didn't look after myself, I'd soon be starving."

This absurd remark in self-defense just made Mummy rock with laughter. That irritated Mrs. Van Daan, who added a string of German-Dutch, Dutch-German expressions, until she became completely tongue-tied; then she rose from her chair and was about to leave the room.

Suddenly her eye fell on me. You should have seen her. Unfortunately, at the very moment that she turned round, I was shaking my head sorrowfully—not on purpose, but quite involuntarily, for I had been following the whole conversation so closely.

Mrs. Van Daan turned round and began to reel off a lot of harsh German, common, and ill-mannered, just like a coarse, red-faced fishwife—it was a marvelous sight. If I could draw, I'd have liked to catch her like this; it was a scream, such a stupid, foolish little person!

Anyhow, I've learned one thing now. You only really get to know people when you've had a jolly good row with them. Then and then only can you judge their true characters!

Yours, Anne

Tuesday, 29 September, 1942

Dear Kitty,

Extraordinary things can happen to people who go into hiding. Just imagine, as there is no bath, we use a washtub and because there is hot water in the office (by which I always mean the whole of the lower floor) all seven of us take it in turns to make use of this great luxury.

But because we are all so different and some are more modest than others, each member of the family has found his own place for carrying out the performance. Peter uses the kitchen in spite of its glass door. When he is going to have a bath, he goes to each one of us in turn and tells us that we must not walk past the kitchen for half an hour. He seems to think this is sufficient. Mr. Van Daan goes right upstairs; to him it is worth the bother of carrying hot water all that way, so as to have the seclusion of his own room. Mrs. Van Daan simply doesn't bathe at all at present; she is waiting to see which is the best place. Daddy has his bath in the private office, Mummy behind a fire guard in the kitchen; Margot and I have chosen the front office for our scrub. The curtains there are drawn on Saturday afternoons, so we wash ourselves in semidarkness.

However, I don't like this place any longer, and since last

week I've been on the lookout for more comfortable quarters. Peter gave me an idea and that was to try the large office W.C. There I can sit down, have the light on, lock the door, pour my own bath water away, and I'm safe from prying eyes.

I tried my beautiful bathroom on Sunday for the first time and although it sounds mad, I think it is the best place of all. Last week the plumber was at work downstairs to move the drains and water pipes from the office W.C. to the passage. This change is a precaution against frozen pipes, in case we should have a cold winter. The plumber's visit was far from pleasant for us. Not only were we unable to draw water the whole day, but we could not go to the W.C. either. Now it is rather indecent to tell you what we did to overcome this difficulty; however, I'm not such a prude that I can't talk about these things.

The day we arrived here, Daddy and I improvised a pottie for ourselves; not having a better receptacle, we sacrificed a glass preserving jar for this purpose. During the plumber's visit, nature's offerings were deposited in these jars in the sitting room during the day, I don't think this was nearly as bad as having to sit still and not talk the whole day. You can't imagine what a trial that was for "Miss Quack-Quack." I have to whisper on ordinary days; but not being able to speak or move was ten times worse. After being flattened by three days of continuous sitting, my bottom was very stiff and painful. Some exercises at bedtime helped.

Yours, Anne

Thursday, 1 October, 1942

Dear Kitty,

I got a terrible shock yesterday. Suddenly at eight o'clock the bell rang loudly. Of course, I thought that someone had come: you'll guess who I mean. But I calmed down a bit when everyone said it must be some urchins or perhaps the postman.

The days are becoming very quiet here. Lewin, a small Jewish chemist and dispenser, works for Mr. Kraler in the kitchen. He knows the whole building well and therefore we are always afraid that he'll take it into his head to have a peep in the old laboratory. We are as quiet as mice. Who, three months ago, would ever have guessed that quicksilver Anne would have to sit still for hours—and, what's more, could?

The twenty-ninth was Mrs. Van Daan's birthday. Although it could not be celebrated in a big way, we managed a little party in her honor, with a specially nice meal, and she received some small presents and flowers. Red carnations from her husband; that seems to be a family tradition. To pause for a moment on the subject of Mrs. Van Daan, I must tell you that her attempts to flirt with Daddy are a source of continual irritation for me. She strokes his face and hair, pulls her skirt right up, and makes so-called witty remarks, trying in this way to attract Pim's attention. Pim, thank goodness, doesn't find her either attractive or funny, so he doesn't play ball. Mummy doesn't behave like that with Mr. Van Daan, I've said that to Mrs. Van Daan's face.

Now and then Peter comes out of his shell and can be quite funny. We have one thing in common, from which everyone usually gets a lot of amusement: we both love dressing up. He appeared in one of Mrs. Van Daan's very narrow dresses and I put on his suit. He wore a hat and I a cap. The grownups were doubled up with laughter and we enjoyed ourselves as much as they did. Elli has bought new skirts for Margot and me at Bijenkorf's. The material is rotten, just like sacking, and they cost 24.00 florins and 7.50 florins respectively. What a difference compared with before the war!

Another nice thing I've been keeping up my sleeve. Elli has written to some secretarial school or other and ordered a correspondence course in shorthand for Margot, Peter, and me. You wait and see what perfect experts we shall be by next year. In any case it's extremely important to be able to write in a code.

Yours, Anne

Saturday, 3 October, 1942

Dear Kitty,

There was another dust-up yesterday. Mummy kicked up a frightful row and told Daddy just what she thought of me. Then she had a awful fit of tears so, of course, off I went too; and I'd got such an awful headache anyway. Finally I told Daddy that I'm much more fond of him than Mummy, to which he replied that I'd get over that. But I don't believe it. I have to simply force myself to stay calm with her. Daddy wishes that I would sometimes volunteer to help Mummy, when she doesn't feel well or has a headache; but I shan't. I am working hard at my French and am now reading *La Belle Nivernaise*.

Yours, Anne

Friday, 9 October, 1942

Dear Kitty,

I've only got dismal and depressing news for you today. Our many Jewish friends are being taken away by the dozen. These people are treated by the Gestapo without a shred of decency, being loaded into cattle trucks and sent to Westerbork, the big Jewish camp in Drente. Westerbork sounds terrible: only one washing cubicle for a hundred people and not nearly enough lavatories. There is no separate accommodation. Men, women, and children all sleep together. One hears of frightful immorality because of this; and a lot of the women, and even girls, who stay there any length of time are expecting babies.

It is impossible to escape; most of the people in the camp are branded as inmates by their shaven heads and many also by their Jewish appearance.

If it is as bad as this in Holland whatever will it be like in the distant and barbarous regions they are sent to? We assume that most of them are murdered. The English radio speaks of their being gassed.

Perhaps that is the quickest way to die. I feel terribly upset. I couldn't tear myself away while Miep told these dreadful stories; and she herself was equally wound up for that matter. Just recently for instance, a poor old crippled Jewess was sitting on her doorstep; she had been told to wait there by the Gestapo, who had gone to fetch a car to take her away. The poor old thing was terrified by the guns that were shooting at English planes overhead, and by the glaring beams of the searchlights. But Miep did not dare take her in; no one would undergo such a risk. The Germans strike without the slightest mercy. Elli too is very quiet: her boy friend has got to go to Germany. She is afraid that the airmen who fly over our homes will drop their bombs, often weighing a million kilos, on Dirk's head. Jokes such as "he's not likely to get a million" and "it only takes one bomb" are in rather bad taste. Dirk is certainly not the only one who has to go: trainloads of boys leave daily. If they stop at a small station en route, sometimes some of them manage to get out unnoticed and escape; perhaps a few manage it. This, however, is not the end of my bad news. Have you ever heard of hostages? That's the latest thing in penalties for sabotage. Can you imagine anything so dreadful?

Prominent citizens—innocent people—are thrown into prison to await their fate. If the saboteur can't be traced, the Gestapo simply put about five hostages against the wall. Announcements of their deaths appear in the papers frequently. These outrages are described as "fatal accidents." Nice people, the Germans! To think that I was once one of them too! No, Hitler took away our nationality long ago. In fact, Germans and Jews are the greatest enemies in the world.

Yours, Anne

Friday, 16 October, 1942

Dear Kitty,

I'm terribly busy. I've just translated a chapter out of *La Belle Nivernaise* and made notes of new words. Then a per-fectly foul math problem and three pages of French grammar. I flatly refuse to do these math problems every day. Daddy agrees that they're vile. I'm almost better at them than he is, though neither of us are much good and we often have to fetch Margot. I'm the furthest on of the three of us in short-hand.

Yesterday I finished *The Assault*. It's quite amusing, but doesn't touch *Joop ter Heul*. As a matter of fact, I think Cissy van Marxveldt is a first-rate writer. I shall definitely let my children read her books. Mummy, Margot, and I are as thick as thieves again. It's really much better. Margot and I got in the same bed together last evening; it was a frightful squash, but that was just the fun of it. She asked if she could read my diary. I said "Yes—at least, bits of it"; and then I asked if I could read hers and she said "Yes." Then we got on to the subject of the future. I asked her what she wanted to be. But she wouldn't say and made a great secret of it. I gathered something about teaching; I'm not sure if I'm right, but I think so. Really, I shouldn't be so curious!

This morning I was lying on Peter's bed, having chased him off at first. He was furious with me, not that I cared very much. He might be a bit more friendly with me for once; after all I did give him an apple yesterday.

I asked Margot if she thought I was very ugly. She said that I was quite attractive and that I had nice eyes. Rather vague, don't you think?

Till next time,

Yours, Anne

Tuesday, 20 October, 1942

Dear Kitty,

My hand still shakes, although it's two hours since we had the shock. I should explain that there are five fire extinguishers in the house. We knew that someone was coming to fill them, but no one had warned us when the carpenter, or whatever you call him, was coming.

The result was that we weren't making any attempt to keep quiet, until I heard hammering outside on the landing opposite our cupboard door. I thought of the carpenter at once and warned Elli, who was having a meal with us, that she shouldn't go downstairs. Daddy and I posted ourselves at the door so as to hear when the man left. After he'd been working for a quarter of an hour, he laid his hammer and tools down on top of our cupboard (as we thought) and knocked at our door. We turned absolutely white. Perhaps he had heard something after all and wanted to investigate our secret den. It seemed like it. The knocking, pulling, pushing, and wrenching went on. I nearly fainted at the thought that this utter stranger might discover our beautiful secret hiding place. And just as I thought my last hour was at hand, I heard Mr. Koophuis say, "Open the door, it's only me." We opened it immediately. The hook that holds the cupboard, which can be undone by people who know the secret, had got jammed. That was why no one had been able to warn us about the carpenter. The man had now gone downstairs and Koophuis wanted to fetch Elli, but couldn't open the cupboard again. It was a great relief to me, I can tell you. In my imagination the man who I thought was trying to get in had been growing and growing in size until in the end he appeared to be a giant and the greatest fascist that ever walked the earth.

Well! Well! Luckily everything was okay this time. Meanwhile we had great fun on Monday. Miep and Henk spent the night here. Margot and I went in Mummy and Daddy's room for the night, so that the Van Santens could have our room. The meal tasted divine. There was one small interruption. Daddy's lamp blew a fuse, and all of a sudden we were sitting in darkness. What was to be done? There was some fuse wire in the house, but the fuse box is right at the very back of the dark storeroom—not such a nice job after dark. Still the men ventured forth and after ten minutes we were able to put the candles away again.

I got up early this morning. Henk had to leave at half past eight. After a cozy breakfast Miep went downstairs. It was pouring and she was glad not to have to cycle to the office. Next week Elli is coming to stay for a night.

Yours, Anne

Thursday, 29 October, 1942

Dear Kitty,

I am awfully worried, Daddy is ill. He has a high temperature and a red rash, it looks like measles. Think of it, we can't even call a doctor! Mummy is letting him have a good sweat. Perhaps that will send his temperature down.

This morning Miep told us all that all the furniture has been removed from the Van Daans' home. We haven't told Mrs. Van Daan yet. She's such a bundle of nerves already, and we don't feel like listening to another moan over all the lovely china and beautiful chairs that she left at home. We had to leave almost all our nice things behind; so what's the good of grumbling about it now?

I'm allowed to read more grown-up books lately. I'm now reading Eva's Youth by Nico van Suchtelen. I can't see much difference between this and the schoolgirl love stories. It is true there are bits about women selling themselves to unknown men in back streets. They ask a packet of money for it. I'd die of shame if anything like that happened to me. Also it says that Eva has a monthly period. Oh, I'm so longing to have it too; it seems so important.

Daddy has brought the plays of Goethe and Schiller from the big cupboard. He is going to read to me every evening. We've started with Don Carlos.

Following Daddy's good example, Mummy has pressed her prayer book into my hand. For decency's sake I read some of the prayers in German; they are certainly beautiful but they don't convey much to me. Why does she force me to be pious, just to oblige her?

Tomorrow we are going to light the fire for the first time. I expect we shall be suffocated with smoke. The chimney hasn't been swept for ages, let's hope the thing draws.

Yours, Anne

Saturday, 7 November, 1942

Dear Kitty,

Mummy is frightfully irritable and that always seems to herald unpleasantness for me. Is it just chance that Daddy and Mummy never rebuke Margot and that they always drop on me for everything? Yesterday evening, for instance: Margot was reading a book with lovely drawings in it; she got up and went upstairs, put the book down ready to go on with it later. I wasn't doing anything, so picked up the book and started looking at the pictures. Margot came back, saw "her" book in my hands, wrinkled her forehead and asked for the book back. Just because I wanted to look a little further on, Margot got more and more angry. Then Mummy joined in: "Give the book to Margot; she was reading it," she said. Daddy came into the room. He didn't even know what it was all about, but saw the injured look on Margot's face and promptly dropped on me: "I'd like to see what you'd say if Margot ever started looking at one of your books!" I gave way at once, laid the book down, and left the room—offended, as they thought. It so happened I was neither offended nor cross, just miserable. It wasn't right of Daddy to judge without knowing what the squabble was about. I would have given Margot the book myself, and much more quickly, if Mummy and Daddy hadn't interfered. They took Margot's part at once, as though she were the victim of some great injustice.

It's obvious that Mummy would stick up for Margot; she and Margot always do back each other up. I'm so used to that that I'm utterly indifferent to both Mummy's jawing and Margot's moods.

I love them; but only because they are Mummy and Margot.

With Daddy it's different. If he holds Margot up as an example, approves of what she does, praises and caresses her, then something gnaws at me inside, because I adore Daddy. He is the one I look up to. I don't love anyone in the world but him. He doesn't notice that he treats Margot differently from me. Now Margot is just the prettiest, sweetest, most beautiful girl in the world. But all the same I feel I have some right to be taken seriously too. I have always been the dunce, the ne'er-do-well of the family, I've always had to pay double for my deeds, first with the scolding and then again because of the way my feelings are hurt. Now I'm not satisfied with this apparent favoritism any more. I want something from Daddy that he is not able to give me.

I'm not jealous of Margot, never have been. I don't envy her good looks or her beauty. It is only that I long for Daddy's real love: not only as his child, but for me—Anne, myself.

I cling to Daddy because it is only through him that I am able to retain the remnant of family feeling. Daddy doesn't understand that I need to give vent to my feelings over Mummy sometimes. He doesn't want to talk about it; he simply avoids anything which might lead to remarks about Mummy's failings. Just the same, Mummy and her failings are something I find harder to bear than anything else. I don't know how to keep it all to myself. I can't always be drawing attention to her untidiness, her sarcasm, and her lack of sweetness, neither can I believe that I'm always in the wrong.

We are exact opposites in everything; so naturally we are bound to run up against each other. I don't pronounce judgment on Mummy's character, for that is something I can't judge. I only look at her as a mother, and she just doesn't succeed in being that to me; I have to be my own mother. I've drawn myself apart from them all; I am my own skipper and later on I shall see where I come to land. All this comes about particularly because I have in my mind's eye an image of what a perfect mother and wife should be; and in her whom I must call "Mother" I find no trace of that image.

I am always making resolutions not to notice Mummy's bad example. I want to see only the good side of her and to seek in myself what I cannot find in her. But it doesn't work; and the worst of it is that neither Daddy nor Mummy understands this gap in my life, and I blame them for it. I wonder if anyone can ever succeed in making their children absolutely content.

Sometimes I believe that God wants to try me, both now and later on; I must become good through my own efforts, without examples and without good advice. Then later on I shall be all the stronger. Who besides me will ever read these letters? From whom but myself shall I get comfort? As I need comforting often, I frequently feel weak, and dissatisfied with myself; my shortcomings are too great. I know this, and every day I try to improve myself, again and again.

My treatment varies so much. One day Anne is so sensible and is allowed to know everything; and the next day I hear that Anne is just a silly little goat who doesn't know anything at all and imagines that she's learned a wonderful lot from books. I'm not a baby or a spoiled darling any more, to be laughed at, whatever she does. I have my own views, plans, and ideas, though I can't put them into words yet. Oh, so many things bubble up inside me as I lie in bed, having to put up with people I'm fed up with, who always misinterpret my intentions. That's why in the end I always come back to my diary. That is where I start and finish, because Kitty is always patient. I'll promise her that I shall persevere, in spite of everything, and find my own way through it all, and swallow my tears. I only wish I could see the results already or occasionally receive encouragement from someone who loves me.

Don't condemn me; remember rather that sometimes I too can reach the bursting point.

Yours, Anne

Monday, 9 November, 1942

Dear Kitty,

Yesterday was Peter's birthday, he was sixteen. He had some nice presents. Among other things a game of Monopoly, a razor, and a lighter. Not that he smokes much; it's really just for show.

The biggest surprise came from Mr. Van Daan when, at one o'clock, he announced that the British had landed in Tunis, Algiers, Casablanca, and Oran. "This is the beginning of the end," everyone was saying, but Churchill, the British Prime Minister, who had probably heard the same thing in England, said: "This is not the end. It is not even the beginning of the end. But it is, perhaps, the end of the beginning." Do you see the difference? There is certainly reason for optimism. Stalingrad, the Russian town which they've already been defending for three months, still hasn't fallen into German hands.

But to return to affairs in our secret den. I must tell you something about our food supply. As you know, we have some real greedy pigs on the top floor. We get our bread from a nice baker, a friend of Koophuis. We don't get so much as we used to at home, naturally. But it's sufficient. Four ration cards have also been bought illegally. Their price is going up all the time; it has now gone up from twenty-seven florins to thirty-three. And all that for a little slip of printed paper! In order to have something in the house that will keep, apart from our 150 tins of vegetables, we have bought 270 pounds of dried peas and beans. They are not all for us, some are for the office people. They are in sacks which hang on hooks in our little passage (inside the hidden door). Owing to the weight of the contents, a few stitches in the sacks burst open. So we decided it would be better to put our winter store in the attic and Peter was given the job of dragging it all up there.

He had managed to get five of the six sacks upstairs intact, and he was just busy pulling up number six, when the bottom seam of the sack split and a shower—no, a positive hailstorm of brown beans came pouring down and rattled down the stairs. There were about fifty pounds in the sack and the noise was enough to waken the dead. Downstairs they thought the old house with all its contents was coming down on them. (Thank God there were no strangers in the house.) It gave Peter a moment's fright. But he was soon roaring with laughter, especially when he saw me standing at the bottom of the stairs, like a little island in the middle of a sea of beans! I was entirely surrounded up to my ankles in beans. Quickly we started to pick them up. But beans are so slippery and small that they seemed to roll into all the possible and impossible corners and holes. Now, every time anyone goes downstairs they bend down once or twice, in order to be able to present Mrs. Van Daan with a handful of beans.

I'd almost forgotten to mention that Daddy is quite better again.

Yours, Anne

P.S. The news has just come over the radio that Algiers has fallen. Morocco, Casablanca, and Oran have been in British hands for several days. Now we're waiting for Tunis.

Tuesday, 10 November, 1942

Dear Kitty,

Great news—we want to take in an eighth person. Yes, really! We've always thought that there was quite enough room and food for one more. We were only afraid of giving Koophuis and Kraler more trouble. But now that the appalling stories we hear about Jews are getting even worse, Daddy got hold of the two people who had to decide, and they thought it was an excellent plan. "It is just as dangerous for seven as for eight," they said, and quite rightly. When this was settled, we ran through our circle of friends, trying to think of a single person who would fit in well with our "family." It wasn't difficult to hit on someone. After Daddy had refused all members of the Van Daan family, we chose a dentist called Albert Dussel, whose wife was fortunate enough to be out of the country when war broke out. He is known to be quiet, and so far as we and Mr. Van Daan can judge from a superficial acquaintance, both families think he is a congenial person. Miep knows him too, so she will be able to make arrangements for him to join us. If he comes, he will have to sleep in my room instead of Margot, who will use the camp bed.

Yours, Anne

Thursday, 12 November, 1942

Dear Kitty,

Dussell was awfully pleased when Miep told him that she had got a hiding place for him. She urged him to come as soon as possible. Preferably Saturday. He thought that this was rather doubtful, since he had to bring his card index up to date first, see to a couple of patients, and settle his accounts. Miep came to us with this news this morning. We thought it was unwise of him to put it off. All these preparations entail explanations to a number of people, whom we would rather keep out of it. Miep is going to ask if he can't manage to come on Saturday after all.

Dussel said no; now he is coming on Monday. I must say I think it's pretty crazy that he doesn't jump at the proposal—whatever it is. If he were to get picked up outside, would he still be able to do his card index, settle his finances, and see to his patients? Why delay then? I think it's stupid of Daddy to have given in. No other news——

Yours, Anne

Tuesday, 17 November, 1942

Dear Kitty,

Dussel has arrived. All went well. Miep had told him that he must be at a special place in front of the Post Office at eleven o'clock, where a man would meet him. Dussel was standing at the rendezvous dead on time. Mr. Koophuis, who knows Dussel too, went up to him and told him that the said gentleman could not come, but asked whether he would just go to Miep at the office. Koophuis got into a tram and went back to the office, while Dussel walked in the same direction. At twenty past eleven Dussel tapped at the office door. Miep helped him off with his coat, so that the yellow star would not be seen, and took him to the private office, where Koophuis engaged him in conversation until the charwoman had gone. Then Miep went upstairs with Dussel under the pretext that the private office was needed for something, opened the swinging cupboard, and stepped inside before the eyes of the dumfounded Dussel.

We all sat around the table upstairs, waiting with coffee and cognac to greet the newcomer. Miep showed him into our sitting room first. He recognized our furniture at once, and had not the remotest idea that we were there, above his head. When Miep told him he nearly passed out with surprise. But luckily Miep didn't give him much time and took him straight upstairs.

Dussel sank into a chair, speechless, and looked at us all for a while, as if he had to really take it all in first. After a while he stuttered "But . . . *aber, sind* you not in Belgium then? *Ist der Militar nicht* come, *das Auto,* the escape is *sie nicht* successful?"

We explained everything to him, that we had spread the story about the soldiers and the car on purpose to put people, and especially the Germans, on the wrong track, should they try to find us.

Dussel was again struck dumb by such ingenuity and, when he had explored further our superpractical exquisite little "Secret Annexe," he could do nothing but gaze about him in astonishment.

We all had lunch together. Then he had a little nap and joined us for tea, tidied up his things a bit (Miep had brought them beforehand), and began to feel more at home. Especially when he received the following typed "Secret Annexe Rules" (Van Daan product).

PROSPECTUS AND GUIDE TO THE "SECRET ANNEXE"

Special institution as temporary residence for Jews and suchlike.

Open all the year round. Beautiful, quiet, free from woodland surroundings, in the heart of Amsterdam. Can be reached by trams 13 and 17, also by car or bicycle. In special cases also on foot, if the Germans prevent the use of transport.

Board and lodging: Free.

Special fat-free diet.

Running water in the bathroom (alas, no bath) and down various inside and outside walls.

Ample storage room for all types of goods.

Own radio center, direct communication with London, New York, Tel Aviv, and numerous other stations. This appliance is only for residents' use after six o'clock in the evening. No stations are forbidden, on the understanding that German stations are only listened to in special cases, such as classical music and the like.

Rest hours: 10 o'clock in the evening until 7:30 in the morning. 10:15 on Sundays. Residents may rest during the day, conditions permitting, as the directors indicate. For reasons of public security rest hours must be strictly observed!!

Holidays (outside the home): postponed indefinitely.

Use of language: Speak softly at all times, by order! All civilized languages are permitted, therefore no German!

Lessons: One written shorthand lesson per week. English, French, Mathematics, and History at all times.

Small Pets—Special Department (permit is necessary): Good treatment available (vermin excepted).

Mealtimes: breakfast, every day except Sundays and Bank Holidays, 9 A.M. Sundays and Bank Holidays, 11:30 A.M. approximately.

Lunch: (not very big): 1:15 P.M. to 1:45 P.M.

Dinner: cold and/or hot: no fixed time (depending on the news broadcast).

Duties: Residents must always be ready to help with office work.

Baths: The washtub is available for all residents from 9 A.M. on Sundays. The W.C., kitchen, private office or main office, whichever preferred, are available.

Alcoholic Beverages: only with doctor's prescription.

END

Yours, Anne

Thursday, 19 November, 1942

Dear Kitty,

Dussel is a very nice man, just as we had all imagined. Of course he thought it was all right to share my little room.

Quite honestly I'm not so keen that a stranger should use my things, but one must be prepared to make some sacrifices for a good cause, so I shall make my little offering with a good will. "If we can save someone, then everything else is of secondary importance," says Daddy, and he's absolutely right.

The first day that Dussel was here, he immediately asked me all sorts of questions: When does the charwoman come? When can one use the bathroom? When is one allowed to use the lavatory? You may laugh, but these things are not so simple in a hiding place. During the day we mustn't make any noise that might be heard downstairs; and if there is some stranger—such as the charwoman for example—then we have to be extra careful. I explained all this carefully to Dussel. But one thing amazed me: he is very slow on the uptake. He asks everything twice over and still doesn't seem to remember. Perhaps that will wear off in time, and it's only that he's thoroughly upset by the sudden change.

Apart from that, all goes well. Dussell has told us a lot about the outside world, which we have missed for so long now. He had very sad news. Countless friends and acquaintances have gone to a terrible fate. Evening after evening the green and gray army lorries trundle past. The Germans ring at every front door to inquire if there are any Jews living in the house. If there are, then the whole family has to go at once. If they don't find any, they go on to the next house. No one has a chance of evading them unless one goes into hiding. Often they go around with lists, and only ring when they know they can get a good haul. Sometimes they let them off for cash—so much per head. It seems like the slave hunts of olden times. But it's certainly no joke; it's much too tragic for that. In the evenings when it's dark, I often see rows of good, innocent people accompanied by crying children, walking on and on, in charge of a couple of these chaps, bullied and knocked about until they almost drop. No one is spared—old people, babies, expectant mothers, the sick—each and all join in the march of death.

How fortunate we are here, so well cared for and undisturbed. We wouldn't have to worry about all this misery were it not that we are so anxious about all those dear to us whom we can no longer help.

I feel wicked sleeping in a warm bed, while my dearest friends have been knocked down or have fallen into a gutter somewhere out in the cold night. I get frightened when I think of close friends who have now been delivered into the hands of the cruelest brutes that walk the earth. And all because they are Jews!

Yours, Anne

Friday, 20 November, 1942

Dear Kitty,

None of us really knows how to take it all. The news about the Jews had not really penetrated through to us until now, and we thought it best to remain as cheerful as possible. Every now and then, when Miep lets out something about what has happened to a friend, Mummy and Mrs. Van Daan always begin to cry, so Miep thinks it better not to tell us any more. But Dussel was immediately plied with questions from all sides, and the stories he told us were so gruesome and dreadful that one can't get them out of one's mind.

Yet we shall still have our jokes and tease each other, when these horrors have faded a bit in our minds. It won't do us any good, or help those outside, to go on being as gloomy as we are at the moment. And what would be the object of making our "Secret Annexe" into a "Secret Annexe of Gloom"? Must I keep thinking about those other people, whatever I am doing? And if I want to laugh about something, should I stop myself quickly and feel ashamed that I am cheerful? Ought I then to cry the whole day long? No, that I can't do. Besides, in time this gloom will wear off.

Added to this misery there is another, but of a purely personal kind; and it pales into insignificance beside all the wretchedness I've just told you about. Still, I can't refrain from telling you that lately I have begun to feel deserted. I am surrounded by too great a void. I never used to feel like this, my fun and amusements, and my girl friends, completely filled my thoughts. Now I either think about unhappy things, or about myself. And at long last I have made the discovery that Daddy, although he's such a darling, still cannot take the place of my entire little world of bygone days. But why do I bother you with such foolish things? I'm very ungrateful, Kitty; I know that. But it often makes my head swim if I'm jumped upon too much, and then on top of that have to think about all those other miseries!

Yours, Anne

Saturday, 28 November, 1942

Dear Kitty,

We have used too much electricity, more than our ration. Result: the utmost economy and the prospect of having it cut off. No light for a fortnight; a pleasant thought, that, but who knows, perhaps it won't happen after all! It's too dark to read in the afternoons after four or half past. We pass the time in all sorts of crazy ways: asking riddles, physical training in the dark, talking English and French, criticizing books. But it all begins to pall in the end. Yesterday evening I discovered something new: to peer through a powerful pair of field glasses into the lighted rooms of the houses at the back. In the daytime we can't allow even as much as a centimeter's chink to appear between our curtains, but it can't do any harm after dark. I never knew before that neighbors could be such interesting people. At any rate, ours are. I found one couple having a meal, one family was in the act of taking a home movie; and the dentist opposite was just attending to an old lady, who was awfully scared.

It was always said about Mr. Dussel that he could get on wonderfully with children and that he loved them all. Now he shows himself in his true colors; a stodgy, old-fashioned disciplinarian, and preacher of long, drawn-out sermons on manners.

As I have the unusual good fortune (!) to share my bedroom—alas, a small one—with His Lordship, and as I'm generally considered to be the most badly behaved of the three young people, I have a lot to put up with and have to pretend to be deaf in order to escape the old, much-repeated tickings-off and warnings. All this wouldn't be too bad, if he wasn't such a frightful sneak and he didn't pick on Mummy of all people to sneak to every time. When I've already just had a dose from him, Mummy goes over it all again, so I get a gale aft as well as fore. Then, if I'm really lucky, I'm called on to give an account of myself to Mrs. Van Daan and then I get a veritable hurricane!

Honestly, you needn't think it's easy to be the "badly brought-up" central figure of a hypercritical family in hiding. When I lie in bed at night and think over the many sins and shortcomings attributed to me, I get so confused by it all that I either laugh or cry: it depends what sort of mood I am in.

Then I fall asleep with a stupid feeling of wishing to be different from what I am or from what I want to be; perhaps to behave differently from the way I want to behave, or do behave. Oh, heavens above, now I'm getting you in a muddle too. Forgive me, but I don't like crossing things out, and in these days of paper shortage we are not allowed to throw paper away. Therefore I can only advise you not to read the last sentence again, and certainly not to try to understand it, because you won't succeed anyhow!

Yours, Anne

Monday, 7 December, 1942

Dear Kitty,

Chanuka and St. Nicholas Day came almost together this year—just one day's difference. We didn't make much fuss about

Chanuka: we just gave each other a few little presents and
then we had the candles. Because of the shortage of candles
we only had them alight for ten minutes, but it is all right as
long as you have the song. Mr. Van Daan has made a wooden
candlestick, so that too was all properly arranged.

Saturday, the evening of St. Nicholas Day, was much more
fun. Miep and Elli had made us very inquisitive by whisper-
ing all the time with Daddy, so naturally we guessed that
something was on.

And so it was. At eight o'clock we all filed down the wooden
staircase through the passage in pitch-darkness (it made me
shudder and wish that I was safely upstairs again) into the
little dark room. There, as there are no windows, we were
able to turn on a light. When that was done, Daddy opened
the big cupboard. "Oh! how lovely," we all cried. A large
basket decorated with St. Nicholas paper stood in the corner
and on top there was a mask of Black Peter.

We quickly took the basket upstairs with us. There was a
nice little present for everyone, with a suitable poem attached.
I got a doll, whose skirt is a bag for odds and ends; Daddy
got book ends, and so on. In any case it was a nice idea and
as none of us had ever celebrated St. Nicholas, it was a good
way of starting.

Yours, Anne

Thursday, 10 December, 1942

Dear Kitty,

Mr. Van Daan used to be in the meat, sausage, and spice
business. It was because of his knowledge of this trade that he
was taken on in Daddy's business. Now he is showing the
sausagy side of himself, which, for us, is by no means disagreeable.

We had ordered a lot of meat (under the counter, of course)
for preserving in case we should come upon hard times. It was
fun to watch, first the way the pieces of meat went through
the mincer, two or three times, then how all the accompanying
ingredients were mixed with the minced meat, and then how
the intestine was filled by means of a spout, to make the
sausages. We fried the sausage meat and ate it with sauerkraut
for supper that evening, but the Gelderland sausages had to be

thoroughly dried first, so we hung them over a stick tied to the ceiling with string. Everyone who came into the room began to laugh when they caught a glimpse of the row of sausages on show. They looked terribly funny!

The room was in a glorious mess. Mr. Van Daan was wearing one of his wife's aprons swathed round his substantial person (he looked fatter than he is!) and was busy with the meat. Hands smothered in blood, red face, and the soiled apron, made him look like a butcher. Mrs. Van Daan was trying to do everything at once, learning Dutch from a book, stirring the soup, watching the meat being done, sighing and complaining about her injured rib. That's what happens to elderly ladies (!) who do such idiotic exercises to reduce their large behinds!

Dussel had inflammation in one eye and was bathing it with camomile tea by the fire. Pim, who was sitting on a chair in a beam of sunlight that shone through the window, kept being pushed from one side to the other. In addition, I think his rheumatism was bothering him, because he sat rather hunched up with a miserable look on his face, watching Mr. Van Daan at work. He looked exactly like some shriveled-up old man from an old people's home. Peter was doing acrobatics round the room with his cat. Mummy, Margot, and I were peeling potatoes; and, of course, all of us were doing everything wrong because we were so busy watching Mr. Van Daan.

Dussel has opened his dental practice. For the fun of it, I must just tell you about his first patient. Mummy was ironing; and Mrs. Van Daan was the first to face the ordeal. She went and sat on a chair in the middle of the room. Dussel began to unpack his case in an awfully important way, asked for some eau de cologne as a disinfectant and vaseline to take the place of wax.

He looked in Mrs. Van Daan's mouth and found two teeth which, when touched, just made her crumple up as if she was going to pass out, uttering incoherent cries of pain. After a lengthy examination (in Mrs. Van Daan's case, lasting in actual fact not more than two minutes) Dussel began to scrape away at one of the holes. But, no fear—it was out of the question— the patient flung her arms and legs about wildly in all directions until at one point Dussel let go of the scraper—that remained stuck in Mrs. Van Daan's tooth.

Then the fat was really in the fire! She cried (as far as it was possible with such an instrument in one's mouth), tried to pull the thing out of her mouth, and only succeeded in pushing it further in. Mr. Dussel stood with his hands against his sides calmly watching the little comedy. The rest of the audience lost all control and roared with laughter. It was rotten of us, because I for one am quite sure that I should have screamed even louder. After much turning, kicking, screaming, and calling out, she got the instrument free at last and Mr. Dussel went on with his work, as if nothing had happened!

This he did so quickly that Mrs. Van Daan didn't have time to start any fresh tricks. But he'd never had so much help in all his life before. Two assistants are pretty useful: Van Daan and I performed our duties well. The whole scene looked like a picture from the Middle Ages entitled "A Quack at Work." In the meantime, however, the patient hadn't much patience; she had to keep an eye on "her" soup and "her" meal. One thing is certain, Mrs. Van Daan won't be in such a hurry to allow herself to be treated again!

Yours, Anne

Sunday, 13 December, 1942

Dear Kitty,

I'm sitting cozily in the main office, looking outside through a slit in the curtain. It is dusk but still just light enough to write to you.

It is a very queer sight, as I watch the people walking by; it looks just as if they are all in a terrible hurry and nearly trip over their own toes. With cyclists, now, one simply can't keep pace with their speed. I can't even see what sort of person is riding on the machine.

The people in this neighborhood don't look very attractive. The children especially are so dirty you wouldn't want to touch them with a barge pole. Real slum kids with running noses. I can hardly understand a word they say.

Yesterday afternoon Margot and I were having a bath here and I said, "Supposing we were to take the children who are walking past, one by one, hoist them up with a fishing rod, give them each a bath, wash and mend their clothes, and then let them go again, then . . ." Margot interrupted me, "By tomorrow they would look just as filthy and ragged as before."

But I'm just talking nonsense; besides, there are other things to see—cars, boats, and rain. I like particularly the screech of the trams as they go by.

There is no more variety in our thoughts than there is for ourselves. They go round and round like a roundabout—from Jews to food and from food to politics. By the way, talking of Jews, I saw two Jews through the curtain yesterday. I could hardly believe my eyes; it was a horrible feeling, just as if I'd betrayed them and was now watching them in their misery. There is a houseboat immediately opposite, where a bargeman lives with his family. He has a small yapping dog. We only know the little dog by his bark and his tail, which we can see when he runs round the deck. Ugh! Now it's started to rain and most of the people are hidden under umbrellas. I see nothing but raincoats and occasionally the back of someone's hat. Really I don't need to see more. I'm gradually getting to know all the women at a glance, blown out with potatoes, wearing a red or a green coat, troddendown heels and with a bag under their arms. Their faces either look grim or kind—depending on their husbands' dispositions.

Yours, Anne

Tuesday, 22 December, 1942

Dear Kitty,

The "Secret Annexe" has heard the joyful news that each person will receive an extra quarter of a pound of butter for Christmas. It says half a pound in the newspapers, but that's only for the lucky mortals who get their ration books from the government, not for Jews who have gone into hiding, who can only afford to buy four illegal ration books, instead of eight.

We are all going to bake something with our butter. I made some biscuits and two cakes this morning. Everyone is very busy upstairs and Mummy has told me I must not go there to work or read, until the household jobs are done.

Mrs. Van Daan is in bed with her bruised rib, complains the whole day long, allows herself to be given fresh dressings all the time, and isn't satisfied with anything. I shall be glad when she's on her feet again and tidies up her own things, because I must say this for her; she's exceptionally industrious and tidy, all the while she is healthy in mind and body. She is cheerful too.

Just as if I didn't hear enough "ssh-ssh" during the day, for making too much noise, my gentleman bedroom companion now repeatedly calls out "ssh-ssh" to me at night too. According to him, I am not even allowed to turn over! I refuse to take the slightest notice of him, and shall go "ssh-ssh" back at him the next time.

He makes me furious, on Sundays especially, when he turns the light on early to do his exercises. It seems to take simply hours, while I, poor tormented creature, feel the chairs, which are placed at the head of my bed to lengthen it, slide backwards and forwards continually under my sleepy head. When he has ended with a couple of violent arm-waving exercises to loosen his muscles, His Lordship begins his toilet. His pants are hanging up, so to and fro he must go to collect them. But he forgets his tie, which is lying on the table. Therefore once more he pushes and bumps past the chairs to get it.

But I won't bore you any longer on the subject of old men. It won't make things any better and all my plans of revenge (such as disconnecting the lamp, shutting the door, hiding his clothes) must be abandoned in order to keep the peace. Oh, I'm becoming so sensible! One must apply one's reason to everything here, learning to obey, to hold your tongue, to help, to be good, to give in, and I don't know what else. I'm afraid I shall use up all my brains too quickly, and I haven't got so very many. Then I shall not have any left for when the war is over.

Yours, Anne

Wednesday, 13 January, 1943

Dear Kitty,

Everything has upset me again this morning, so I wasn't able to finish a single thing properly.

It is terrible outside. Day and night more of those poor miserable people are being dragged off, with nothing but a rucksack and a little money. On the way they are deprived even of these possessions. Families are torn apart, the men, women, and children all being separated. Children coming home from school find that their parents have disappeared.

Women return from shopping to find their homes shut up and their families gone.

The Dutch people are anxious too, their sons are being sent to Germany. Everyone is afraid.

And every night hundreds of planes fly over Holland and go to German towns, where the earth is plowed up by their bombs, and every hour hundreds and thousands of people are killed in Russia and Africa. No one is able to keep out of it, the whole globe is waging war and although it is going better for the Allies, the end is not yet in sight.

And as for us, we are fortunate. Yes, we are luckier than millions of people. It is quiet and safe here, and we are, so to speak, living on capital. We are even so selfish as to talk about "after the war," brighten up at the thought of having new clothes and new shoes, whereas we really ought to save every penny, to help other people, and save what is left from the wreckage after the war.

The children here run about in just a thin blouse and clogs; no coat, no hat, no stockings, and no one helps them. Their tummies are empty, they chew an old carrot to stay the pangs, go from their cold homes out into the cold street and, when they get to school, find themselves in an even colder class-room. Yes, it has even got so bad in Holland that countless children stop the passers-by and beg for a piece of bread. I could go on for hours about all the suffering the war has brought, but then I would only make myself more dejected. There is nothing we can do but wait as calmly as we can till the misery comes to an end. Jews and Christians wait, the whole earth waits; and there are many who wait for death.

Yours, Anne

Saturday, 30 January, 1943

Dear Kitty,

I'm boiling with rage, and yet I mustn't show it. I'd like to stamp my feet, scream, give Mummy a good shaking, cry, and I don't know what else, because of the horrible words, mocking looks, and accusations which are leveled at me repeatedly every day, and find their mark, like shafts from a tightly strung bow, and which are just as hard to draw from my body.

I would like to shout to Margot, Van Daan, Dussel—and

Daddy too—"Leave me in peace, let me sleep one night at least without my pillow being wet with tears, my eyes burning and my head throbbing. Let me get away from it all, preferably away from the world!" But I can't do that, they mustn't know my despair, I can't let them see the wounds which they have caused, I couldn't bear their sympathy and their kindhearted jokes, it would only make me want to scream all the more. If I talk, everyone thinks I'm showing off; when I'm silent they think I'm ridiculous; rude if I answer, sly if I get a good idea, lazy if I'm tired, selfish if I eat a mouthful more than I should, stupid, cowardly, crafty, etc., etc. The whole day long I hear nothing else but that I am an insufferable baby, and although I laugh about it and pretend not to take any notice, I *do* mind. I would like to ask God to give me a different nature, so that I didn't put everyone's back up. But that can't be done. I've got the nature that has been given to me and I'm sure it can't be bad. I do my very best to please everybody, far more than they'd ever guess. I try to laugh it all off, because I don't want to let them see my trouble. More than once, after a whole string of undeserved rebukes, I have flared up at Mummy: "I don't care what you say anyhow. Leave me alone: I'm a hopeless case anyway." Naturally, I was then told I was rude and was virtually ignored for two days; and then, all at once, it was quite forgotten, and I was treated like everyone else again. It is impossible for me to be all sugar one day and spit venom the next. I'd rather choose the golden mean (which is not so golden), keep my thoughts to myself, and try for *once* to be just as disdainful to them as they are to me. Oh, if only I could!

Yours, Anne

Friday, 5 February, 1943

Dear Kitty,

Although I haven't written anything about our rows for a long time, there still isn't any change. The discord, long accepted by us, struck Mr. Dussel as a calamity at first. But he is getting used to it now and tries not to think about it. Margot and Peter aren't a bit what you would call "young," they are both so staid and quiet. I show up terribly against them and am always hearing, "You don't find Margot and Peter doing that

—why don't you follow their example?" I simply loathe it. I might tell you I don't want to be in the least like Margot. She is much too soft and passive for my liking, and allows everyone to talk her around, and gives in about everything. I want to be a stronger character! But I keep such ideas to myself: they would only laugh at me, if I came along with this as an explanation of my attitude. The atmosphere at table is usually strained, though luckily the outbursts are sometimes checked by "the soup eaters"! The "soup eaters" are the people from the office who come in and are served with a cup of soup. This afternoon Mr. Van Daan was talking about Margot eating so little again. "I suppose you do it to keep slim," he added, teasing her. Mummy, who always defends Margot, said loudly: "I can't bear your stupid chatter any longer." Mr. Van Daan turned scarlet, looked straight in front of him, and said nothing. We often laugh about things; just recently Mrs. Van Daan came out with some perfect nonsense. She was recalling the past, how well she and her father got on together and what a flirt she was. "And do you know," she went on, "if a man gets a bit aggressive, my father used to say, then you must say to him 'Mr. So and So, remember I am a lady!' and he will know what you mean." We thought that was a good joke and burst out laughing. Peter too, although usually so quiet, sometimes gives cause for mirth. He is blessed with a passion for foreign words, although he does not always know their meaning. One afternoon we couldn't go to the lavatory because there were visitors in the office; however, Peter had to pay an urgent call. So he didn't pull the plug. He put a notice up on the lavatory door to warn us, with "S.V.P. gas" on it. Of course he meant to put "Beware of gas"; but he thought the other looked more genteel. He hadn't got the faintest notion it meant "if you please."

Yours, Anne

Saturday, 27 February, 1943

Dear Kitty,

Pim is expecting the invasion any day. Churchill has had pneumonia, but is improving slowly. The freedom-loving Gandhi of India is holding his umpteenth fast. Mrs. Van Daan claims to be fatalistic. But who is the most scared when the guns go off? No one else but Petronella.

Henk brought a copy of the bishop's letter to churchgoers for us to read. It was very fine and inspiring. "Do not rest, people of the Netherlands, everyone is fighting with his own weapons to free the country, the people, and their religion." "Give help, be generous, and do not dismay!" is what they cry from the pulpit, just like that. Will it help? It won't help the people of our religion.

You'd never guess what has happened to us now. The owner of these premises has sold the house without informing Kraler and Koophuis. One morning the new owner arrived with an architect to have a look at the house. Luckily, Mr. Koophuis was present and showed the gentlemen everything except the "Secret Annexe." He professed to have forgotten the key of the communicating door. The new owner didn't question any further. It will be all right as long as he doesn't come back and want to see the "Secret Annexe," because then it won't look too good for us.

Daddy has emptied a card index box for Margot and me, and put cards in it. It is to be a book card system; then we both write down which books we have read, who they are by, etc. I have procured another little notebook for foreign words.

Lately Mummy and I have been getting on better together, but we still *never* confide in each other. Margot is more catty than ever and Daddy has got something he is keeping to himself, but he remains the same darling.

New butter and margarine rationing at table! Each person has their little bit of fat put on their plate. In my opinion the Van Daans don't divide it at all fairly. However, my parents are much too afraid of a row to say anything about it. Pity, *I* think you should always give people like them tit for tat.

Yours, Anne

Wednesday, 10 March, 1943

Dear Kitty,

We had a short circuit last evening, and on top of that the guns kept banging away all the time. I still haven't got over my fear of everything connected with shooting and planes, and I creep into Daddy's bed nearly every night for comfort.

I know it's very childish but you don't know what it is like. The A.A. guns roar so loudly that you can't hear yourself speak. Mrs. Van Daan, the fatalist, was nearly crying, and said in a very timid little voice, "Oh, it is so unpleasant! Oh they are shooting so hard," by which she really means "I'm so frightened."

It didn't seem nearly so bad by candlelight as in the dark. I was shivering, just as if I had a temperature, and begged Daddy to light the candle again. He was relentless, the light remained off. Suddenly there was a burst of machine-gun fire, and that is ten times worse than guns. Mummy jumped out of bed and, to Pim's annoyance, lit the candle. When he complained her answer was firm: "After all, Anne's not exactly a veteran soldier," And that was the end of it.

Have I already told you about Mrs. Van Daan's other fears? I don't think so. If I am to keep you informed of all that happens in the "Secret Annexe," you must know about this too. One night Mrs. Van Daan thought she heard burglars in the attic; she heard loud footsteps and was so frightened that she woke her husband. Just at that moment the burglars disappeared and the only sounds that Mr. Van Daan could hear were the heartbeats of the frightened fatalist herself. "Oh, Putti [Mr. Van Daan's nickname], they are sure to have taken the sausages and all our peas and beans. And Peter, I wonder if he is still safely in bed?" "They certainly won't have stolen Peter. Listen, don't worry and let me go to sleep." But nothing came of that. Mrs. Van Daan was far too nervous to sleep another wink. A few nights after that the whole Van Daan family was woken by ghostly sounds. Peter went up to the attic with a torch—and scamper—scamper! What do you think it was running away? A swarm of enormous rats! When we knew who the thieves were, we let Mouschi sleep in the attic and the uninvited guests didn't come back again; at least not during the night.

Peter went up to the loft a couple of evenings ago to fetch some old newspapers. He had to hold the trap door firmly to get down the steps. He put his hand down without looking . . . and went tumbling down the ladder from the sudden shock and pain. Without knowing it he had put his hand on a large rat, and it had bitten him hard. By the time he reached us, as white as a sheet and with his knees knocking, the blood had soaked through his pajamas. And no wonder; it's not very pleasant to stroke a large rat; and to get bitten into the bargain is really dreadful.

Yours, Anne

Friday, 12 March, 1943

Dear Kitty,

May I introduce someone to you: Mama Frank, champion of youth! Extra butter for the young; the problems of modern youth; Mummy defends youth in everything and after a certain amount of squabbling she always gets her way. A bottle of preserved sole has gone bad: gala dinner for Mouschi and Boche. You haven't met Boche yet, although she was here before we went into hiding. She is the warehouse and office cat and keeps down the rats in the storerooms. Her odd political name requires an explanation. For some time the firm had two cats; one for the warehouse and one for the attic. Now it occasionally happened that the two cats met; and the result was always a terrific fight. The aggressor was always the warehouse cat; yet it was always the attic cat who managed to win—just like among nations. So the storehouse cat was named the German or "Boche" and the attic cat the English or "Tommy." Tommy was got rid of later; we are all entertained by Boche when we go downstairs.

We have eaten so many kidney beans and haricot beans that I can't bear the sight of them any more. The mere thought of them makes me feel quite sick. Bread is no longer served in the evenings now. Daddy has just said that he doesn't feel in a good mood. His eyes look so sad again—poor soul!

I can't drag myself away from a book called *The Knock at the Door* by Ina Boudier-Bakker. The story of the family is exceptionally well written. Apart from that, it is about war, writers, the emancipation of women; and quite honestly I'm not awfully interested.

Horrible air raids on Germany. Mr. Van Daan is in a bad mood; the cause—cigarette shortage. Discussions over the question of whether we should, or should not, use our canned vegetables ended in our favor.

I can't get into a single pair of shoes any more, except ski boots, which are not much use about the house. A pair of rush sandals costing 6.50 florins lasted me just one week, after which they were out of action. Perhaps Miep will scrounge something under the counter. I must cut Daddy's hair. Pim maintains that he will never have another barber after the war, as I do the job so well. If only I didn't snip his ear so often!

Yours, Anne

Thursday, 18 March, 1943

Dear Kitty,
Turkey is in the war. Great excitement. Waiting in suspense for the news.

Yours, Anne

Friday, 19 March, 1943

Dear Kitty,
An hour later joy was followed by disappointment. Turkey is not in the war yet. It was only a cabinet minister talking about them soon giving up their neutrality. A newspaper in the Dam[1] was crying, "Turkey on England's side." The news-papers were torn out of his hands. This is how the joyful news reached us too; 500- and 1000-guilder notes have been declared no longer valid. It is a trap for black marketeers and suchlike, but even more for people who have got other kinds of "black" money, and for people in hiding. If you wish to hand in a 1000-guilder note you must be able to declare, and prove, ex-actly how you got it. They may still be used to pay taxes, but only until next week. Dussel has received an old-fashioned foot-operated dentist's drill, I expect he'll soon give me a thorough check-over. The "Führer aller Germanen" has been talking to wounded soldiers. Listening-in to it was pitiful. Question and answer went something like this:
"My name is Heinrich Scheppel."
"Wounded where?"
"Near Stalingrad."
"What kind of wound?"
"Two feet frozen off and a broken joint in the left arm."
This is exactly what the frightful puppet show on the radio was like. The wounded seemed to be proud of their wounds

[1]A square in front of the Royal Palace.

—the more the better. One of them felt so moved at being able to shake hands with the Führer (that is, if he still had a hand!) that he could hardly get the words out of his mouth.

Yours, Anne

Thursday, 25 March, 1943

Dear Kitty,

Yesterday Mummy, Daddy, Margot, and I were sitting pleasantly together when suddenly Peter came in and whispered something in Daddy's ear. I heard something about "a barrel fallen over in the warehouse" and "someone fumbling about at the door." Margot had heard it too; but when Daddy and Peter went off immediately, she tried to calm me down a bit, because I was naturally as white as a sheet and very jittery.

The three of us waited in suspense. A minute or two later Mrs. Van Daan came upstairs; she'd been listening to the wireless in the private office. She told us that Pim had asked her to turn off the wireless and go softly upstairs. But you know what that's like, if you want to be extra quiet, then each step of the old stairs creaks twice as loudly. Five minutes later Pim and Peter appeared again, white to the roots of their hair, and told us their experiences.

They had hidden themselves under the stairs and waited, with no result at first. But suddenly, yes, I must tell you, they heard two loud bumps, just as if two doors were banged here in the house. Pim was upstairs in one leap. Peter warned Dussel first, who finally landed upstairs with a lot of fuss and noise. Then we all went up in stockinged feet to the Van Daans on the next floor. Mr. Van Daan had a bad cold and had already gone to bed, so we all drew up closely around his bed and whispered our suspicions to him.

Each time Mr. Van Daan coughed loudly, Mrs. Van Daan and I were so scared that we thought we were going to have a fit. That went on until one of us got the bright idea of giving him some codeine, which soothed the cough at once. Again we waited and waited, but we heard no more and finally we all came to the conclusion that the thieves had taken to their heels when they heard footsteps in the house, which was otherwise so silent.

Now it was unfortunate that the wireless downstairs was still turned to England, and that the chairs were neatly arranged round it. If the door had been forced, and the air-raid wardens had noticed and warned the police, then the results might have been very unpleasant. So Mr. Van Daan got up and put on his coat and hat and followed Daddy cautiously downstairs, Peter took up the rear, armed with a large hammer in case of emergencies. The ladies upstairs (including Margot and me) waited in suspense, until the gentlemen reappeared five minutes later and told us that all was quiet in the house.

We arranged that we would not draw any water or pull the plug in the lavatory. But as the excitement had affected most of our tummies, you can imagine what the atmosphere was like when we had each paid a visit in succession.

When something like that happens, heaps of other things seem to come at the same time, as now. Number One was that the clock at the Westertoren, which I always find so reassuring, did not strike. Number Two was that, Mr. Vossen having left earlier than usual the previous evening, we didn't know definitely whether Elli had been able to get hold of the key, and had perhaps forgotten to shut the door. It was still evening and we were still in a state of uncertainty, although we certainly did feel a bit reassured by the fact that from about eight o'clock, when the burglar had alarmed the house, until half past ten we had not heard a sound. On further reflection it also seemed very unlikely to us that a thief would have forced open a door so early in the evening, while there were still people about in the street. Moreover, one of us got the idea that it was possible that the caretaker of the warehouse next door was still at work since, in the excitement, and with the thin walls, one can easily make a mistake, and what's more, one's imagination can play a big part at such critical moments.

So we all went to bed; but none of us could get to sleep. Daddy as well as Mummy and Mr. Dussel were awake, and without much exaggeration I can say that I hardly slept a wink. This morning the men went downstairs to see whether the outside door was still shut, and everything turned out to be quite safe. We gave everyone a detailed description of the nerve-racking event. They all made fun of it, but it is easy to laugh at such things afterwards. Elli was the only one who took us seriously.

Yours, Anne

Saturday, 27 March, 1943

Dear Kitty,

We have finished our shorthand course; now we are beginning to practice speed. Aren't we getting clever? I must tell you more about my time-killing subjects (I call them such, because we have got nothing else to do but make the days go by as quickly as possible, so that the end of our time here comes more quickly); I'm mad on Mythology and especially the Gods of Greece and Rome. They think here that it is just a passing craze, they've never heard of an adolescent kid of my age being interested in Mythology. Well, then, I shall be the first!

Mr. Van Daan has a cold, or rather he has a little tickle in his throat. He makes a tremendous fuss about it. Gargling with camomile tea, painting his throat with tincture of myrrh, rubbing eucalyptus all over his chest, nose, teeth, and tongue; and then getting into an evil mood on top of it all.

Rauter, one of the German big shots, has made a speech. "All Jews must be out of the German-occupied countries before July 1. Between April 1 and May 1 the province of Utrecht must be cleaned out [as if the Jews were cockroaches]. Between May 1 and June 1 the provinces of North and South Holland." These wretched people are sent to filthy slaughterhouses like a herd of sick, neglected cattle. But I won't talk about it, I only get nightmares from such thoughts.

One good little piece of news is that the German department of the Labor Exchange has been set on fire by saboteurs. A few days after, the Registrar's Office went the same way. Men in German police uniforms gagged the guards and managed to destroy important papers.

Yours, Anne

Thursday, 1 April, 1943

Dear Kitty,

I'm really not April-fooling (see the date), but the opposite; today I can easily quote the saying: "Misfortunes never come singly." To begin with, Mr. Koophuis, the one who always cheers us up, has had hemorrhage of the stomach and has got to stay in bed for at least three weeks. Secondly, Elli has flu. Thirdly, Mr. Vossen is going to the hospital next week. He has probably got an abdominal ulcer. And fourthly, some important business conferences, the main points of which Daddy had discussed in detail with Mr. Koophuis, were due to be held, but now there isn't time to explain everything thoroughly to Mr. Kraler.

The gentlemen who had been expected duly arrived; even before they came Daddy was trembling with anxiety as to how the talks would go. "If only I could be there, if only I was downstairs," he cried. "Why don't you go and lie with one ear pressed against the floor, then you'll be able to hear everything." Daddy's face cleared, and at half past ten yesterday morning Margot and Pim (two ears are better than one!) took up their positions on the floor. The talks were not finished in the morning, but by the afternoon Daddy was not in a fit state to continue the listening campaign. He was half paralyzed from remaining in so unusual and uncomfortable a position. I took his place at half past two, as soon as we heard voices in the passage. Margot kept me company. The talk at times was so long-winded and boring that quite suddenly I fell asleep on the cold hard linoleum floor. Margot did not dare to touch me for fear they might hear us, and talking was out of the question. I slept for a good half hour and then woke with a shock, having forgotten every word of the important discussions. Luckily Margot had paid more attention.

Yours, Anne

Friday, 2 April, 1943

Dear Kitty,

Oh Dear: I've got another terrible black mark against my name. I was lying in bed yesterday evening waiting for Daddy to come and say my prayers with me, and wish me good night, when Mummy came into my room, sat on my bed, and asked very nicely, "Anne, Daddy can't come yet, shall I say your prayers with you tonight?" "No, Mummy," I answered.

Mummy got up, paused by my bed for a moment, and walked slowly towards the door. Suddenly she turned around, and with a distorted look on her face said, "I don't want to be cross, love cannot be forced." There were tears in her eyes as she left the room.

I lay still in bed, feeling at once that I had been horrible to push her away so rudely. But I knew too that I couldn't have answered differently. It simply wouldn't work. I felt sorry for Mummy; very, very sorry, because I had seen for the first time in my life that she minds my coldness. I saw the look of sorrow on her face when she spoke of love not being forced. It is hard to speak the truth, and yet it is the truth: she herself has pushed me away, her tactless remarks and her crude jokes, which I don't find at all funny, have now made me insensitive to any love from her side. Just as I shrink at her hard words, so did her heart when she realized that the love between us was gone. She cried half the night and hardly slept at all. Daddy doesn't look at me and if he does for a second, then I read in his eyes the words: "How can you be so unkind, how can you bring yourself to cause your mother such sorrow?"

They expect me to apologize; but this is something I can't apologize for because I spoke the truth and Mummy will have to know it sooner or later anyway. I seem, and indeed am, indifferent both to Mummy's tears and Daddy's looks, because for the first time they are both aware of something which I have always felt. I can only feel sorry for Mummy, who has now had to discover that I have adopted her own attitude. For myself, I remain silent and aloof; and I shall not shrink from the truth any longer, because the longer it is put off, the more difficult it will be for them when they do hear it.

Yours, Anne

Tuesday, 27 April, 1943

Dear Kitty,

Such quarrels that the whole house thunders! Mummy and I, the Van Daans and Daddy, Mummy and Mrs. Van Daan, everyone is angry with everyone else. Nice atmosphere, isn't it? Anne's usual list of failings has been brought out again and fully ventilated.

Mr. Vossen is already in the Binnengasthuis hospital. Mr. Koophuis is up again, the hemorrhage having stopped sooner than usual. He told us that the Registrar's Office received additional damage from the Fire Service who, instead of just quenching the flames, soaked the whole place with water. I'm glad!

The Carlton Hotel is smashed to bits. Two British planes

loaded with incendiary bombs fell right on top of the "Of-
fiziersheim."[1] The whole Vijzelstraat-Singel corner is burned
down. The air raids on German towns are growing in strength
every day. We don't have a single quiet night. I've got dark
rings under my eyes from lack of sleep. Our food is miserable. Dry bread and coffee substitute for breakfast. Dinner:
spinach or lettuce foi a fortnight on end. Potatoes twenty cen-
timeters long and tasting sweet and rotten. Whoever wants
to follow a slimming course should stay in the "Secret Annexe"! They complain bitterly upstairs, but we don't regard
it as such a tragedy. All the men who fought in 1940 or were
mobilized have been called up to work for "der Führer" as
prisoners of war. Suppose they're doing that as a precaution
against invasion.

Yours, Anne

Saturday, 1 May, 1943

Dear Kitty,

If I just think of how we live here, I usually come to the
conclusion that it is a paradise compared with how other Jews
who are not in hiding must be living. Even so, later on, when
everything is normal again, I shall be amazed to think that we,
who were so spick and span at home, should have sunk to such
a low level. By this I mean that our manners have declined.
For instance, ever since we have been here, we have had one
oilcloth on our table which, owing to so much use, is not one of
the cleanest. Admittedly I often try to clean it with a dirty
dishcloth, which is more hole than cloth. The table doesn't do
us much credit either, in spite of hard scrubbing. The Van
Daans have been sleeping on the same flannelette sheet the
whole winter; one can't wash it here because the soap powder
we get on the ration isn't sufficient, and besides it's not good
enough. Daddy goes about in frayed trousers and his tie is beginning to show signs of wear too. Mummy's corsets have split
today and are too old to be repaired, while Margot goes about
in a brassiere two sizes too small for her.

Mummy and Margot have managed the whole winter with
three vests between them, and mine are so small that they
don't even reach my tummy.

[1]German Officers' Club.

Certainly, these are all things which can be overcome. Still, I sometimes realize with a shock: "How are we, now going about in worn-out things, from my pants down to Daddy's shaving brush, ever going to get back to our prewar standards?"

They were banging away so much last night that four times I gathered all my belongings together. Today I have packed a suitcase with the most necessary things for an escape. But Mummy quite rightly says: "Where will you escape to?" The whole of Holland is being punished for the strikes which have been going on in many parts of the country. Therefore a state of siege has been declared and everyone gets one butter coupon less. What naughty little children!

Yours, Anne

Tuesday, 18 May, 1943

Dear Kitty,

I witnessed a terrific air battle between German and British planes. Unfortunately a couple of the Allies had to jump from burning machines. Our milkman, who lives in Halfweg, saw four Canadians sitting by the roadside, one of them spoke fluent Dutch. He asked the milkman to give him a light for his cigarette, and told him that the crew had consisted of six men. The pilot was burned to death, and their fifth man had hidden himself somewhere. The German police came and fetched the four perfectly fit men. I wonder how they managed to have such clear brains after that terrifying parachute trip.

Although it is fairly warm, we have to light our fires every other day, in order to burn vegetable peelings and refuse. We can't put anything in the garbage pails, because we must always think of the warehouse boy. How easily one could be betrayed by being a little careless!

All students who wish either to get their degrees this year or continue their studies, are compelled to sign that they are in sympathy with the Germans and approve of the New Order. Eighty per cent have refused to go against their consciences. Naturally they had to bear the consequences. All the students who do not sign have to go to a labor camp in Germany. What will be left of the youth of the country if they have all got to do hard labor in Germany? Mummy shut the window last night because of all the banging; I was in Pim's bed. Suddenly Mrs.

Van Daan jumped out of bed above us, just as if Mouschi had bitten her. A loud clap followed immediately. It sounded just as if an incendiary bomb had fallen beside my bed. I shrieked out, "Light, light!" Pim turned on the lamp. I expected nothing less than to see the room ablaze within a few minutes. Nothing happened. We all hurried upstairs to see what was going on. Mr. and Mrs. Van Daan had seen a red glow through the open window. He thought that there was a fire in the neighborhood and she thought that our house had caught fire. When the clap came Mrs. Van Daan was already on her feet with her knees knocking. But nothing more happened and we all crept back into our beds.

Before a quarter of an hour had passed the shooting started up again. Mrs. Van Daan sat bolt upright at once and then went downstairs to Mr. Dussel's room, seeking there the rest which she could not find with her spouse. Dussel received her with the words, "Come into my bed, my child!" which sent us off into uncontrollable laughter. The gunfire troubled us no longer, our fear was banished!

Yours, Anne

Sunday, 13 June, 1943

Dear Kitty,

My birthday poem from Daddy is too good to keep from you. As Pim usually writes verses in German, Margot volunteered to translate it. Judge for yourself whether Margot didn't do it brilliantly. After the usual summary of the events of the year, this is how it ran:

> Though youngest here, you are no longer small,
> But life is very hard, since one and all
> Aspire to be your teacher, thus and thus:
> "We have experience, take a tip from us."
> "We know because we did it long ago."
> "Elders are always better, you must know."
> At least that's been the rule since life began!
> Our personal faults are much too small to scan:
> This makes it easier to criticize
> The faults of others, which seem double size.
> Please bear with us, your parents, for we try

To judge you fairly and with sympathy.
Correction sometimes take against your will,
Though it's like swallowing a bitter pill,
Which must be done if we're to keep the peace,
While time goes by till all this suffering cease.
You read and study nearly all the day,
Who might have lived in such a different way.
You're never bored and bring us all fresh air.
Your only moan is this: "What can I wear?
I have no knickers, all my clothes are small,
My vest might be a loincloth, that is all!
To put on shoes would mean to cut off toes,
Oh dear, I'm worried by so many woes!"

There was also a bit about food that Margot could not translate into rhyme, so I shall leave it out. Don't you think my
birthday poem is good? I have been thoroughly spoiled in
other ways and received a lot of lovely things. Among other
things a fat book on my pet subject—the mythology of Greece
and Rome. I can't complain of a shortage of sweets either—
everyone has broken into their last reserves. As the Benjamin
of the family in hiding, I am really more honored than I deserve.

Yours, Anne

Tuesday, 15 June, 1943

Dear Kitty,
   Lots of things have happened, but I often think that all my
uninteresting chatter bores you very much and that you are
glad not to receive too many letters. So I shall give you the
news in brief.
   Mr. Vossen has not been operated on for his duodenal ulcer.
When he was on the operating table and they had opened him
up, the doctors saw that he had cancer, which was far too advanced to operate. So they stitched him up again, kept him in
bed for three weeks and gave him good food, and finally sent
him home again. I do pity him terribly and think it is rotten
that we can't go out, otherwise I should certainly visit him
frequently to cheer him up. It is a disaster for us that good old
Vossen won't be able to keep us in touch with all that goes on,

and all he hears in the warehouse. He was our best helper and
security adviser; we miss him very much indeed.

It will be our turn to hand in our radio next month. Koophuis
has a clandestine baby set at home that he will let us have to
take the place of our big Phillips. It certainly is a shame to have
to hand in our lovely set, but in a house where people are
hiding, one daren't, under any circumstances, take wanton
risks and so draw the attention of the authorities. We shall have
the little radio upstairs. On top of hidden Jews, clandestine
money and clandestine buying, we can add a clandestine radio.
Everyone is trying to get hold of an old set and to hand that in
instead of their "source of courage." It is really true that as the
news from outside gets worse, so the radio with its miraculous
voice helps us to keep up our morale and to say again, "Chins
up, stick it out, better times will come!"

Yours, Anne

Sunday, 11 July, 1943

Dear Kitty,

To return to the "upbringing" theme for the umpteenth time,
I must tell you that I really am trying to be helpful, friendly,
and good, and to do everything I can so that the rain of rebukes
dies down to a light summer drizzle. It is mighty difficult to be
on such model behavior with people you can't bear, especially
when you don't mean a word of it. But I do really see that I
get on better by shamming a bit, instead of my old habit of
telling everyone exactly what I think (although no one ever
asked my opinion or attached the slightest importance to it).

I often lose my cue and simply can't swallow my rage at
some injustice, so that for four long weeks we hear nothing
but an everlasting chatter about the cheekiest and most shame-
less girl on earth. Don't you think that sometimes I've cause
for complaint? It's a good thing I'm not a grouser, because then
I might get sour and bad-tempered.

I have decided to let my shorthand go a bit, firstly to give
me more time for my other subjects and secondly because of
my eyes. I'm so miserable and wretched as I've become very
shortsighted and ought to have had glasses for a long time already (phew, what an owl I shall look!) but you know, of
course, in hiding one cannot. Yesterday everyone talked of noth-

ing but Anne's eyes, because Mummy had suggested sending me to the oculist with Mrs. Koophuis. I shook in my shoes somewhat at this announcement, for it is no small thing to do. Go out of doors, imagine it, in the street—doesn't bear thinking about! I was petrified at first, then glad. But it doesn't go as easily as that, because all the people who would have to approve such a step could not reach an agreement quickly. All the difficulties and risks had first to be carefully weighed, although Miep would have gone with me straight away.

In the meantime I got out my gray coat from the cupboard, but it was so small that it looked as if it belonged to my younger sister.

I am really curious to know what will come of it all, but I don't think the plan will come off because the British have landed in Sicily now and Daddy is once again hoping for a "quick finish."

Elli gives Margot and me a lot of office work; it makes us both feel quite important and is a great help to her. Anyone can file away correspondence and write in the sales book, but we take special pains.

Miep is just like a pack mule, she fetches and carries so much. Almost every day she manages to get hold of some vegetables for us and brings everything in shopping bags on her bicycle. We always long for Saturdays when our books come. Just like little children receiving a present.

Ordinary people simply don't know what books mean to us, shut up here. Reading, learning, and the radio are our amusements.

Yours, Anne

Tuesday, 13 July, 1943

Dear Kitty,

Yesterday afternoon, with Daddy's permission, I asked Dussel whether he would please be so good (being really very polite) as to allow me to use the little table in our room twice a week in the afternoons, from four o'clock till half past five. I sit there every day from half past two till four, while Dussel sleeps, but otherwise the room plus table are out of bounds. Inside, in our common room, there is much too much going on;

it is impossible to work there, and besides, Daddy likes to sit at the writing table and work too sometimes.

So it was quite a reasonable request, and the question was put very politely. Now honestly what do you think the very learned Dussel replied: "No." Just plain "No!" I was indignant and refused to be put off like that, so I asked him the reason for his "No." But I was sent away with a flea in my ear. This was the barrage which followed:

"I have to work too, and if I can't work in the afternoons, then there is no time left for me at all. I must finish my task, otherwise I've started it all for nothing. Anyway, you don't work seriously at anything. Your mythology, now just what kind of work is that; knitting and reading are not work either. I am at the table and shall stay there." My reply was:

"Mr. Dussel, I do work seriously and there is nowhere else for me to work in the afternoons. I beg of you to kindly reconsider my request!"

With these words the offended Anne turned her back on the very learned doctor, ignoring him completely. I was seething with rage, and thought Dussel frightfully rude (which he certainly was) and myself very friendly. In the evening when I could get hold of Pim, I told him how it had gone off and discussed what I should do next, because I was not going to give in, and preferred to clear it up myself. Pim told me how I ought to tackle the problem, but warned me that it would be better to leave it till the next day, as I was so het up. I let his advice go to the winds, and waited for Dussel after the dishes were done. Pim sat in the room next to us, which had a calming influence on me. I began: "Mr. Dussel, I don't suppose you see any point in discussing the matter any more, but I must ask you to do so." Dussel then remarked with his sweetest smile: "I am always, and at all times, prepared to discuss this matter, but it has already been settled."

I went on talking, though continually interrupted by Dussel. "When you first came here we arranged that this room should be for both of us; if we were to divide it fairly, you would have the morning and I all the afternoon! But I don't even ask that much, and I think that my two afternoons are really perfectly reasonable." At this Dussel jumped up as if someone had stuck a needle into him. "You can't talk about your rights here at all. And where am I to go, then? I shall ask Mr. Van Daan whether he will build a little compartment in the attic, then I can go and sit there. I simply can't work anywhere. With you one always gets trouble. If your sister Margot, who after all has more reason to ask such a thing, would have come to me with the same questions, I should not think of refusing, but you . . ." Then followed the business about the mythology and the knitting, and Anne was insulted again. However, she did not show it and let Dussel finish speaking: "But you, one simply can't talk to you. You are so outrageously selfish, as long as you can get what you want, you don't mind pushing everyone else to one side, I've never seen such a child. But after all, I suppose I shall be obliged to give you your own way, because otherwise I shall be told later on that Anne Frank failed her exam because Mr. Dussel would not give up the table for her."

It went on and on and finally it was such a torrent I could hardly keep pace with it. At one moment I thought, "In a minute I'll give him such a smack in the face that he'll fly up to the ceiling together with his lies," but the next moment I said to myself, "Keep calm! Such a fellow isn't worth getting worked up about."

After giving final vent to his fury, Master Dussel left the room with an expression of mixed wrath and triumph, his coat stuffed with food. I dashed to Daddy and told him all that he had not already heard of the story. Pim decided to talk to Dussel the same evening, which he did. They talked for over half an hour. The theme of the conversation was something like this: first of all they talked about whether Anne should sit at the table, yes or no. Daddy said that he and Dussel had already discussed the subject once before, when he had professed to agree with Dussel, in order not to put him in the wrong in front of the young. But Daddy had not thought it fair then. Dussel thought that I should not speak as if he was an intruder who tried to monopolize everything, but Daddy stuck up for me firmly over that, because he had heard for himself that I had not breathed a word of such a thing.

To and fro it went, Daddy defending my selfishness and my "trifling" work, Dussel grumbling continually.

Finally, Dussel had to give in after all, and I had the opportunity of working undisturbed until five o'clock for two afternoons a week. Dussel looked down his nose very much, didn't speak to me for two days and still had to go and sit at the table from five till half past—frightfully childish.

A person of fifty-four who is still so pedantic and small-minded must be so by nature, and will never improve.

Yours, Anne

Friday, 16 July, 1943

Dear Kitty,

Burglars again, but real this time! This morning Peter went to the warehouse at seven o'clock as usual, and at once noticed that both the warehouse door and the door opening on to the street were ajar. He told Pim, who tuned the radio in the private office to Germany and locked the door. Then they went upstairs together.

The standing orders for such times were observed as usual: no taps to be turned on; therefore, no washing, silence, everything to be finished by eight o'clock and no lavatory. We were all very glad that we had slept so well and not heard anything. Not until half past eleven did we learn from Mr. Koophuis that the burglars had pushed in the outer door with a crowbar and had forced the warehouse door. However, they did not find much to steal, so they tried their luck upstairs. They stole two cashboxes containing forty florins, postal orders and checkbooks and then, worst of all, all the coupons for 150 kilos of sugar.

Mr. Koophuis thinks that they belonged to the same gang as the ones who tried all three doors six weeks ago. They were unsuccessful then.

It has caused rather a stir in the building, but the "Secret Annexe" can't seem to go on without sensations like this. We were very glad that the typewriters and money in our wardrobe, where they are brought upstairs every evening, were safe.

Yours, Anne

Monday, 19 July, 1943

Dear Kitty,

North Amsterdam was very heavily bombed on Sunday. The destruction seems to be terrible. Whole streets lie in ruins, and it will take a long time before all the peope are dug out. Up till now there are two hundred dead and countless wounded; the hospitals are crammed. You hear of children lost in the smoldering ruins, looking for their parents. I shudder when I recall the dull droning rumble in the distance, which for us marked the approaching destruction.

Yours, Anne

Friday, 23 July, 1943

Dear Kitty,

Just for fun I'm going to tell you each person's first wish, when we are allowed to go outside again. Margot and Mr. Van Daan long more than anything for a hot bath filled to overflowing and want to stay in it for half an hour. Mrs. Van Daan wants most to go and eat cream cakes immediately. Dussel thinks of nothing but seeing Lotje, his wife; Mummy of her cup of coffee; Daddy is going to visit Mr. Vossen first; Peter the town and a cinema, while I should find it so blissful, I shouldn't know where to start! But most of all, I long for a home of our own, to be able to move freely and to have some help with my work again at last, in other words—school.

Elli has offered to get us some fruit. It costs next to nothing—grapes f.5.00 per kilo, gooseberries f.0.70 per pound, *one* peach f.0.50, one kilo melon f.1.50.[1] Then you see in the newspapers every evening in bold letters, "Play fair and keep prices down!"

Yours, Anne

Monday, 26 July, 1943

Dear Kitty,

Nothing but tumult and uproar yesterday, we are still very het up about it all. You might really ask, does a day go by without some excitement?

We had the first warning siren while we were at breakfast, but we don't give a hoot about that, it only means that the planes are crossing the coast.

After breakfast I went and lay down for an hour as I had a bad headache, then I went downstairs. It was about two

[1]Equivalent prices, in order, would be approximately $1.40, twenty-one cents, fourteen cents, and forty-two cents.

o'clock. Margot had finished her office work at half past two: she had not packed her things together when the sirens began to wail, so upstairs I went again with her. It was high time, for we had not been upstairs five minutes when they began shooting hard, so much so that we went and stood in the passage. And yes, the house rumbled and shook, and down came the bombs.

I clasped my "escape bag" close to me, more because I wanted to have something to hold than with an idea of escaping, because there's nowhere we can go. If ever we come to the extremity of fleeing from here, the street would be just as dangerous as an air raid. This one subsided after half an hour, but the activity in the house increased. Peter came down from his lookout post in the attic, Dussel was in the main office, Mrs. Van Daan felt safe in the private office, Mr. Van Daan had been watching from the loft, and we on the little landing dispersed ourselves too: I went upstairs to see rising above the harbor the columns of smoke Mr. Van Daan had told us about. Before long you could smell burning, and outside it looked as if a thick mist hung everywhere. Although such a big fire is not a pleasant sight, luckily for us it was all over, and we went about our respective tasks. That evening at dinner: another air raid alarm! It was a nice meal, but my hunger vanished, simply at the sound of the alarm. Nothing happened and three quarters of an hour later it was all clear. The dishes were stacked ready to be done: air-raid warning, ack-ack fire, an awful lot of planes. "Oh, dear me, twice in one day, that's too much," we all thought, but that didn't help at all; once again the bombs rained down, the other side this time, on Schiphol,[1] according to the British. The planes dived and climbed, we heard the hum of their engines and it was very gruesome. Each moment I thought: "One's falling now. Here it comes."

I can assure you that when I went to bed at nine o'clock I couldn't hold my legs still. I woke up at the stroke of twelve: planes. Dussel was undressing. I didn't let that put me off, and at the first shot, I leaped out of bed, wide awake. Two hours with Daddy and still they kept coming. Then they ceased firing and I was able to go to bed. I fell asleep at half past two.

[1] Amsterdam airport.

Seven o'clock. I sat up in bed with a start. Mr. Van Daan was with Daddy. Burglars was my first thought. I heard Mr. Van Daan say "everything." I thought that everything had been stolen. But no, this time it was wonderful news, such as we have not heard for months, perhaps in all the war years. "Mussolini has resigned, the King of Italy has taken over the government." We jumped for joy. After the terrible day yesterday, at last something good again and—hope. Hope for it to end, hope for peace.

Kraler called in and told us that Fokkers has been badly damaged. Meanwhile we had another air-raid alarm with planes over head and one more warning siren. I'm just about choked with alarms, very tired and don't feel a bit like work. But now the suspense over Italy will awaken the hope that it will soon end, perhaps even this year.

Yours, Anne

Thursday, 29 July, 1943

Dear Kitty,

Mrs. Van Daan, Dussel, and I were doing the dishes and I was extraordinarily quiet, which hardly ever happens, so they would have been sure to notice.

In order to avoid questions I quickly sought a fairly neutral topic, and thought that the book *Henry from the Other Side* would meet the need. But I had made a mistake. If Mrs. Van Daan doesn't pounce on me, then Mr. Dussel does. This was what it came to: Mr. Dussel had specially recommended us this book as being excellent. Margot and I thought it was anything but excellent. The boy's character was certainly well drawn, but the rest—I had better gloss over that. I said something to that effect while we were washing the dishes, but that brought me a packet of trouble.

"How can you understand the psychology of a man! Of a child is not so difficult (!). You are much too young for a book like that; why, even a man of twenty would not be able to grasp it." (Why did he so especially recommend this book to Margot and me?) Now Dussel and Mrs. Van Daan continued together: "You know much too much about things that are unsuitable for you, you've been brought up all wrong. Later on, when you are older, you won't enjoy anything, then you'll say:

'I read that in books twenty years ago.' You had better make haste, if you want to get a husband or fall in love—or everything is sure to be a disappointment to you. You are already proficient in the theory, it's only the practice that you still lack!"

I suppose it's their idea of a good upbringing to always try to set me against my parents, because that is what they often do. And to tell a girl of my age nothing about "grown-up" subjects is an equally fine method! I see the results of that kind of upbringing frequently and all too clearly.

I could have slapped both their faces at that moment as they stood there making a fool of me. I was beside myself with rage and I'm just counting the days until I'm rid of "those" people.

Mrs. Van Daan is a nice one! She sets a fine example . . . she certainly sets one—a bad one. She is well known as being very pushing, selfish, cunning, calculating, and is never content. I can also add vanity and coquetry to the list. There is no question about it, she is an unspeakably disagreeable person. I could write whole chapters about Madame, and who knows, perhaps I will someday. Anyone can put on a fine coat of varnish outside. Mrs. Van Daan is friendly to strangers and especially men, so it is easy to make a mistake when you have only known her for a short time. Mummy thinks she is too stupid to waste words over, Margot too unimportant, Pim too ugly (literally and figuratively), and I, after long observation—for I was never prejudiced from the start—have come to the conclusion that she is all three and a lot more! She has so many bad qualities, why should I even begin about one of them?

Yours, Anne

P.S.—Will the reader take into consideration that when this story was written the writer had not cooled down from her fury!

Tuesday, 3 August, 1943

Dear Kitty,

Political news excellent. In Italy the Fascist party has been banned. The people are fighting the Fascists in many places— even the army is actually taking part in the battle. Can a country like that wage war against England?

We've just had a third air raid; I clenched my teeth together to make myself feel courageous. Mrs. Van Daan, who has always said, "A terrible end is better than no end at all," is the greatest coward of us all now. She was shaking like a leaf this morning and even burst into tears. When her husband, with whom she has just made it up after a week's squabbling, comforted her, the expression on her face alone almost made me feel sentimental.

Mouschi has proved that keeping cats has disadvantages as well as advantages. The whole house is full of fleas, and the plague gets worse every day. Mr. Koophuis has scattered yellow powder in every nook and corner, but the fleas don't seem to mind a bit. It's making us all quite nervous; one keeps imagining an itch on one's arms, legs, and various parts of the body, which is why quite a lot of us are doing gymnastics, so as to be able to look at the back of our necks or legs while standing up. Now we're being paid back for not being more supple—we're too stiff to even turn our heads properly. We gave up real gymnastics long ago.

Yours, Anne

Wednesday, 4 August, 1943

Dear Kitty,

Now that we have been in the "Secret Annexe" for over a year, you know something of our lives, but some of it is quite indescribable. There is so much to tell, everything is so different from ordinary times and from ordinary people's lives. But still, to give you a closer look into our lives, now and again I intend to give you a description of an ordinary day. Today I'm beginning with the evening and night.

Nine o'clock in the evening. The bustle of going to bed in the "Secret Annexe" begins and it is always really quite a business. Chairs are shoved about, beds are pulled down, blankets unfolded, nothing remains where it is during the day. I sleep on the little divan, which is not more than one and a half meters long. So chairs have to be used to lengthen it. A quilt, sheets, pillows, blankets, are all fetched from Dussel's bed where they remain during the day. One hears terrible creaking in the next room: Margot's concertina-bed being pulled out. Again, divan, blankets, and pillows, everything is done to make the wooden slats a bit more comfortable. It sounds like thunder above, but it is only Mrs. Van Daan's bed. This is shifted to the window, you see, in order to give Her Majesty in the pink bed jacket fresh air to tickle her dainty nostrils!

After Peter's finished, I step into the washing cubicle, where I give myself a thorough wash and general toilet; it occasionally happens (only in the hot weeks or months) that there is a tiny flea floating in the water. Then teeth cleaning, hair curling, manicure, and my cotton-wool pads with hydrogen peroxide (to bleach black mustache hairs)—all this in under half an hour.

Half past nine. Quickly into dressing gown, soap in one hand, pottie, hairpins, pants, curlers, and cotton wool in the other, I hurry out of the bathroom; but usually I'm called back once for the various hairs which decorate the washbasin in graceful curves, but which are not approved of by the next person.

Ten o'clock. Put up the blackout. Good night! For at least a quarter of an hour there is creaking of beds and a sighing of broken springs, then all is quiet, at least that is if our neighbors upstairs don't quarrel in bed.

Half past eleven. The bathroom door creaks. A narrow strip of light falls into the room. A squeak of shoes, a large coat, even larger than the man inside it—Dussel returns from his night work in Kraler's office. Shuffling on the floor for ten minutes, crackle of paper (that is the food which has to be stowed away), and a bed is made. Then the form disappears again and one only hears suspicious noises from the lavatory from time to time.

Three o'clock. I have to get up for a little job in the metal pot under my bed, which is on a rubber mat for safety's sake in case of leakage. When this has to take place, I always hold my breath, as it clatters into the tin like a brook from a mountain. Then the pot is returned to its place and the figure in the white nightgown, which evokes the same cry from Margot every evening: "Oh, that indecent nightdress!" steps back into bed.

Then a certain person lies awake for about a quarter of an hour, listening to the sounds of the night. Firstly, to whether there might not be a burglar downstairs, then to the various beds, above, next door, and in my room, from which one is usually able to make out how the various members of the household are sleeping, or how they pass the night in wakefulness.

The latter is certainly not pleasant, especially when it concerns a member of the family by the name of Dussel. First, I hear a sound like a fish gasping for breath, this is repeated nine or ten times, then with much ado and interchanged with little smacking sounds, the lips are moistened, followed by a lengthy twisting and turning in bed and rearranging of pillows. Five minutes' perfect peace and then the same sequence of events unfolds itself at least three times more, after the doctor has soothed himself to sleep again for a little while. It can also happen that we get a bit of shooting in the night, varying between one o'clock and four. I never really realize it, until from habit I am already standing at my bedside. Sometimes I'm so busy dreaming that I'm thinking about French irregular verbs or a quarrel upstairs. It is some time before I begin to realize that guns are firing and that I am still in the room. But it usually happens as described abɔve. I quickly grab a pillow and handkerchief, put on my dressing gown and slippers, and scamper to Daddy, like Margot wrote in this birthday poem:

> The first shot sounds at dead of night.
> Hush, look! A door creaks open wide,
> A little girl glides into sight,
> Clasping a pillow to her side.

Once landed in the big bed, the worst is over, except if the firing gets very bad.

Quarter to seven. Trrrrr—the alarm clock that raises its voice at any hour of the day (if one asks for it and sometimes when one doesn't). Crack—ping—Mrs. Van Daan has turned it off. Creak—Mr. Van Daan gets up. Puts on water and then full speed to the bathroom.

Quarter past seven. The door creaks again. Dussel can go to the bathroom. Once alone, I take down the blackout—and a new day in the "Secret Annexe" has begun.

Yours, Anne

Thursday, 5 August, 1943

Dear Kitty,

Today I am going to take lunchtime.

It is half past twelve. The whole mixed crowd breathes again.

The warehouse boys have gone home now. Above one can hear the noise of Mrs. Van Daan's vacuum cleaner on her beautiful, and only, carpet. Margot goes with a few books under her arm for her Dutch lesson "for children who make no progress," because that's Dussel's attitude. Pim goes into a corner with his inseparable Dickens to try and find peace somewhere. Mummy hurries upstairs to help the industrious housewife, and I go to the bathroom to tidy it up a bit, and myself at the same time.

Quarter to one. The place is filling up. First Mr. Van Santen, then Koophuis or Kraler, Elli and sometimes Miep as well.

One o'clock. We're all sitting listening to the B.B.C., seated around the baby wireless; these are the only times when the members of the "Secret Annexe" do not interrupt each other, because now someone is speaking whom even Mr. Van Daan can't interrupt.

Quarter past one. The great share-out. Everyone from below gets a cup of soup and if there is ever a pudding, some of that as well. Mr. Van Santen is happy and goes to sit on the divan or lean against the writing table. Newspaper, cup, and usually the cat, beside him. If one of the three is missing he's sure to protest. Koophuis tells us the latest news from town, he is certainly an excellent source of information. Kraler comes helter-skelter upstairs—a short, firm knock on the door and in he comes rubbing his hands, according to his mood, in a good temper and talkative, or bad-tempered and quiet.

Quarter to two. Everyone rises from the table and goes about his own business. Margot and Mummy to the dishes. Mr. and Mrs. Van Daan to their divan. Peter up to the attic. Daddy to the divan downstairs. Dussel to his bed and Anne to her work. Then follows the most peaceful hour; everyone is asleep, no one is disturbed. Dussel dreams of lovely food—the expression on his face gives this away, but I don't look long because the time goes so fast and at four o'clock the pedantic doctor is standing, clock in hand, because I'm one minute late in clearing the table for him.

Yours, Anne

Monday, 9 August, 1943

Dear Kitty,

To continue the "Secret Annexe" daily timetable. I shall now describe the evening meal:

Mr. Van Daan begins. He is first to be served, takes a lot of everything if it is what he likes. Usually talks at the same time, always gives his opinion as the only one worth listening to, and once he has spoken it is irrevocable. Because if anyone *dares* to question it, then he flares up at once. Oh, he can spit like a cat—I'd rather not argue, I can tell you—if you've *once* tried you don't try again. He has the best opinion, he knows the most about everything. All right then, he has got brains, but "self-satisfaction" has reached a high grade with this gentleman.

Madame. Really, I should remain silent. Some days, especially if there is a bad mood coming on, you can't look at her face. On closer examination, she is the guilty one in all the arguments. Not the subject! Oh, no, everyone prefers to remain aloof over that, but one could perhaps call her the "kindler." Stirring up trouble, that's fun. Mrs. Frank against Anne; Margot against Daddy doesn't go quite so easily.

But now at table, Mrs. Van Daan doesn't go short, although she thinks so at times. The tiniest potatoes, the sweetest mouthful, the best of everything; picking over is her system. The others will get their turn, as long as I have the best. Then talking. Whether anyone is interested, whether they are listening or not, that doesn't seem to matter. I suppose she thinks: "Everyone is interested in what Mrs. Van Daan says." Coquettish smiles, behaving as if one knew everything, giving everyone a bit of advice and encouragement, that's *sure* to make a good impression. But if you look longer, then the good soon wears off.

One, she is industrious, two, gay, three, a coquette—and, occasionally, pretty. This is Petronella Van Daan.

The third table companion. One doesn't hear much from him. Young Mr. Van Daan is very quiet and doesn't draw much attention to himself. As for appetite: a Danaïdean vessel, which is never full and after the heartiest meal declares quite calmly that he could have eaten double.

Number four—Margot. Eats like a little mouse and doesn't talk at all. The only things that go down are vegetables and fruit. "Spoiled" is the Van Daans' judgment; "not enough fresh air and games" our opinion.

Beside her—Mummy. Good appetite, very talkative. No one has the impression, as Mrs. Van Daan: this is the housewife. What is the difference? Well, Mrs. Van Daan does the cooking, and Mummy washes up and polishes.

Numbers six and seven. I won't say much about Daddy and me. The former is the most unassuming of all at table. He looks first to see if everyone else has something. He needs nothing himself, for the best things are for the children. He is the perfect example, and sitting beside him, the "Secret Annexe's" "bundle of nerves."

Dr. Dussel. Helps himself, never looks up, eats and doesn't talk. And if one must talk, then for heaven's sake let it be about food. You don't quarrel about it, you only brag. Enormous helpings go down and the word "No" is never heard, never when the food is good, and not often when it's bad. Trousers wrapping his chest, red coat, black bedroom slippers, and horn-rimmed spectacles. That is how one sees him at the little table, always working, alternated only by his afternoon nap, food, and—his favorite spot—the lavatory. Three, four, five times a day someone stands impatiently in front of the door and wriggles, hopping from one foot to the other, hardly able to contain himself. Does it disturb him? Not a bit! From quarter past seven till half past, from half past twelve till one o'clock, from two till quarter past, from four till quarter past, from six till quarter past, and from half past eleven until twelve. One can make a note of it—these are the regular "sitting times." He won't come off or pay any heed to an imploring voice at the door, giving warning of approaching disaster!

Number nine isn't a member of the "Secret Annexe" family, but rather a companion in the house and at table. Elli has a healthy appetite. Leaves nothing on her plate and is not picky-and-choosy. She is easy to please and that is just what gives us pleasure. Cheerful and good-tempered, willing and good-natured, these are her characteristics.

Yours, Anne

Tuesday, 10 August, 1943

Dear Kitty,

New idea. I talk more to myself than to the others at meal-times, which is to be recommended for two reasons. Firstly, because everyone is happy if I don't chatter the whole time, and secondly, I needn't get annoyed about other people's opinions. I don't think my opinions are stupid and the others do; so it is better to keep them to myself. I do just the same if I have to eat something that I simply can't stand. I put my plate in front of me, pretend that it is something delicious, look at it as little as possible, and before I know where I am, it is gone. When I get up in the morning, also a very unpleasant process, I jump out of bed thinking to myself: "You'll be back in a second," go to the window, take down the blackout, sniff at the crack of the window until I feel a bit of fresh air, and I'm awake. The bed is turned down as quickly as possible and then the temptation is removed. Do you know what Mummy calls this sort of thing? "The Art of Living"—that's an odd expression. For the last week we've all been in a bit of a muddle about time, because our dear and beloved Westertoren clock bell has apparently been taken away for war purposes, so that neither by day nor night do we ever know the exact time. I still have some hope that they will think up a substitute (tin, copper or some such thing) to remind the neighborhood of the clock.

Whether I'm upstairs or down, or wherever I am, my feet are the admiration of all, glittering in a pair of (for these days) exceptionally fine shoes. Miep managed to get hold of them secondhand for 27.50 florins, wine-colored suede leather with fairly high wedge heels. I feel as if I'm on stilts and look much taller than I am.

Dussel has indirectly endangered our lives. He actually let Miep bring a forbidden book for him, one which abuses Mussolini and Hitler. On the way she happened to be run into by an S.S. car. She lost her temper, shouted, "Miserable wretches," and rode on. It is better not to think of what might have happened if she had had to go to their headquarters.

Yours, Anne

Wednesday, 18 August, 1943

Dear Kitty,

The title for this piece is: "The communal task of the day: potato peeling!"

One person fetches the newspapers, another the knives (keeping the best for himself, of course), a third potatoes, and the fourth a pan of water.

Mr. Dussel begins, does not always scrape well, but scrapes incessantly, glancing right and left. Does everyone do it the way he does? No! "Anne, look here; I take the knife in my hand like this, scrape from the top downwards! No, not like that—like this!"

"I get on better like *this*, Mr. Dussel," I remark timidly.

"But still this is the best way. But *du kannst* take *dies* from me. Naturally I don't care a bit, *aber du* must know for yourself." We scrape on. I look slyly once in my neighbor's direction. He shakes his head thoughtfully once more (over me, I suppose) but is silent.

I scrape on again. Now I look to the other side, where Daddy is sitting; for him scraping potatoes is not just a little odd job, but a piece of precision work. When he reads, he has a deep wrinkle at the back of his head, but if he helps prepare potatoes, beans, or any other vegetables, then it seems as if nothing else penetrates. Then he has on his "potato face," and he would never hand over an imperfectly scraped potato; it's out of the question when he makes that face!

I work on again and then just look up for a second; I know it already. Mrs. Van Daan is trying to attract Dussel's attention. First she looks in his direction and Dussel appears not to notice anything. Then she winks an eye; Dussel works on. Then she laughs, Dussel doesn't look up. Then Mummy laughs too; Dussel takes no notice. Mrs. Van Daan has not achieved anything, so she has to think of something else. A pause and then: "Putti, do put on an apron! Tomorrow I shall have to get all the spots out of your suit!"

"I'm not getting myself dirty!"

Another moment's silence.

"Putti, why don't you sit down?"

"I'm comfortable standing up and prefer it!" Pause.

"Putti, look, *du spatst schon!*" ("You are making a mess!")

"Yes, Mammy, I'm being careful."

Mrs. Van Daan searches for another subject. "I say, Putti, why aren't there any English air raids now?"

"Because the weather is bad, Kerli."

"But it was lovely yesterday, and they didn't fly then either."

"Let's not talk about it."

"Why, surely one can talk about it, or give one's opinion?"

"No."

"Why ever not?"

"Do be quiet, mammi'chen."

"Mr. Frank always answers his wife, doesn't he?"

Mr. Van Daan wrestles with himself. This is his tender spot, it's something he can't take and Mrs. Van Daan begins again: "The invasion seems as if it will never come!"

Mr. Van Daan goes white; when Mrs. Van Daan sees this, she turns red, but goes on again: "The British do nothing!" The bomb explodes!

"And now hold your tongue, *donnerwetter-noch-einmal!*"

Mummy can hardly hold back her laughter. I look straight in front of me.

This sort of thing happens nearly every day, unless they have just had a very bad quarrel, because then they both keep their mouths shut.

I have to go up to the attic to fetch some potatoes. Peter is busy there delousing the cat. He looks up, the cat notices—pop— he has disappeared through the open window into the gutter. Peter swears. I laugh and disappear.

Yours, Anne

Friday, 20 August, 1943

Dear Kitty,

The men in the warehouse go home sharp at half past five and then we are free.

Half past five. Elli comes to give us our evening freedom. Immediately we begin to make some headway with our work. First, I go upstairs with Elli, where she usually begins by having a bite from our second course.

Before Elli is seated, Mrs. Van Daan begins thinking of things she wants. It soon comes out: "Oh, Elli, I have only one little wish. . . ." Elli winks at me; whoever comes upstairs, Mrs. Van Daan never misses a single opportunity of letting them know what she wants. That must be one of the reasons why none of them like coming upstairs.

Quarter to six. Elli departs. I go two floors down to have a look around. First to the kitchen, then to the private office, after that the coalhole, to open the trap door for Mouschi. After a long tour of inspection I land up in Kraler's room. Van Daan is looking in all the drawers and portfolios to find the day's post. Peter is fetching the warehouse key and Boche; Pim is hauling the typewriters upstairs; Margot is looking for a quiet spot to do her office work; Mrs. Van Daan puts a kettle on the gas ring; Mummy is coming downstairs with a pan of potatoes; each one knows his own job.

Peter soon returns from the warehouse. The first question is —bread. This is always put in the kitchen cupboard by the Ladies; but it is not there. Forgotten? Peter offers to look in the main office. He crouches in front of the door to make himself as small as possible and crawls towards the steel lockers on hands and knees, so as not to be seen from outside, gets the bread, which had been put there, and disappears; at least, he wants to disappear, but before he quite realizes what has happened, Mouschi has jumped over him and gone and sat right under the writing table.

Peter looks all around—aha, he sees him there, he crawls into the office again and pulls the animal by its tail. Mouschi spits, Peter sighs. What has he achieved? Now Mouschi is sitting right up by the window cleaning himself, very pleased to have escaped Peter. Now Peter is holding a piece of bread under the cat's nose as a last decoy. Mouschi will not be tempted and the door closes. I stood and watched it all through the crack of the door. We work on. Rat, tat, tat. Three taps means a meal!

Yours, Anne

Monday, 23 August, 1943

Dear Kitty,

Continuation of the "Secret Annexe" daily timetable. As the clock strikes half past eight in the morning, Margot and

Mummy are jittery: "Ssh . . . Daddy, quiet, Otto, ssh . . . Pim." "It is half past eight, come back here, you can't run any more water; walk quietly!" These are the various cries to Daddy in the bathroom. As the clock strikes half past eight, he has to be in the living room. Not a drop of water, no lavatory, no walking about, everything quiet. As long as none of the office staff are there, everything can be heard in the warehouse. The door is opened upstairs at twenty minutes past eight and shortly after there are three taps on the floor: Anne's porridge. I climb upstairs and fetch my "puppy-dog" plate. Down in my room again, everything goes at terrific speed: do my hair, put away my noisy tin pottie, bed in place. Hush, the clock strikes! Upstairs Mrs. Van Daan has changed her shoes and is shuffling about in bedroom slippers. Mr. Van Daan, too; all is quiet.

Now we have a little bit of real family life. I want to read or work, Margot as well, also Daddy and Mummy. Daddy is sitting (with Dickens and the dictionary, naturally) on the edge of the sagging, squeaky bed, where there aren't even any decent mattresses: two bolsters on top of each other will also serve the purpose, then he thinks: "Mustn't have them, then I'll manage without!"

Once he is reading he doesn't look up, or about him, laughs every now and then, takes awful trouble to get Mummy interested in a little story. Answer: "I haven't got time now." Looks disappointed for just a second, then reads on again; a little later, when he comes to something extra amusing, he tries it again: "You must read this, Mummy!" Mummy sits on the "Opklap"[1] bed, reads, sews, knits, or works, whatever she feels like. She suddenly thinks of something. Just says it quickly: "Anne, do you know . . . Margot, just jot down . . . !" After a while peace returns once more.

Margot closes her book with a clap. Daddy raises his eyebrows into a funny curve, his reading wrinkle deepens again, and he is lost in his book once more; Mummy begins to chatter with Margot, I become curious and listen too! Pim is drawn into the discussion . . . nine o'clock! Breakfast!

Yours, Anne

[1]Dutch type of bed, which folds against the wall to look like a bookcase with curtains hanging before it.

Friday, 10 September, 1943

Dear Kitty,

Every time I write to you something special seems to have happened, but they are more often unpleasant than pleasant things. However, now there is something wonderful going on. Last Wednesday evening, 8 September, we sat around listening to the seven o'clock news and the first thing we heard was: "Here follows the best news of the whole war. Italy has capitulated!" Italy's unconditional surrender! The Dutch program from England began at quarter past eight. "Listeners, an hour ago, I had just finished writing the chronicle of the day when the wonderful news of Italy's capitulation came in. I can tell you that I have never deposited my notes in the wastepaper basket with such joy!" "God Save the King," the American national anthem, and the "Internationale" were played. As always, the Dutch program was uplifting, but not too optimistic.

Still we have troubles, too; it's about Mr. Koophuis. As you know, we are all very fond of him, he is always cheerful and amazingly brave, although he is never well, has a lot of pain, and is not allowed to eat much or do much walking. "When Mr. Koophuis enters, the sun begins to shine," Mummy said just recently, and she is quite right. Now he has had to go into the hospital for a very unpleasant abdominal operation and will have to stay there for at least four weeks. You really ought to have seen how he said good-by to us just as usual—he might have simply been going out to do a bit of shopping.

Yours, Anne

Thursday, 16 September, 1943

Dear Kitty,

Relations between us here are getting worse all the time. At mealtimes, no one dares to open their mouths (except to allow a mouthful of food to slip in) because whatever is said you either annoy someone or it is misunderstood. I swallow Valerian pills every day against worry and depression, but it doesn't prevent me from being even more miserable the next day. A good hearty laugh would help more than ten Valerian pills, but we've almost forgotten how to laugh. I feel afraid sometimes that from having to be so serious I'll grow a long face and my mouth will droop at the corners. The others don't get any better either, everyone looks with fear and misgivings towards that great terror, winter. Another thing that does not cheer us up is the fact that the warehouseman, V.M., is becoming suspicious about the "Secret Annexe." We really wouldn't mind what V.M. thought of the situation if he wasn't so exceptionally inquisitive, difficult to fob off, and, moreover, not to be trusted. One day Kraler wanted to be extra careful, put on his coat at ten minutes to one, and went to the chemist round the corner. He was back in less than five minutes, and sneaked like a thief up the steep stairs that led straight to us. At a quarter past one he wanted to go again, but Elli came to warn him that V.M. was in the office. He did a right-about turn and sat with us until half past one. Then he took off his shoes and went in stockinged feet to the front attic door, went downstairs step by step, and, after balancing there for a quarter of an hour to avoid creaking, he landed safely in the office, having entered from the outside. Elli had been freed of V.M. in the meantime, and came up to us to fetch Kraler, but he had already been gone a long time; he was still on the staircase with his shoes off. Whatever would the people in the street have thought if they had seen the Manager putting on his shoes outside? Gosh! the Manager in his socks!

Yours, Anne

Wednesday, 29 September, 1943

Dear Kitty,

It is Mrs. Van Daan's birthday. We gave her a pot of jam, as well as coupons for cheese, meat, and bread. From her husband, Dussel, and our protectors she received things to eat and flowers. Such are the times we live in!

Elli had a fit of nerves this week; she had been sent out so often; time and again she had been asked to go and fetch something quickly, which meant yet another errand or made her feel that she had done something wrong. If you just think that she still has to finish her office work downstairs, that Koophuis is ill, Miep at home with a cold, and that she herself has a sprained ankle, love worries, and a grumbling father, then it's no wonder she's at her wit's end. We comforted her and said that if she puts her foot down once or twice and says she has no time, then the shopping lists will automatically get shorter.

There is something wrong with Mr. Van Daan again, I can see it coming on already! Daddy is very angry for some reason or other. Oh, what kind of explosion is hanging over us now? If only I wasn't mixed up so much with all these rows! If I could only get away! They'll drive us crazy before long!

Yours, Anne

Sunday, 17 October, 1943

Dear Kitty,

Koophuis is back again, thank goodness! He still looks rather pale, but in spite of this sets out cheerfully to sell clothes for Van Daan. It is an unpleasant fact that the Van Daans have run right out of money. Mrs. Van Daan won't part with a thing from her pile of coats, dresses, and shoes. Mr. Van Daan's suit isn't easily disposed of, because he wants too much for it. The end of the story is not yet in sight. Mrs. Van Daan will certainly have to part with her fur coat. They've had a terrific row upstairs about it, and now the reconciliation period of "oh, darling Putti" and "precious Kerli" has set in.

I am dazed by all the abusive exchanges that have taken place in this virtuous house during the past month. Daddy goes about with his lips tightly pursed; when anyone speaks to him, he looks up startled, as if he is afraid he will have to patch up some tricky relationship again. Mummy has red patches on her cheeks from excitement. Margot complains of headaches. Dussel can't sleep. Mrs. Van Daan grouses the whole day and I'm going completely crazy! Quite honestly, I sometimes forget who we are quarreling with and with whom we've made it up.

The only way to take one's mind off it all is to study, and I do a lot of that.

Yours, Anne

Friday, 29 October, 1943

Dear Kitty,

There have been resounding rows again between Mr. and Mrs. Van Daan. It came about like this: as I have already told you, the Van Daans are at the end of their money. One day, some time ago now, Koophuis spoke about a furrier with whom he was on good terms; this gave Van Daan the idea of selling his wife's fur coat. It's a fur coat made from rabbit skins, and she has worn it seventeen years. He got 325 florins for it—an enormous sum. However, Mrs. Van Daan wanted to keep the money to buy new clothes after the war, and it took some doing before Mr. Van Daan made it clear to her that the money was urgently needed for the household.

The yells and screams, stamping and abuse—you can't possibly imagine it! It was frightening. My family stood at the bottom of the stairs, holding their breath, ready if necessary to drag them apart! All this shouting and weeping and nervous tension are so unsettling and such a strain, that in the evening I drop into my bed crying, thanking heaven that I sometimes have half an hour to myself.

Mr. Koophuis is away again; his stomach gives him no peace. He doesn't even know whether it has stopped bleeding yet. For the first time, he was very down when he told us that he didn't feel well and was going home.

All goes well with me on the whole, except that I have no appetite. I keep being told: "You don't look at all well." I must say that they are doing their very best to keep me up to the mark. Grape sugar, cod-liver oil, yeast tablets, and calcium have all been lined up.

My nerves often get the better of me: it is especially on Sundays that I feel rotten. The atmosphere is so oppressive, and sleepy and as heavy as lead. You don't hear a single bird singing outside, and a deadly close silence hangs everywhere, catching hold of me as if it will drag me down deep into an underworld.

At such times Daddy, Mummy, and Margot leave me cold. I wander from one room to another, downstairs and up again, feeling like a songbird whose wings have been clipped and who is hurling himself in utter darkness against the bars of his cage. "Go outside, laugh, and take a breath of fresh air," a voice cries within me, but I don't even feel a response any more; I go and lie on the divan and sleep, to make the time pass more quickly, and the stillness and the terrible fear, because there is no way of killing them.

Yours, Anne

Wednesday, 3 November, 1943

Dear Kitty,

In order to give us something to do, which is also educational, Daddy applied for a prospectus from the Teachers' Institute in Leiden. Margot nosed through the thick book at least three times without finding anything to her liking or to suit her purse. Daddy was quicker, and wants a letter written to the Institute asking for a trial lesson in "Elementary Latin."

To give me something new to begin as well, Daddy asked Koophuis for a children's Bible so that I could find out something about the New Testament at last. "Do you want to give Anne a Bible for Chanuka?" asked Margot, somewhat perturbed. "Yes—er, I think St. Nicholas Day is a better occasion," answered Daddy; "Jesus just doesn't go with Chanuka."[1]

Yours, Anne

Monday evening, 8 November, 1943

Dear Kitty,

If you were to read my pile of letters one after another, you would certainly be struck by the many different moods in which they are written. It annoys me that I am so dependent on the atmosphere here, but I'm certainly not the only one—we all find it the same. If I read a book that impresses me, I have to take myself firmly in hand, before I mix with other people; otherwise they would think my mind rather queer. At the moment, as you've probably noticed, I'm going through a spell of being depressed. I really couldn't tell you why it is, but I believe it's just because I'm a coward, and that's what I keep bumping up against.

This evening, while Elli was still here, there was a long, loud, penetrating ring at the door. I turned white at once, got a tummy-ache and heart palpitations, all from fear. At night, when I'm in bed, I see myself alone in a dungeon, without Mummy and Daddy. Sometimes I wander by the roadside, or our "Secret Annexe" is on fire, or they come and take us away at night. I see everything as if it is actually taking place, and this gives me the feeling that it may all happen to me very

[1]See entry for 7 December, 1942.

soon! Miep often says she envies us for possessing such tranquillity here. That may be true, but she is not thinking about
all our fears. I simply can't imagine that the world will ever be
normal for us again. I do talk about "after the war," but then
it is only a castle in the air, something that will never really
happen. If I think back to our old house, my girl friends, the
fun at school, it is just as if another person lived it all, not me.

I see the eight of us with our "Secret Annexe" as if we were
a little piece of blue heaven, surrounded by heavy black rain
clouds. The round, clearly defined spot where we stand is still
safe, but the clouds gather more closely about us and the circle
which separates us from the approaching danger closes more
and more tightly. Now we are so surrounded by danger and
darkness that we bump against each other, as we search desperately for a means of escape. We all look down below, where
people are fighting each other, we look above, where it is quiet
and beautiful, and meanwhile we are cut off by the great dark
mass, which will not let us go upwards, but which stands before
us as an impenetrable wall; it tries to crush us, but cannot
do so yet. I can only cry and implore: "Oh, if only the black
circle could recede and open the way for us!"

Yours, Anne

Thursday, 11 November, 1943

Dear Kitty,
I have a good title for this chapter:

ODE TO MY FOUNTAIN PEN
IN MEMORIAM

My fountain pen has always been one of my most priceless
possessions; I value it highly, especially for its thick nib, for I
can only really write neatly with a thick nib. My fountain pen
has had a very long and interesting pen-life, which I will
briefly tell you about.

When I was nine, my fountain pen arrived in a packet
(wrapped in cotton wool) as "sample without value" all the
way from Aachen, where my Grandmother, the kind donor,
used to live. I was in bed with flu, while February winds
howled round the house. The glorious fountain pen had a red

leather case and was at once shown around to all my friends. I, Anne Frank, the proud owner of a fountain pen! When I was ten I was allowed to take the pen to school and the mistress went so far as to permit me to write with it.

When I was eleven, however, my treasure had to be put away again, because the mistress in the sixth form only allowed us to use school pens and inkpots.

When I was twelve and went to the Jewish Lyceum,[1] my fountain pen received a new case in honor of the great occasion; it could take a pencil as well, and as it closed with a zipper looked much more impressive.

At thirteen the fountain pen came with us to the "Secret Annexe," where it has raced through countless diaries and compositions for me.

Now I am fourteen, we have spent our last year together.

It was on a Friday afternoon after five o'clock. I had come out of my room and wanted to go and sit at the table to write, when I was roughly pushed on one side and had to make room for Margot and Daddy, who wanted to practice their "Latin." The fountain pen remained on the table unused while, with a sigh, its owner contented herself with a tiny little corner of the table and started rubbing beans. "Bean rubbing" is making moldy beans decent again. I swept the floor at a quarter to six and threw the dirt, together with the bad beans, into a newspaper and into the stove. A terrific flame leaped out and I thought it was grand that the fire should burn up so well when it was practically out. All was quiet again, the "Latinites" had finished, and I went and sat at the table to clear up my writing things, but look as I might, my fountain pen was nowhere to be seen. I looked again, Margot looked, but there was not a trace of the thing. "Perhaps it fell into the stove together with the beans," Margot suggested. "Oh, no, of course not!" I answered. When my fountain pen didn't turn up that evening, however, we all took it that it had been burned, all the more as celluloid is terribly inflammable.

And so it was, our unhappy fears were confirmed; when Daddy did the stove the following morning the clip used for fastening was found among the ashes. Not a trace of the gold

[1] A type of secondary school specializing in the classics, common in most continental countries.

nib was found. "Must have melted and stuck to some stone or other," Daddy thought.

I have one consolation, although a slender one: my fountain pen has been cremated, just what I want later!

Yours, Anne

Wednesday, 17 November, 1943

Dear Kitty,

Shattering things are happening. Diphtheria reigns in Elli's home, so she is not allowed to come into contact with us for six weeks. It makes it very awkward over food and shopping, not to mention missing her companionship. Koophuis is still in bed and has had nothing but porridge and milk for three weeks. Kraler is frantically busy.

The Latin lessons Margot sends in are corrected by a teacher and returned, Margot writing in Elli's name. The teacher is very nice, and witty, too. I expect he is glad to have such a clever pupil.

Dussel is very put out, none of us knows why. It began by his keeping his mouth closed upstairs; he didn't utter a word to either Mr. or Mrs. Van Daan. Everyone was struck by it, and when it lasted a couple of days, Mummy took the opportunity of warning him about Mrs. Van Daan, who, if he went on like this, could make things very disagreeable for him.

Dussel said that Mr. Van Daan started the silence, so he was not going to be the one to break it.

Now I must tell you that yesterday was the sixteenth of November, the day he had been exactly one year in the "Secret Annexe." Mummy received a plant in honor of the occasion, but Mrs. Van Daan, who for weeks beforehand had made no bones about the fact that she thought Dussel should treat us to something, received nothing.

Instead of expressing, for the first time, his thanks for our unselfishness in taking him in, he didn't say a word. And when I asked him, on the morning of the sixteenth, whether I should congratulate or condole, he answered that it didn't matter to him. Mummy, who wanted to act as peacemaker, didn't get one step further, and finally the situation remained as it was.

Der Man hat einen grossen Geist
Und ist so klein von Taten![1]

Yours, Anne

Saturday, 27 November, 1943

Dear Kitty,

Yesterday evening, before I fell asleep, who should suddenly appear before my eyes but Lies!

I saw her in front of me, clothed in rags, her face thin and worn. Her eyes were very big and she looked so sadly and reproachfully at me that I could read in her eyes: "Oh, Anne, why have you deserted me? Help, oh, help me, rescue me from this hell!"

And I cannot help her, I can only look on, how others suffer and die, and can only pray to God to send her back to us.

I just saw Lies, no one else, and now I understand. I misjudged her and was too young to understand her difficulties. She was attached to a new girl friend, and to her it seemed as though I wanted to take her away. What the poor girl must have felt like, I know; I know the feeling so well myself!

Sometimes, in a flash, I saw something of her life, but a moment later I was selfishly absorbed again in my own pleasures and problems. It was horrid of me to treat her as I did, and now she looked at me, oh so helplessly, with her pale face and imploring eyes. If only I could help her!

Oh, God, that I should have all I could wish for and that she should be seized by such a terrible fate. I am not more virtuous than she; she, too, wanted to do what was right, why should I be chosen to live and she probably to die? What was the difference between us? Why are we so far from each other now?

Quite honestly, I haven't thought about her for months, yes, almost for a year. Not completely forgotten her, but still I had never thought about her like this, until I saw her before me in all her misery.

Oh, Lies, I hope that, if you live until the end of the war,

[1](The spirit of the man is great,
How puny are his deeds!)

you will come back to us and that I shall be able to take you in and do something to make up for the wrong I did you.

But when I am able to help her again, then she will not need my help so badly as now. I wonder if she ever thinks of me; if so, what would she feel?

Good Lord, defend her, so that at least she is not alone. Oh, if only You could tell her that I think lovingly of her and with sympathy, perhaps that would give her greater endurance.

I must not go on thinking about it, because I don't get any further. I only keep seeing her great big eyes, and cannot free myself from them. I wonder if Lies has real faith in herself, and not only what has been thrust upon her?

I don't even know, I never took the trouble to ask her!

Lies, Lies, if only I could take you away, if only I could let you share all the things I enjoy. It is too late now, I can't help, or repair the wrong I have done. But I shall never forget her again, and I shall always pray for her.

Yours, Anne

Monday, 6 December, 1943

Dear Kitty,

When St. Nicholas' Day approached, none of us could help thinking of the prettily decorated basket we had last year and I, especially, thought it would be very dull to do nothing at all this year. I thought a long time about it, until I invented something, something funny.

I consulted Pim, and a week ago we started composing a little poem for each person.

On Sunday evening at a quarter to eight we appeared upstairs with the large laundry basket between us, decorated with little figures, and bows of pink and blue carbon copy paper. The basket was covered with a large piece of brown paper, on which a letter was pinned. Everyone was rather astonished at the size of the surprise package.

I took the letter from the paper and read:

> "Santa Claus has come once more,
>   Though not quite as he came before;
>   We can't celebrate his day
>   In last year's fine and pleasant way.

For then our hopes were high and bright,
All the optimists seemed right,
None supposing that this year
We would welcome Santa here.
Still, we'll make his spirit live,
And since we've nothing left to give,
We've thought of something else to do
Each please look inside his shoe."

As each owner took his shoe from the basket there was a resounding peal of laughter. A little paper package lay in each shoe with the address of the shoe's owner on it.

Yours, Anne

Wednesday, 22 December, 1943

Dear Kitty,

A bad attack of flu has prevented me from writing to you until today. It's wretched to be ill here. When I wanted to cough—one, two, three—I crawled under the blankets and tried to stifle the noise. Usually the only result was that the tickle wouldn't go away at all; and milk and honey, sugar or lozenges had to be brought into operation. It makes me dizzy to think of all the cures that were tried on me. Sweating, compresses, wet cloths on my chest, dry cloths on my chest, hot drinks, gargling, throat painting, lying still, cushion for extra warmth, hot-water bottles, lemon squashes, and, in addition, the thermometer every two hours!

Can anyone really get better like this? The worst moment of all was certainly when Mr. Dussel thought he'd play doctor, and came and lay on my naked chest with his greasy head, in order to listen to the sounds within. Not only did his hair tickle unbearably, but I was embarrassed, in spite of the fact that he once, thirty years ago, studied medicine and has the title of Doctor. Why should the fellow come and lie on my heart? He's not my lover, after all! For that matter, he wouldn't hear whether it's healthy or unhealthy inside me anyway; his ears need syringing first, as he's becoming alarmingly hard of hearing.

But that is enough about illness. I'm as fit as a fiddle again, one centimeter taller, two pounds heavier, pale, and with a real appetite for learning.

There is not much news to tell you. We are all getting on well together for a change! There's no quarreling—we haven't had such peace in the home for at least half a year. Elli is still parted from us.

We received extra oil for Christmas, sweets and syrup; the "chief present" is a brooch, made out of a two-and-a-half-cent piece, and shining beautifully. Anyway, lovely, but indescribable. Mr. Dussel gave Mummy and Mrs. Van Daan a lovely cake which he had asked Miep to bake for him. With all her work, she has to do that as well! I have also something for Miep and Elli. For at least two months I have saved the sugar from my porridge, you see, and with Mr. Koophuis's help I'll have it made into fondants.

It is drizzly weather, the stove smells, the food lies heavily on everybody's tummy, causing thunderous noises on all sides! The war at a standstill, morale rotten.

Yours, Anne

Friday, 24 December, 1943

Dear Kitty,

I have previously written about how much we are affected by atmospheres here, and I think that in my own case this trouble is getting much worse lately.

"*Himmelhoch jauchzend und zum Tode betrübt*"[1] certainly fits here. I am "*Himmelhoch jauchzend*" if I only think how lucky we are here compared with other Jewish children, and "*zum Tode betrübt*" comes over me when, as happened today, for example, Mrs. Koophuis comes and tells us about her daughter Corry's hockey club, canoe trips, theatrical performances, and friends. I don't think I'm jealous of Corry, but I couldn't help feeling a great longing to have lots of fun myself for once, and to laugh until my tummy ached. Especially at this time of the year with all the holidays for Christmas and the New Year, and we are stuck here like outcasts. Still, I really ought not to write this, because it seems ungrateful and I've certainly been exaggerating. But still, whatever you think

---

[1] A famous line from Goëthe: "On top of the world, or in the depths of despair."

of me, I can't keep everything to myself, so I'll remind you of my opening words—"Paper is patient."

When someone comes in from outside, with the wind in their clothes and the cold on their faces, then I could bury my head in the blankets to stop myself thinking: "When will we be granted the privilege of smelling fresh air?" And because I must not bury my head in the blankets, but the reverse—I must keep my head high and be brave, the thoughts will come, not once, but oh, countless times. Believe me, if you have been shut up for a year and a half, it can get too much for you some days. In spite of all justice and thankfulness, you can't crush your feelings. Cycling, dancing, whistling, looking out into the world, feeling young, to know that I'm free—that's what I long for; still, I mustn't show it, because I sometimes think if all eight of us began to pity ourselves, or went about with dis-contented faces, where would it lead us? I sometimes ask my-self, "Would anyone, either Jew or non-Jew, understand this about me, that I am simply a young girl badly in need of some rollicking fun?" I don't know, and I couldn't talk about it to anyone, because then I know I should cry. Crying can bring such relief.

In spite of all my theories, and however much trouble I take, each day I miss having a real mother who understands me. That is why with everything I do and write I think of the "Mumsie" that I want to be for my children later on. The "Mumsie" who doesn't take everything that is said in general conversation so seriously, but who does take what *I* say seri-ously. I have noticed, though I can't explain how, that the word "Mumsie" tells you everything. Do you know what I've found? To give me the feeling of calling Mummy something which sounds like "Mumsie" I often call her "Mum"; then from that comes "Mums": the incomplete "Mumsie," as it were, whom I would so love to honor with the extra "ie" and yet who does not realize it. It's a good thing, because it would only make her unhappy.

That's enough about that, writing has made my *"zum Tode betrübt"* go off a bit.

Yours, Anne

Saturday, 25 December, 1943

Dear Kitty,

During these days, now that Christmas is here, I find myself thinking all the time about Pim, and what he told me about the love of his youth. Last year I didn't understand the meaning of his words as well as I do now. If he'd only talk about it again, perhaps I would be able to show him that I understand.

I believe that Pim talked about it because he who "knows the secrets of so many other hearts" had to express his own feelings for once; because otherwise Pim never says a word about himself, and I don't think Margot has any idea of all Pim has had to go through. Poor Pim, he can't make *me* think that he has forgotten everything. He will never forget this. He has become very tolerant. I hope that I shall grow a bit like him, without having to go through all that.

Yours, Anne

Monday, 27 December, 1943

Dear Kitty,

On Friday evening for the first time in my life I received something for Christmas. Koophuis, Kraler and the girls had prepared a lovely surprise again. Miep has made a lovely Christmas cake, on which was written "Peace 1944." Elli had provided a pound of sweet biscuits of prewar quality. For Peter, Margot, and me a bottle of yoghourt, and a bottle of beer for each of the grownups. Everything was so nicely done up, and there were pictures stuck on the different packages. Otherwise Christmas passed by quickly for us.

Yours, Anne

Wednesday, 29 December, 1943

Dear Kitty,

I was very unhappy again last evening. Granny and Lies came into my mind. Granny, oh, darling Granny, how little we understood of what she suffered, or how sweet she was. And besides all this, she knew a terrible secret which she carefully kept to herself the whole time.[1] How faithful and good

[1] A severe internal disease.

Granny always was; she would never have let one of us down. Whatever it was, however naughty I had been, Granny always stuck up for me.

Granny, did you love me or didn't you understand me either? I don't know. No one ever talked about themselves to Granny. How lonely Granny must have been, how lonely in spite of us! A person can be lonely even if he is loved by many people, because he is still not the "One and Only" to anyone.

And Lies, is she still alive? What is she doing? Oh, God, protect her and bring her back to us. Lies, I see in you all the time what my lot might have been, I keep seeing myself in your place. Why then should I often be unhappy over what happens here? Shouldn't I always be glad, contented, and happy, except when I think about her and her companions in distress? I am selfish and cowardly. Why do I always dream and think of the most terrible things—my fear makes me want to scream out loud sometimes. Because still, in spite of everything, I have not enough faith in God. He has given me so much —which I certainly do not deserve—and I still do so much that is wrong every day. If you think of your fellow creatures, then you only want to cry, you could really cry the whole day long. The only thing to do is to pray that God will perform a miracle and save some of them. And I hope that I am doing that enough!

Yours, Anne

Sunday, 2 January, 1944

Dear Kitty,

This morning when I had nothing to do I turned over some of the pages of my diary and several times I came across letters dealing with the subject "Mummy" in such a hotheaded way that I was quite shocked, and asked myself: "Anne, is it really you who mentioned hate? Oh, Anne, how could you!" I remained sitting with the open page in my hand, and thought about it and how it came about that I should have been so brimful of rage and really so filled with such a thing as hate that I had to confide it all in you. I have been trying to understand the Anne of a year ago and to excuse her, because my conscience isn't clear as long as I leave you with these accusations, without being able to explain, on looking back, how it happened.

I suffer now—and suffered then—from moods which kept my head under water (so to speak) and only allowed me to see the things subjectively without enabling me to consider quietly the words of the other side, and to answer them as the words of one whom I, with my hotheaded temperament, had offended or made unhappy.

I hid myself within myself, I only considered myself and quietly wrote down all my joys, sorrows, and contempt in my diary. This diary is of great value to me, because it has become a book of memoirs in many places, but on a good many pages I could certainly put "past and done with."

I used to be furious with Mummy, and still am sometimes. It's true that she doesn't understand me, but I don't understand her either. She did love me very much and she was tender, but as she landed in so many unpleasant situations through me, and was nervous and irritable because of other worries and difficulties, it is certainly understandable that she snapped at me.

I took it much too seriously, was offended, and was rude and aggravating to Mummy, which, in turn, made her unhappy. So it was really a matter of unpleasantness and misery rebounding all the time. It wasn't nice for either of us, but it is passing.

I just didn't want to see all this, and pitied myself very much; but that, too, is understandable. Those violent outbursts on paper were only giving vent to anger which in a normal life could have been worked off by stamping my feet a couple of times in a locked room, or calling Mummy names behind her back.

The period when I caused Mummy to shed tears is over. I have grown wiser and Mummy's nerves are not so much on edge. I usually keep my mouth shut if I get annoyed, and so does she, so we appear to get on much better together. I can't really love Mummy in a dependent childlike way—I just don't have that feeling.

I soothe my conscience now with the thought that it is better for hard words to be on paper than that Mummy should carry them in her heart.

Yours, Anne

Wednesday, 5 January, 1944

Dear Kitty,

I have two things to confess to you today, which will take a long time. But I must tell someone and you are the best one to tell, as I know that, come what may, you always keep a secret.

The first is about Mummy. You know that I've grumbled a lot about Mummy, yet still tried to be nice to her again. Now it is suddenly clear to me what she lacks. Mummy herself has told us that she looked upon us more as her friends than her daughters. Now that is all very fine, but still, a friend can't take a mother's place. I need my mother as an example which I can follow, I want to be able to respect her. I have the feeling that Margot thinks differently about these things and would never be able to understand what I've just told you. And Daddy avoids all arguments about Mummy.

I imagine a mother as a woman who, in the first place, shows great tact, especially towards her children when they reach our age, and who does not laugh at me if I cry about something —not pain, but other things—like "Mums" does.

One thing, which perhaps may seem rather fatuous, I have never forgiven her. It was on a day that I had to go to the dentist. Mummy and Margot were going to come with me, and agreed that I should take my bicycle. When we had finished at the dentist, and were outside again, Margot and Mummy told me that they were going into the town to look at something or buy something—I don't remember exactly what. I wanted to go, too, but was not allowed to, as I had my bicycle with me. Tears of rage sprang into my eyes, and Mummy and Margot began laughing at me. Then I became so furious that I stuck my tongue out at them in the street just as an old woman happened to pass by, who looked very shocked! I rode home on my bicycle, and I know I cried for a long time.

It is queer that the wound that Mummy made then still burns, when I think of how angry I was that afternoon.

The second is something that is very difficult to tell you, because it is about myself.

Yesterday I read an article about blushing by Sis Heyster. This article might have been addressed to me personally. Although I don't blush very easily, the other things in it certainly all fit me. She writes roughly something like this—that a girl in the years of puberty becomes quiet within and begins to think about the wonders that are happening to her body.

I experience that, too, and that is why I get the feeling lately of being embarrassed about Margot, Mummy, and Daddy. Funnily enough, Margot, who is much more shy than I am, isn't at all embarrassed.

I think what is happening to me is so wonderful, and not only what can be seen on my body, but all that is taking place inside. I never discuss myself or any of these things with anybody; that is why I have to talk to myself about them.

Each time I have a period—and that has only been three times—I have the feeling that in spite of all the pain, unpleasantness, and nastiness, I have a sweet secret, and that is why, although it is nothing but a nuisance to me in a way, I always long for the time that I shall feel that secret within me again.

Sis Heyster also writes that girls of this age don't feel quite certain of themselves, and discover that they themselves are individuals with ideas, thoughts, and habits. After I came here, when I was just fourteen, I began to think about myself sooner than most girls, and to know that I am a "person." Sometimes, when I lie in bed at night, I have a terrible desire to feel my breasts and to listen to the quiet rhythmic beat of my heart.

I already had these kinds of feelings subconsciously before I came here, because I remember that once when I slept with a girl friend I had a strong desire to kiss her, and that I did do so. I could not help being terribly inquisitive over her body, for she had always kept it hidden from me. I asked her whether, as a proof of our friendship, we should feel one another's breasts, but she refused. I go into ecstasies every time I see the naked figure of a woman, such as Venus, for example. It strikes me as so wonderful and exquisite that I have difficulty in stopping the tears rolling down my cheeks.

If only I had a girl friend!

Yours, Anne

Thursday, 6 January, 1944

Dear Kitty,

My longing to talk to someone became so intense that some-how or other I took it into my head to choose Peter.

Sometimes if I've been upstairs into Peter's room during the day, it always struck me as very snug, but because Peter is so retiring and would never turn anyone out who became a nuisance, I never dared stay long, because I was afraid he might think me a bore. I tried to think of an excuse to stay in his room and get him talking, without it being too noticeable, and my chance came yesterday. Peter has a mania for cross-word puzzles at the moment and hardly does anything else. I helped him with them and we soon sat opposite each other at his little table, he on the chair and me on the divan.

It gave me a queer feeling each time I looked into his deep blue eyes, and he sat there with that mysterious laugh playing round his lips. I was able to read his inward thoughts. I could see on his face that look of helplessness and uncertainty as to how to behave, and, at the same time, a trace of his sense of manhood. I noticed his shy manner and it made me feel very gentle; I couldn't refrain from meeting those dark eyes again and again, and with my whole heart I almost beseeched him: oh, tell me, what is going on inside you, oh, can't you look beyond this ridiculous chatter?

But the evening passed and nothing happened, except that I told him about blushing—naturally not what I have written but just so that he would become more sure of himself as he grew older.

When I lay in bed and thought over the whole situation, I found it far from encouraging, and the idea that I should beg for Peter's patronage was simply repellent. One can do a lot to satisfy one's longings, which certainly sticks out in my case, for I have made up my mind to go and sit with Peter more often and to get him talking somehow or other.

Whatever you do, don't think I'm in love with Peter—not a bit of it! If the Van Daans had had a daughter instead of a son, I should have tried to make friends with her too.

I woke at about five to seven this morning and knew at once, quite positively, what I had dreamed. I sat on a chair and opposite me sat Peter . . . Wessel. We were looking together at a book of drawings by Mary Bos. The dream was so vivid that I can still partly remember the drawings. But that was not all—the dream went on. Suddenly Peter's eyes met mine and I looked into those fine, velvet brown eyes for a long time. Then Peter said very softly, "If I had only known, I would have come to you long before!" I turned around brusquely because the emotion was too much for me. And after that I felt a soft, and oh, such a cool kind cheek against mine and it felt so good, so good. . . .

I awoke at this point, while I could still feel his cheek against mine and felt his brown eyes looking deep into my heart, so deep, that there he read how much I had loved him and how much I still love him. Tears sprang into my eyes once more, and I was very sad that I had lost him again, but at the same time glad because it made me feel quite certain that Peter was still the chosen one.

It is strange that I should often see such vivid images in my dreams here. First I saw Gramdma[1] so clearly one night that I could even distinguish her thick, soft, wrinkled velvety skin. Then Granny appeared as a guardian angel; then followed Lies, who seems to be a symbol to me of the sufferings of all my girl friends and all Jews. When I pray for her, I pray for all Jews and all those in need. And now Peter, my darling Peter—never before have I had such a clear picture of him in my mind. I don't need a photo of him, I can see him before my eyes, and oh, so well!

Yours, Anne

Friday, 7 January, 1944

Dear Kitty,

What a silly ass I am! I am quite forgetting that I have never told you the history of myself and all my boys friends.

When I was quite small—I was even still at a kindergarten —I became attached to Karel Samson. He had lost his father, and he and his mother lived with an aunt. One of Karel's cousins, Robby, was a slender, good-looking dark boy, who aroused more admiration than the little, humorous fellow, Karel. But looks did not count with me and I was very fond of Karel for years.

---

[1]Grandma is grandmother on Father's side, Granny on Mother's side.

We used to be together a lot for quite a long time, but for the rest, my love was unreturned.

Then Peter crossed my path, and in my childish way I really fell in love. He liked me very much, too, and we were inseparable for one whole summer. I can still remember us walking hand in hand through the streets together, he in a white cotton suit and me in a short summer dress. At the end of the summer holidays he went into the first form of the high school and I into the sixth form of the lower school. He used to meet me from school and, vice versa, I would meet him. Peter was a very good-looking boy, tall, handsome, and slim, with an earnest, calm, intelligent face. He had dark hair, and wonderful brown eyes, ruddy cheeks, and a pointed nose. I was mad about his laugh, above all, when he looked so mischievous and naughty!

I went to the country for the holidays; when I returned, Peter had in the meantime moved, and a much older boy lived in the same house. He apparently drew Peter's attention to the fact that I was a childish little imp, and Peter gave me up. I adored him so that I didn't want to face the truth. I tried to hold on to him until it dawned on me that if I went on running after him I should soon get the name of being boy-mad. The years passed. Peter went around with girls of his own age and didn't even think of saying "Hello" to me any more; but I couldn't forget him.

I went to the Jewish Secondary School. Lots of boys in our class were keen on me—I thought it was fun, felt honored, but was otherwise quite untouched. Then later on, Harry was mad about me, but, as I've already told you, I never fell in love again.

There is a saying "Time heals all wounds," and so it was with me. I imagined that I had forgotten Peter and that I didn't like him a bit any more. The memory of him, however, lived so strongly in my subconscious mind that I admitted to myself sometimes I was jealous of the other girls, and that was why I didn't like him any more. This morning I knew that nothing has changed; on the contrary, as I grew older and more mature my love grew with me. I can quite understand now that Peter thought me childish, and yet it still hurt that he had so completely forgotten me. His face was shown so clearly to me, and now I know that no one else could remain with me like he does.

I am completely upset by the dream. When Daddy kissed

me this morning, I could have cried out: "Oh, if only you were Peter!" I think of him all the time and I keep repeating to myself the whole day, "Oh, Petel, darling, darling Petel . . . !"

Who can help me now? I must live on and pray to God that He will let Peter cross my path when I come out of here, and that when he reads the love in my eyes he will say, "Oh, Anne, if I had only known, I would have come to you long before!"

I saw my face in the mirror and it looks quite different. My eyes look so clear and deep, my cheeks are pink—which they haven't been for weeks—my mouth is much softer; I look as if I am happy, and yet there is something so sad in my expression and my smile slips away from my lips as soon as it has come. I'm not happy, because I might know that Peter's thoughts are not with me, and yet I still feel his wonderful eyes upon me and his cool soft cheek against mine.

Oh, Petel, Petel, how will I ever free myself of your image? Wouldn't any other in your place be a miserable substitute? I love you, and with such a great love that it can't grow in my heart any more but has to leap out into the open and suddenly manifest itself in such a devastating way!

A week ago, even yesterday, if anyone had asked me, "Which of your friends do you consider would be the most suitable to marry?" I would have answered, "I don't know"; but now I would cry, "Petel, because I love him with all my heart and soul. I give myself completely!" But one thing, he may touch my face, but no more.

Once, when we spoke about sex, Daddy told me that I couldn't possibly understand the longing yet; I always knew that I did understand it and now I understand it fully. Nothing is so beloved to me now as he, my Petel.

Yours, Anne

Wednesday, 12 January, 1944

Dear Kitty,

Elli has been back a fortnight. Miep and Henk were away from their work for two days—they both had tummy upsets.

I have a craze for dancing and ballet at the moment, and practice dance steps every evening diligently. I have made a supermodern dance frock from a light blue petticoat edged with lace belonging to Mansa. A ribbon is threaded through round the top and ties in a bow in the center, and a pink corded ribbon completes the creation. I tried in vain to convert my gym shoes into real ballet shoes. My stiff limbs are well on the way to becoming supple again like they used to be. One terrific exercise is to sit on the floor, hold a heel in each hand, and then lift both legs up in the air. I have to have a cushion under me, otherwise my poor little behind has a rough time.

Everyone here is reading the book *Cloudless Morn.* Mummy thought it exceptionally good; there are a lot of youth problems in it. I thought to myself rather ironically: "Take a bit more trouble with your own young people first!"

I believe Mummy thinks there could be no better relationship between parents and their children, and that no one could take a greater interest in their children's lives than she. But quite definitely she only looks at Margot, who I don't think ever had such problems and thoughts as I do. Still, I wouldn't dream of pointing out to Mummy that, in the case of her daughters, it isn't at all as she imagines, because she would be utterly amazed and wouldn't know how to change anyway; I want to save her the unhappiness it would cause her, especially as I know that for me everything would remain the same anyway.

Mummy certainly feels that Margot loves her much more than I do, but she thinks that this just goes in phases! Margot has grown so sweet; she seems quite different from what she used to be, isn't nearly so catty these days and is becoming a real friend. Nor does she any longer regard me as a little kid who counts for nothing.

I have an odd way of sometimes, as it were, being able to see myself through someone else's eyes. Then I view the affairs of a certain "Anne" at my ease, and browse through the pages of her life as if she were a stranger. Before we came here, when I didn't think about things as much as I do now, I used at times to have the feeling that I didn't belong to Mansa, Pim, and Margot, and that I would always be a bit of an outsider. Sometimes I used to pretend I was an orphan, until I reproached and punished myself, telling myself it was all my own fault that I played this self-pitying role, when I was really so fortunate. Then came the time that I used to force myself to be friendly. Every morning, as soon as someone came downstairs I hoped that it would be Mummy who would say good morning to me; I greeted her warmly, because I really longed for her to look lovingly at me. Then she made some remark or other that seemed unfriendly, and I would go off to school again feeling thoroughly disheartened. On the way home I would make excuses for her because she had so many worries, arrive home very cheerful, chatter nineteen to the dozen, until I began repeating myself, and left the room wearing a pensive expression, my satchel under my arm. Sometimes I decided to remain cross, but when I came home from school I always had so much news that my resolutions were gone with the wind and Mummy, whatever she might be doing, had to lend an ear to all my adventures. Then the time came once more when I didn't listen for footsteps on the staircase any longer, and at night my pillow was wet with tears.

Everything grew much worse at that point; *enfin,* you know all about it.

Now God has sent me a helper—Peter . . . I just clasp my pendant, kiss it, and think to myself, "What do I care about the lot of them! Peter belongs to me and no one knows anything about it." This way I can get over all the snubs I receive. Who would ever think that so much can go on in the soul of a young girl?

Yours, Anne

Saturday, 15 January, 1944

Dear Kitty,

There is no point in telling you every time the exact details of our rows and arguments. Let it suffice to tell you that we have divided up a great many things, such as butter and meat, and that we fry our own potatoes. For some time now we've been eating whole-meal bread between meals as an extra, because by four o'clock in the afternoon we are longing for our supper so much that we hardly know how to control our rumbling tummies.

Mummy's birthday is rapidly approaching. She got some extra sugar from Kraler, which made the Van Daans jealous as Mrs. Van Daan had not been favored in this way for her birthday. But what's the use of annoying each other with yet more unkind words, tears, and angry outbursts. You can be sure of one thing, Kitty, that we are even more fed up with them than ever! Mummy has expressed the wish—one which cannot come true just now—not to see the Van Daans for a fortnight.

I keep asking myself, whether one would have trouble in the long run, whoever one shared a house with. Or did we strike it extra unlucky? Are most people so selfish and stingy then? I think it's all to the good to have learned a bit about human beings, but now I think I've learned enough. The war goes on just the same, whether or not we choose to quarrel, or long for freedom and fresh air, and so we should try to make the best of our stay here. Now I'm preaching, but I also believe that if I stay here for very long I shall grow into a dried-up old beanstalk. And I did so want to grow into a real young woman!

Yours, Anne

Saturday, 22 January, 1944

Dear Kitty,

I wonder whether you can tell me why it is that people always try so hard to hide their real feelings? How is it that I always behave quite differently from what I should in other people's company?

Why do we trust one another so little? I know there must be a reason, but still I sometimes think it's horrible that you find you can never really confide in people, even in those who are nearest to you.

It seems as if I've grown up a lot since my dream the other night. I'm much more of an "independent being." You'll certainly be amazed when I tell you that even my attitude towards the Van Daans has changed. I suddenly see all the arguments and the rest of it in a different light, and am not as prejudiced as I was.

How can I have changed so much? Yes, you see it suddenly struck me that if Mummy had been different, a real Mumsie, the relationship might have been quite, quite different. It's true that Mrs. Van Daan is by no means a nice person, but still I do think that half the quarrels could be avoided if it weren't for the fact that when the conversation gets tricky Mummy is a bit difficult too.

Mrs. Van Daan has one good side, and that is that you can

talk to her. Despite all her selfishness, stinginess, and under-handedness, you can make her give in easily, as long as you don't irritate her and get on the wrong side of her. This way doesn't work every time, but if you have patience you can try again and see how far you get.

All the problems of our "upbringing," of our being spoiled, the food—it could have been quite different if we'd remain perfectly open and friendly, and not always only on the lookout for something to seize on.

I know exactly what you'll say, Kitty: "But, Anne, do these words really come from *your* lips? From you, who have had to listen to so many harsh words from the people upstairs, from you, the girl who has suffered so many injustices?" And yet they come from me.

I want to start afresh and try to get to the bottom of it all, not be like the saying "the young always follow a bad example." I want to examine the whole matter carefully myself and find out what is true and what is exaggerated. Then if I myself am disappointed in them, I can adopt the same line as Mummy and Daddy; if not, I shall try first of all to make them alter their ideas and if I don't succeed I shall stick to my own opinions and judgment. I shall seize every opportunity to discuss openly all our points of argument with Mrs. Van Daan and not be afraid of declaring myself neutral, even at the cost of being called a "know-all." It is not that I shall be going against my own family, but from today there will be no more unkind gossip on my part.

Until now I was immovable! I always thought the Van Daans were in the wrong, but we too are partly to blame. We have certainly been right over the subject matter; but handling of others from intelligent people (which we consider ourselves to be!) one expects more insight. I hope that I have acquired a bit of insight and will use it well when the occasion arises.

Yours, Anne

Monday, 24 January, 1944

Dear Kitty,

Something has happened to me; or rather, I can hardly describe it as an event, except that I think it is pretty crazy. Whenever anyone used to speak of sexual problems at home or at school, it was something either mysterious or revolting. Words which had any bearing on the subject were whispered, and often if someone didn't understand he was laughed at. It struck me as very odd and I thought, "Why are people so secretive and tiresome when they talk about these things?" But as I didn't think that I could change things, I kept my mouth shut as much as possible, or sometimes asked girl friends for information. When I had learned quite a lot and had also spoken about it with my parents, Mummy said one day, "Anne, let me give you some good advice; never speak about this subject to boys and don't reply if they begin about it." I remember exactly what my answer was: I said, "No, of course not! The very idea!" And there it remained.

When we first came here, Daddy often told me about things that I would really have preferred to hear from Mummy, and I found out the rest from books and things I picked up from conversations. Peter Van Daan was never as tiresome over this as the boys at school—once or twice at first perhaps—but he never tried to get me talking.

Mrs. Van Daan told us that she had never talked about these things to Peter, and for all she knew neither had her husband. Apparently she didn't even know how much he knew.

Yesterday, when Margot, Peter, and I were peeling potatoes, somehow the conversation turned to Boche. "We still don't know what sex Boche is, do we?" I asked.

"Yes, certainly," Peter answered. "He's a tom."

I began to laugh. "A tomcat that's expecting, that's marvelous!"

Peter and Margot laughed too over this silly mistake. You see, two months ago, Peter had stated that Boche would soon be having a family, her tummy was growing visibly. However, the fatness appeared to come from the many stolen bones, because the children didn't seem to grow fast, let alone make their appearance!

Peter just had to defend himself. "No," he said, "You can go with me yourself to look at him. Once when I was playing around with him, I noticed quite clearly that he's a tom."

I couldn't control my curiosity, and went with him to the warehouse. Boche, however, was not receiving visitors, and was nowhere to be seen. We waited for a while, began to get cold, and went upstairs again. Later in the afternoon I heard

Peter go downstairs for the second time. I mustered up all my courage to walk through the silent house alone, and reached the warehouse. Boche stood on the packing table playing with Peter, who had just put him on the scales to weigh him.

"Hello, do you want to see him?" He didn't make any lengthy preparations, but picked up the animal, turned him over on to his back, deftly held his head and paws together, and the lesson began. "These are the male organs, these are just a few stray hairs, and that is his bottom." The cat did another half turn and was standing on his white socks once more.

If any other boy had shown me "the male organs," I would never have looked at him again. But Peter went on talking quite normally on what is otherwise such a painful subject, without meaning anything unpleasant, and finally put me sufficiently at my ease for me to be normal too. We played with Boche, amused ourselves, chattered together, and then sauntered through the large warehouse towards the door.

"Usually, when I want to know something, I find it in some book or other, don't you?" I asked.

"Why on earth? I just ask upstairs. My father knows more than me and has had more experience in such things."

We were already on the stairs, so I kept my mouth shut after that.

"Things may alter," as Brer Rabbit said. Yes. Really I shouldn't have discussed these things in such a normal way with a girl. I know too definitely that Mummy didn't mean it that way when she warned me not to discuss the subject with boys. I wasn't quite my usual self for the rest of the day though, in spite of everything. When I thought over our talk, it still seemed rather odd. But at least I'm wiser about one thing, that there really are young people—and of the opposite sex too— who can discuss these things naturally without making fun of them.

I wonder if Peter really does ask his parents much. Would he honestly behave with them as he did with me yesterday? Ah, what would I know about it!

Yours, Anne

Thursday, 27 January, 1944

Dear Kitty,

Lately I have developed a great love for family trees and
genealogical tables of the royal families, and have come to
the conclusion that, once you begin, you want to delve still
deeper into the past, and can keep on making fresh and interesting discoveries. Although I am extraordinarily industrious
over my lessons, and can already follow the English Home
Service quite well on the wireless, I still devote many Sundays
to sorting and looking over my large collection of film stars,
which is quite a respectable size by now.

I am awfully pleased whenever Mr. Kraler brings the
Cinema and Theater with him on Mondays. Although this
little gift is often called a waste of money by the less worldly
members of the household, they are amazed each time at
how accurately I can state who is in a certain film, even after
a year. Elli, who, on her days off, often goes to the movies
with her boy friend, tells me the titles of the new films each
week; and in one breath I rattle off the names of the stars who
appear in them, together with what the reviews say. Not so
long ago, Mum said that I wouldn't need to go to a cinema
later on because I knew the plots, the names of the stars, and
the opinions of the reviews all by heart.

If ever I come sailing in with a new hair style, they all look
disapprovingly at me, and I can be quite sure that someone
will ask which glamorous star I'm supposed to be imitating.
They only half believe me if I reply that it's my own inven-
tion.

But to continue about the hair style—it doesn't stay put for
more than half an hour; then I'm so tired of the remarks people
pass that I quickly hasten to the bathroom and restore my
ordinary house-garden-kitchen hair style.

Yours, Anne

Friday, 28 January, 1944

Dear Kitty,

I asked myself this morning whether you don't sometimes
feel rather like a cow who has had to chew over all the old
pieces of news again and again, and who finally yawns loudly

and silently wishes that Anne would occasionally dig up something new.

Alas, I know it's dull for you, but try to put yourself in my place, and imagine how sick I am of the old cows who keep having to be pulled out of the ditch again. If the conversation at mealtimes isn't over politics or a delicious meal, then Mummy or Mrs. Van Daan trot out one of the old stories of their youth, which we've heard so many times before; or Dussel twaddles on about his wife's extensive wardrobe, beautiful race horses, leaking rowboats, boys who can swim at the age of four, muscular pains and nervous patients. What it all boils down to is this —that if one of the eight of us opens his mouth, the other seven can finish the story for him! We all know the point of every joke from the start, and the storyteller is alone in laughing at his witticisms. The various milkmen, grocers, and butchers of the two ex-housewives have already grown beards in our minds, so often have they been praised to the skies or pulled to pieces; it is impossible for anything in the conversation here to be fresh or new.

Still, all this would be bearable if the grownups didn't have their little way of telling the stories, with which Koophuis, Henk, or Miep oblige the company, ten times over and adding their own little frills and furbelows, so that I often have to pinch my arm under the table to prevent myself from putting them right. Little children such as Anne must never, under any circumstances, know better than the grownups, however many blunders they make, and to whatever extent they allow their imaginations to run away with them.

One favorite subject of Koophuis's and Henk's is that of people in hiding and in the underground movement. They know very well that anything to do with other people in hiding interests us tremendously, and how deeply we can sympathize with the sufferings of people who get taken away, and rejoice with the liberated prisoner.

We are quite as used to the idea of going into hiding, or "underground," as in bygone days one was used to Daddy's bedroom slippers warming in front of the fire.

There are a great number of organizations, such as "The Free Netherlands," which forge identity cards, supply money to people "underground," find hiding places for people, and work for young men in hiding, and it is amazing how much noble, unselfish work these people are doing, risking their own lives to help and save others. Our helpers are a very good example. They have pulled us through up till now and we hope they will bring us safely to dry land. Otherwise, they will have to share the same fate as the many others who are being searched for. Never have we heard *one* word of the burden which we certainly must be to them, never has one of them complained of all the trouble we give.

They all come upstairs every day, talk to the men about business and politics, to the women about food and wartime difficulties, and about newspapers and books with the children. They put on the brightest possible faces, bring flowers and presents for birthdays and bank holidays, are always ready to help and do all they can. That is something we must never forget; although others may show heroism in the war or against the Germans, our helpers display heroism in their cheerfulness and affection.

The wildest tales are going around, but still they are usually founded on fact. For instance, Koophuis told us this week that in Gelderland two football elevens met, and one side consisted solely of members of the "underground" and the other was made up of members of the police. New ration books are being handed out in Hilversum. In order that the many people in hiding may also draw rations, the officials have given instructions to those of them in the district to come at a certain time, so that they can collect their documents from a separate little table. Still, they'll have to be careful that such impudent tricks do not reach the ears of the Germans.

Yours, Anne

Thursday, 3 February, 1944

Dear Kitty,

Invasion fever in the country is mounting daily. If you were here, on the one hand, you would probably feel the effect of all these preparations just as I do and, on the other, you would laugh at us for making such a fuss—who knows—perhaps for nothing.

All the newspapers are full of the invasion and are driving people mad by saying that "In the event of the English landing in Holland, the Germans will do all they can to defend the country; if necessary they will resort to flooding." With this, maps have been published, on which the parts of Holland that will be under water are marked. As this applies to large parts of Amsterdam, the first question was, what shall we do if the water in the streets rises to one meter? The answers given by different people vary considerably.

"As walking or cycling is out of the question, we shall have to wade through the stagnant water."

"Of course not, one will have to try and swim. We shall all put on our bathing suits and caps and swim under water as much as possible, then no one will see that we are Jews."

"Oh, what nonsense! I'd like to see the ladies swimming, if the rats started biting their legs!" (That was naturally a man: just see who screams the loudest!)

"We shan't be able to get out of the house anyway; the warehouse will definitely collapse if there is a flood, it is so wobbly already."

"Listen, folks, all joking apart, we shall try and get a boat."

"Why bother? I know something much better. We each get hold of a wooden packing case from the attic and row with a soup ladle!"

"I shall walk on stilts: I used to be an expert at it in my youth."

"Henk Van Santen won't need to, he's sure to take his wife on his back, then she'll be on stilts."

This gives you a rough idea, doesn't it, Kit?

This chatter is all very amusing, but the truth may be otherwise. A second question about the invasion was bound to arise: what do we do if the Germans evacuate Amsterdam?

"Leave the city too, and disguise ourselves as best we can."

"Don't go, whatever happens, stay put! The only thing to do is to remain here! The Germans are quite capable of driving the whole population right into Germany, where they will all die."

"Yes, naturally, we shall stay here, since this is the safest place. We'll try and fetch Koophuis and his family over here to come and live with us. We'll try and get hold of a sack of wood wool, then we can sleep on the floor. Let's ask Miep and Koophuis to start bringing blankets here."

"We'll order some extra corn in addition to our sixty pounds. Let's get Henk to try and obtain more peas and beans; we have about sixty pounds of beans and ten pounds of peas in the house at present. Don't forget that we've got fifty tins of vegetables."

"Mummy, just count up how much we've got of other food, will you?"

"Ten tins of fish, forty tins of milk, ten kilos of milk powder, three bottles of salad oil, four preserving jars of butter, four ditto of meat, two wicker-covered bottles of strawberries, two bottles of raspberries, twenty bottles of tomatoes, ten pounds of rolled oats, eight pounds of rice; and that's all.

"Our stock's not too bad, but if you think that we may be having visitors as well and drawing from reserves each week, then it seems more than it actually is. We have sufficient coal and firewood in the house, also candles. Let's all make little moneybags, which could easily be hidden in our clothing, in case we want to take money with us.

"We'll make lists of the most important things to take, should we have to run for it, and pack rucksacks now in readiness. If it gets that far, we'll put two people on watch, one in the front and one in the back loft. I say, what's the use of collecting such stocks of food, if we haven't any water, gas, or electricity?"

"Then we must cook on the stove. Filter and boil our water. We'll clean out some large wicker bottles and store water in them."

I hear nothing but this sort of talk the whole day long, invasion and nothing but invasion, arguments about suffering from hunger, dying, bombs, fire extinguishers, sleeping bags, Jewish vouchers, poisonous gases, etc., etc. None of it is exactly cheering. The gentlemen in the "Secret Annexe" give pretty straightforward warnings; an example is the following conversation with Henk:

"Secret Annexe": "We are afraid that if the Germans withdraw, they will take the whole population with them."

Henk: "That is impossible, they haven't the trains at their disposal."

"S.A.": "Trains? Do you really think they'd put civilians in carriages? Out of the question. They could use 'shank's mare.'" (*Per pedes apostolorum,* Dussel always says.)

H.: "I don't believe a word of it, you look on the black side of everything. What would be their object in driving all the civilians along with them?"

"S.A.": "Didn't you know that Goebbels said, 'If we have to withdraw, we shall slam the doors of all the occupied countries behind us'?"

H.: "They have said so much already."

"S.A.": "Do you think the Germans are above doing such a thing or too humane? What they think is this: 'If we have got to go down, then everybody in our clutches will go down with us.'"

H.: "Tell that to the Marines; I just don't believe it!"

"S.A.": "It's always the same song; no one will see danger approaching until it is actually on top of him."

H.: "But you know nothing definite; you just simply suppose."

"S.A.": "We have all been through it ourselves, first in Germany, and then here. And what is going on in Russia?"

H.: "You mustn't include the Jews. I don't think anyone knows what is going on in Russia. The English and the Russians are sure to exaggerate things for propaganda purposes, just like the Germans."

"S.A.": "Out of the question, the English have always told the truth over the wireless. And suppose they do exaggerate the news, the facts are bad enough anyway, because you can't deny that many millions of peace-loving people were just simply murdered or gassed in Poland and Russia."

I will spare you further examples of these conversations; I myself keep very quiet and don't take any notice of all the fuss and excitement. I have now reached the stage that I don't care much whether I live or die. The world will still keep on turning without me; what is going to happen, will happen, and anyway it's no good trying to resist.

I trust to luck and do nothing but work, hoping that all will end well.

Yours, Anne

Saturday, 12 February, 1944

Dear Kitty,

The sun is shining, the sky is a deep blue, there is a lovely breeze and I'm longing—so longing—for everything. To talk, for freedom, for friends, to be alone. And I do so long . . . to cry! I feel as if I'm going to burst, and I know that it would

get better with crying; but I can't, I'm restless, I go from one
room to the other, breathe through the crack of a closed window, feel my heart beating, as if it is saying, "Can't you satisfy
my longings at last?"

I believe that it's spring within me, I feel that spring is
awakening, I feel it in my whole body and soul. It is an effort
to behave normally, I feel utterly confused, don't know what
to read, what to write, what to do, I only know that I am
longing . . . !

Yours, Anne

Sunday, 13 February, 1944

Dear Kitty,

Since Saturday a lot has changed for me. It came about like
this. I longed—and am still longing—but . . . now something
has happened, which has made it a little, just a little, less.

To my great joy—I will be quite honest about it—already this
morning I noticed that Peter kept looking at me all the time.
Not in the ordinary way, I don't know how, I just can't explain.

I used to think that Peter was in love with Margot, but yesterday I suddenly had the feeling that it is not so. I made a special
effort not to look at him too much, because whenever I did, he
kept on looking too and then—yes, then—it gave me a lovely
feeling inside, but which I mustn't feel too often.

I desperately want to be alone. Daddy has noticed that I'm
not quite my usual self, but I really can't tell him everything.
"Leave me in peace, leave me alone," that's what I'd like to
keep crying out all the time. Who knows, the day may come
when I'm left alone more than I would wish!

Yours, Anne

Monday, 14 February, 1944

Dear Kitty,

On Sunday evening everyone except Pim and me was sitting beside the wireless in order to listen to the "Immortal
Music of the German Masters." Dussel fiddled with the knobs
continually. This annoyed Peter, and the others too. After
restraining himself for half an hour, Peter asked somewhat ir-
ritably if the twisting and turning might stop. Dussel answered

in his most hoity-toity manner, "I'm getting it all right." Peter became angry, was rude, Mr. Van Daan took his side, and Dussel had to give in. That was all.

The reason in itself was very unimportant, but Peter seems to have taken it very much to heart. In any case, when I was rummaging about in the bookcase in the attic, he came up to me and began telling me the whole story. I didn't know anything about it, but Peter soon saw that he had found an attentive ear and got fairly into his stride.

"Yes, and you see," he said, "I don't easily say anything, because I know beforehand that I'll only become tongue-tied. I begin to stutter, blush, and twist around what I want to say, until I have to break off because I simply can't find the words. That's what happened yesterday, I wanted to say something quite different, but once I had started, I got in a hopeless muddle and that's frightful. I used to have a bad habit; I wish I still had it now. If I was angry with anyone, rather than argue it out I would get to work on him with my fists. I quite realize that this method doesn't get me anywhere; and that is why I admire you. You are never at a loss for a word, you say exactly what you want to say to people and are never the least bit shy."

"I can tell you, you're making a big mistake," I answered. "I usually say things quite differently from the way I meant to say them, and then I talk too much and far too long, and that's just as bad."

I couldn't help laughing to myself over this last sentence. However, I wanted to let him go on talking about himself, so I kept my amusement to myself, went and sat on a cushion on the floor, put my arms around my bent knees, and looked at him attentively.

I am very glad that there is someone else in the house who can get into the same fits of rage as I get into. I could see it did Peter good to pull Dussel to pieces to his heart's content, without fear of my telling tales. And as for me, I was very pleased, because I sensed a real feeling of fellowship, such as I can only remember having had with my girl friends.

Yours, Anne

Wednesday, 16 February, 1944

Dear Kitty,

It's Margot's birthday. Peter came at half past twelve to look at the presents and stayed talking much longer than was strictly necessary—a thing he'd have never done otherwise. In the afternoon I went to get some coffee and, after that, potatoes, because I wanted to spoil Margot for just that one day in the year. I went through Peter's room; he took all his papers off the stairs at once and I asked whether I should close the trap door to the attic. "Yes," he replied, "knock when you come back, then I'll open it for you."

I thanked him, went upstairs, and searched at least ten minutes in the large barrel for the smallest potatoes. Then my back began to ache and I got cold. Naturally I didn't knock, but opened the trap door myself, but still he came to meet me most obligingly, and took the pan from me.

"I've looked for a long time, these are the smallest I could find," I said.

"Did you look in the big barrel?"

"Yes, I've been over them all."

By this time I was standing at the bottom of the stairs and he looked searchingly in the pan which he was still holding. "Oh, but these are first-rate," he said, and added when I took the pan from him, "I congratulate you!" At the same time he gave me such a gentle warm look which made a tender glow within me. I could really see that he wanted to please me, and because he couldn't make a long complimentary speech he spoke with his eyes. I understood him, oh, so well, and was very grateful. It gives me pleasure even now when I recall those words and that look he gave me.

When I went downstairs, Mummy said that I must get some more potatoes, this time for supper. I willingly offered to go upstairs again.

When I came into Peter's room, I apologized at having to disturb him again. When I was already on the stairs he got up, and went and stood between the door and the wall, firmly took hold of my arm, and wanted to hold me back by force.

"I'll go," he said. I replied that it really wasn't necessary and that I didn't have to get particularly small ones this time. Then he was convinced and let my arm go. On the way down, he came and opened the trap door and took the pan again. When I reached the door, I asked, "What are you doing?" "French," he replied. I asked if I might glance through the exercises, washed my hands, and went and sat on the divan opposite him.

We soon began talking, after I'd explained some of the French to him. He told me that he wanted to go to the Dutch East Indies and live on a plantation later on. He talked about his home life, about the black market, and then he said that he felt so useless. I told him that he certainly had a very strong inferiority complex. He talked about the Jews. He would have found it much easier if he'd been a Christian and if he could be one after the war. I asked if he wanted to be baptized, but that wasn't the case either. Who was to know whether he was a Jew when the war was over? he said.

This gave me rather a pang; it seems such a pity that there's always just a tinge of dishonesty about him. For the rest we chatted very pleasantly about Daddy, and about judging people's characters and all kinds of things, I can't remember exactly what now.

It was half past four by the time I left.

In the evening he said something else that I thought was nice. We were talking about a picture of a film star that I'd given him once, which has now been hanging in his room for at least a year and a half. He liked it very much and I offered to give him a few more sometime. "No," he replied, "I'd rather leave it like this. I look at these every day and they have grown to be my friends."

Now I understand more why he always hugs Mouschi. He needs some affection, too, of course.

I'd forgotten something else that he talked about. He said, "I don't know what fear is, except when I think of my own shortcomings. But I'm getting over that too."

Peter has a terrible inferiority complex. For instance, he always thinks that he is so stupid, and we are so clever. If I help him with his French, he thanks me a thousand times. One day I shall turn around and say: "Oh, shut up, you're much better at English and geography!"

Yours, Anne

Friday, 18 February, 1944

Dear Kitty,

Whenever I go upstairs now I keep on hoping that I shall see "him." Because my life now has an object, and I have something to look forward to, everything has become more pleasant.

At least the object of my feelings is always there, and I needn't be afraid of rivals, except Margot. Don't think I'm in love, because I'm not, but I do have the feeling all the time that something fine can grow up between us, something that gives confidence and friendship. If I get half a chance, I go up to him now. It's not like it used to be when he didn't know how to begin. It's just the opposite—he's still talking when I'm half out of the room.

Mummy doesn't like it much, and always says I'll be a nuisance and that I must leave him in peace. Honestly, doesn't she realize that I've got some intuition? She looks at me so queerly every time I go into Peter's little room. If I come downstairs from there, she asks me where I've been. I simply can't bear it, and think it's horrible.

Yours, Anne

Saturday, 19 February, 1944

Dear Kitty,

It is Saturday again and that really speaks for itself.

The morning was quiet. I helped a bit upstairs, but I didn't have more than a few fleeting words with "him." At half past two, when everyone had gone to their own rooms, either to sleep or to read, I went to the private office, with my blanket and everything, to sit at the desk and read or write. It was not long before it all became too much for me, my head drooped on to my arm, and I sobbed my heart out. The tears streamed down my cheeks and I felt desperately unhappy. Oh, if only "he" had come to comfort me. It was four o'clock by the time I went upstairs again. I went for some potatoes, with fresh hope in my heart of a meeting, but while I was still smartening up my hair in the bathroom, he went down to see Boche in the warehouse.

Suddenly I felt the tears coming back and I hurried to the

lavatory, quickly grabbing a pocket mirror as I passed. There I sat then, fully dressed, while the tears made dark spots on the red of my apron, and I felt very wretched.

This is what was going through my mind. Oh, I'll never reach Peter like this. Who knows, perhaps he doesn't like me at all and doesn't need anyone to confide in. Perhaps he only thinks about me in a casual sort of way. I shall have to go on alone once more, without friendship and without Peter. Perhaps soon I'll be without hope, without comfort, or anything to look forward to again. Oh, if I could nestle my head against his shoulder and not feel so hopelessly alone and deserted! Who knows, perhaps he doesn't care about me at all and looks at the others in just the same way. Perhaps I only imagined that it was especially for me? Oh, Peter, if only you could see or hear me. If the truth were to prove as bad as that, it would be more than I could bear.

However, a little later fresh hope and anticipation seemed to return, even though the tears were still streaming down my cheeks.

Yours, Anne

Wednesday, 23 February, 1944

Dear Kitty,

It's lovely weather outside and I've quite perked up since yesterday. Nearly every morning I go to the attic where Peter works to blow the stuffy air out of my lungs. From my favorite spot on the floor I look up at the blue sky and the bare chestnut tree, on whose branches little raindrops shine, appearing like silver, and at the seagulls and other birds as they glide on the wind.

He stood with his head against a thick beam, and I sat down. We breathed the fresh air, looked outside, and both felt that the spell should not be broken by words. We remained like this for a long time, and when he had to go up to the loft to chop wood, I knew that he was a nice fellow. He climbed the ladder, and I followed; then he chopped wood for about a quarter of an hour, during which time we still remained silent. I watched him from where I stood, he was obviously doing his best to show off his strength. But I looked out of the open window too, over a large area of Amsterdam, over all the roofs and on to the horizon, which was such a pale blue that it was hard to see the dividing line. "As long as this exists," I thought, "and I may live to see it, this sunshine, the cloudless skies, while this lasts, I cannot be unhappy."

The best remedy for those who are afraid, lonely, or unhappy is to go outside, somewhere where they can be quite alone with the heavens, nature, and God. Because only then does one feel that all is as it should be and that God wishes to see people happy, amidst the simple beauty of nature. As long as this exists, and it certainly always will, I know that then there will always be comfort for every sorrow, whatever the circumstances may be. And I firmly believe that nature brings solace in all troubles.

Oh, who knows, perhaps it won't be long before I can share this overwhelming feeling of bliss with someone who feels the way I do about it.

Yours, Anne

A thought:

We miss so much here, so very much and for so long now: I miss it too, just as you do. I'm not talking of outward things, for we are looked after in that way; no, I mean the inward things. Like you, I long for freedom and fresh air, but I believe now that we have ample compensation for our privations. I realized this quite suddenly when I sat in front of the window this morning. I mean inward compensation.

When I looked outside right into the depth of Nature and God, then I was happy, really happy. And Peter, so long as I have that happiness here, the joy in nature, health and a lot more besides, all the while one has that, one can always recapture happiness.

Riches can all be lost, but that happiness in your own heart can only be veiled, and it will still bring you happiness again, as long as you live. As long as you can look fearlessly up into the heavens, as long as you know that you are pure within and that you will still find happiness.

Sunday, 27 February, 1944

Dearest Kitty,

From early in the morning till late at night, I really do hardly anything else but think of Peter. I sleep with his image before my eyes, dream about him and he is still looking at me when I awake.

I have a strong feeling that Peter and I are really not so different as we would appear to be, and I will tell you why. We both lack a mother. His is too superficial, loves flirting and doesn't trouble much about what he thinks. Mine does bother about me, but lacks sensitiveness, real motherliness.

Peter and I both wrestle with our inner feelings, we are still uncertain and are really too sensitive to be roughly treated. If we are, then my reaction is to "get away from it all." But as that is impossible, I hide my feelings, throw my weight about the place, am noisy and boisterous, so that everyone wishes that I was out of the way.

He, on the contrary, shuts himself up, hardly talks at all, is quiet, day-dreams and in this way carefully conceals his true self.

But how and when will we finally reach each other? I don't know quite how long my common sense will keep this longing under control.

Yours, Anne

Monday, 28 February, 1944

Dearest Kitty,

It is becoming a bad dream—in daytime as well as at night. I see him nearly all the time and can't get at him, I mustn't show anything, must remain gay while I'm really in despair.

Peter Wessel and Peter Van Daan have grown into one Peter, who is beloved and good, and for whom I long desperately.

Mummy is tiresome, Daddy sweet and therefore all the more tiresome, Margot the most tiresome because she expects me to wear a pleasant expression; and all I want is to be left in peace.

Peter didn't come to me in the attic. He went up to the loft instead and did some carpentry. At every creak and every knock some of my courage seemed to seep away and I grew more unhappy. In the distance a bell was playing "Pure in body, pure in soul."[1] I'm sentimental—I know. I'm desperate and silly—I know that too. Oh, help me!

Yours, Anne

[1] The bells in old clock towers play tunes.

Wednesday, 1 March, 1944

Dear Kitty,

My own affairs have been pushed into the background by —a burglary. I'm becoming boring with all my burglars, but what can I do, they seem to take such a delight in honoring Kolen & Co. with their visits. This burglary is much more complicated than the one in July 1943.

When Mr. Van Daan went to Kraler's office at half past seven, as usual, he saw that the communicating glass doors and the office door were open. Surprised at this, he walked through and was even more amazed to see that the doors of the little dark room were open too, and that there was a terrible mess in the main office. "There has been a burglar," he thought to himself at once, and to satisfy himself he went straight downstairs to look at the front door, felt the Yale lock, and found everything closed. "Oh, then both Peter and Elli must have been very slack this evening," he decided. He remained in Kraler's room for a while, then switched off the lamp, and went upstairs, without worrying much about either the open doors or the untidy office.

This morning Peter knocked at our door early and came with the not so pleasant news that the front door was wide open. He also told us that the projector and Kraler's new portfolio had both disappeared from the cupboard. Peter was told to close the door. Van Daan told us of his discoveries the previous evening and we were all awfully worried.

What must have happened is that the thief had a skeleton key, because the lock was quite undamaged. He must have crept into the house quite early and closed the door behind him, hidden himself when disturbed by Mr. Van Daan, and when he departed fled with his spoils, leaving the door open in his haste. Who can have our key? Why didn't the thief go to the warehouse? Might it be one of our own warehousemen, and would he perhaps betray us, since he certainly heard Van Daan and perhaps even saw him?

It is all very creepy, because we don't know whether this same burglar may not take it into his head to visit us again. Or perhaps it gave him a shock to find that there was someone walking about in the house?

Yours, Anne

Thursday, 2 March, 1944

Dear Kitty,

Margot and I were both up in the attic today; although we were not able to enjoy it together as I had imagined, still I do know that she shares my feelings over most things.

During dish washing Elli began telling Mummy and Mrs. Van Daan that she felt very discouraged at times. And what help do you think they gave her? Do you know what Mummy's advice was? She should try to think of all the other people who are in trouble! What is the good of thinking of misery when one is already miserable oneself? I said this too and was told, "You keep out of this sort of conversation."

Aren't the grownups idiotic and stupid? Just as if Peter, Margot, Elli, and I don't all feel the same about things, and only a mother's love or that of a very, very good friend can help us. These mothers here just don't understand us at all. Perhaps Mrs. Van Daan does a little more than Mummy. Oh, I would have so liked to say something to poor Elli, something that I know from experience would have helped her. But Daddy came between us and pushed me aside.

Aren't they all stupid! We aren't allowed to have any opinions. People can tell you to keep your mouth shut, but it doesn't stop you having your own opinion. Even if people are still very young, they shouldn't be prevented from saying what they think.

Only great love and devotion can help Elli, Margot, Peter, and me, and none of us gets it. And no one, especially the stupid "know-alls" here, can understand us, because we are much more sensitive and much more advanced in our thoughts than anyone here would ever imagine in their wildest dreams.

Mummy is grumbling again at the moment—she is obviously jealous because I talk more to Mrs. Van Daan than to her nowadays.

I managed to get hold of Peter this afternoon and we talked for at least three quarters of an hour. Peter had the greatest difficulty in saying anything about himself; it took a long time to draw him out. He told me how often his parents quarrel over politics, cigarettes, and all kinds of things. He was very shy.

Then I talked to him about my parents. He defended Daddy: he thought him a "first-rate chap." Then we talked about "upstairs" and "downstairs" again; he was really rather amazed that we don't always like his parents. "Peter," I said, "you know I'm always honest, so why shouldn't I tell you that we can see their faults too." And among other things I also said, "I would so like to help you, Peter; can't I? You are in such an awkward position and, although you don't say anything, it doesn't mean that you don't care."

"Oh, I would always welcome your help."

"Perhaps you would do better to go to Daddy, he wouldn't let anything go any further, take it from me; you can easily tell him!"

"Yes, he is a real pal."

"You're very fond of him, aren't you?" Peter nodded and I went on: "And he is of you too!"

He looked up quickly and blushed, it was really moving to see how these few words pleased him.

"Do you think so?" he asked.

"Yes," I said, "you can easily tell by little things that slip out now and then!"

Peter is a first-rate chap, too, just like Daddy!

Yours, Anne

Friday, 3 March, 1944

Dear Kitty,

When I looked into the candle this evening[1] I felt calm and happy. Oma seems to be in the candle and it is Oma too who shelters and protects me and who always makes me feel happy again.

But . . . there is someone else who governs all my moods and that is . . . Peter. When I went up to get potatoes today and was still standing on the stepladder with the pan, he at once asked, "What have you been doing since lunch?" I went and sat on the steps and we started talking. At a quarter past five (an hour later) the potatoes, which had been sitting on the floor in the meantime, finally reached their destinations.

Peter didn't say another word about his parents; we just talked about books and about the past. The boy has such warmth in his eyes; I believe I'm pretty near to being in love

[1] In Jewish homes candles are lit on the Sabbath eve.

with him. He talked about that this evening. I went into his room, after peeling the potatoes, and said that I felt so hot.

"You can tell what the temperature is by Margot and me; if it's cold we are white, and if it is hot we are red in the face," I said.

"In love?" he asked.

"Why should I be in love?" My answer was rather silly.

"Why not?" he said, and then we had to go for supper.

Would he have meant anything by that question? I finally managed to ask him today whether he didn't find my chatter a nuisance; he only said: "It's okay, I like it!"

To what extent this answer was just shyness, I am not able to judge.

Kitty, I'm just like someone in love, who can only talk about her darling. And Peter really is a darling. When shall I be able to tell him so? Naturally, only if he thinks I'm a darling too. But I'm quite capable of looking after myself, and he knows that very well. And he likes his tranquillity, so I have no idea how much he likes me. In any case, we are getting to know each other a bit. I wish we dared to tell each other much more already. Who knows, the time may come sooner than I think! I get an understanding look from him about twice a day, I wink back, and we both feel happy.

I certainly seem quite mad to be talking about him being happy, and yet I feel pretty sure that he thinks just the same as I do.

Yours, Anne

Saturday, 4 March, 1944

Dear Kitty,

This is the first Saturday for months and months that hasn't been boring, dreary, and dull. And Peter is the cause.

This morning I went to the attic to hang up my apron, when Daddy asked whether I'd like to stay and talk some French. I agreed. First we talked French, and I explained something to Peter; then we did some English. Daddy read out loud to us from Dickens and I was in the seventh heaven, because I sat on Daddy's chair very close to Peter.

I went downstairs at eleven o'clock. When I came upstairs again at half past eleven, he was already waiting for me on the stairs. We talked until a quarter to one. If, as I leave the room, he gets a chance after a meal, for instance, and if no one can hear, he says: "Good-by, Anne, see you soon."

Oh, I am so pleased! I wonder if he is going to fall in love with me after all? Anyway, he is a very nice fellow and no one knows what lovely talks I have with him!

Mrs. Van Daan quite approves when I go and talk to him, but she asked today teasingly, "Can I really trust you two up there together?"

"Of course," I protested, "really you quite insult me!"

From morn till night I look forward to seeing Peter.

Yours, Anne

Monday, 6 March, 1944

Dear Kitty,

I can tell by Peter's face that he thinks just as much as I do, and when Mrs. Van Daan yesterday evening said scoffingly: "The thinker!" I was irritated. Peter flushed and looked very embarrassed, and I was about to explode.

Why can't these people keep their mouths shut?

You can't imagine how horrible it is to stand by and see how lonely he is and yet not be able to do anything. I can so well imagine, just as if I were in his place, how desperate he must feel sometimes in quarrels and in love. Poor Peter, he needs love very much!

When he said he didn't need any friends how harsh the words sounded to my ears. Oh, how mistaken he is! I don't believe he meant it a bit.

He clings to his solitude, to his affected indifference and his grown-up ways, but it's just an act, so as never, never to show his real feelings. Poor Peter, how long will he be able to go on playing this role? Surely a terrible outburst must follow as the result of this superhuman effort?

Oh, Peter, if only I could help you, if only you would let me! Together we could drive away your loneliness and mine!

I think a lot, but I don't say much. I am happy if I see him and if the sun shines when I'm with him. I was very excited yesterday; while I was washing my hair, I knew that he was sitting in the room next to ours. I couldn't do anything about it; the more quiet and serious I feel inside, the more noisy I become outwardly.

Who will be the first to discover and break through this armor? I'm glad after all that the Van Daans have a son and not a daughter, my conquest could never have been so difficult, so beautiful, so good, if I had not happened to hit on someone of the opposite sex.

Yours, Anne

P.S. You know that I'm always honest with you, so I must tell you that I actually live from one meeting to the next. I keep hoping to discover that he too is waiting for me all the time and I'm thrilled if I notice a small shy advance from his side. I believe he'd like to say a lot just like I would; little does he know that it's just his clumsiness that attracts me.

Yours, Anne

Tuesday, 7 March, 1944

Dear Kitty,

If I think now of my life in 1942, it all seems so unreal. It was quite a different Anne who enjoyed that heavenly existence from the Anne who has grown wise within these walls. Yes, it was a heavenly life. Boy friends at every turn, about twenty friends and acquaintances of my own age, the darling of nearly all the teachers, spoiled from top to toe by Mummy and Daddy, lots of sweets, enough pocket money, what more could one want?

You will certainly wonder by what means I got around all these people. Peter's word "attractiveness" is not altogether true. All the teachers were entertained by my cute answers, my amusing remarks, my smiling face, and my questioning looks. That is all I was—a terrible flirt, coquettish and amusing. I had one or two advantages, which kept me rather in favor. I was industrious, honest, and frank. I would never have dreamed of cribbing from anyone else. I shared my sweets generously, and I wasn't conceited.

Wouldn't I have become rather forward with so much admiration? It was a good thing that in the midst of, at the height of, all this gaiety, I suddenly had to face reality, and it took me at least a year to get used to the fact that there was no more admiration forthcoming.

How did I appear at school? The one who thought of new jokes and pranks, always "king of the castle," never in a bad mood, never a crybaby. No wonder everyone liked to cycle with me, and I got their attentions.

Now I look back at that Anne as an amusing, but very superficial girl, who has nothing to do with the Anne of to-day. Peter said quite rightly about me: "If ever I saw you, you were always surrounded by two or more boys and a whole troupe of girls. You were always laughing and always the center of everything!"

What is left of this girl? Oh, don't worry, I haven't forgotten how to laugh or to answer back readily. I'm just as good, if not better, at critizing people, and I can still flirt if . . . I wish. That's not it though, I'd like that sort of life again for an evening, a few days, or even a week; the life which seems so carefree and gay. But at the end of that week, I should be dead beat and would be only too thankful to listen to anyone who began to talk about something sensible. I don't want followers, but friends, admirers who fall not for a flattering smile but for what one does and for one's character.

I know quite well that the circle around me would be much smaller. But what does that matter, as long as one still keeps a few sincere friends?

Yet I wasn't entirely happy in 1942 in spite of everything; I often felt deserted, but because I was on the go the whole day long, I didn't think about it and enjoyed myself as much as I could. Consciously or unconsciously, I tried to drive away the emptiness I felt with jokes and pranks. Now I think seriously about life and what I have to do. One period of my life is over forever. The carefree schooldays are gone, never to return.

I don't even long for them any more; I have outgrown them, I can't just only enjoy myself as my serious side is always there.

I look upon my life up till the New Year, as it were, through a powerful magnifying glass. The sunny life at home, then coming here in 1942, the sudden change, the quarrels, the bickerings. I couldn't understand it, I was taken by surprise, and the only way I could keep up some bearing was by being impertinent.

The first half of 1943: my fits of crying, the loneliness, how I slowly began to see all my faults and shortcomings, which are so great and which seemed much greater then. During the day I deliberately talked about anything and everything that was farthest from my thoughts, tried to draw Pim to me; but couldn't. Alone I had to face the difficult task of changing myself, to stop the everlasting reproaches, which were so oppressive and which reduced me to such terrible despondency.

Things improved slightly in the second half of the year, I became a young woman and was treated more like a grownup. I started to think, and write stories, and came to the conclusion that the others no longer had the right to throw me about like an india-rubber ball. I wanted to change in accordance with my own desires. But *one* thing that struck me even more was when I realized that even Daddy would never become my confidant over everything. I didn't want to trust anyone but myself any more.

At the beginning of the New Year: the second great change, my dream. . . . And with it I discovered my longing, not for a girl friend, but for a boy friend. I also discovered my inward happiness and my defensive armor of superficiality and gaiety. In due time I quieted down and discovered my boundless desire for all that is beautiful and good.

And in the evening, when I lie in bed and end my prayers with the words, "I thank you, God, for all that is good and dear and beautiful," I am filled with joy. Then I think about "the good" of going into hiding, of my health and with my whole being of the "dearness" of Peter, of that which is still embryonic and impressionable and which we neither of us dare to name or touch, of that which will come sometime; love, the future, happiness and of "the beauty" which exists in the world; the world, nature, beauty and all, all that is exquisite and fine.

I don't think then of all the misery, but of the beauty that still remains. This is one of the things that Mummy and I are so entirely different about. Her counsel when one feels melancholy is: "Think of all the misery in the world and be thankful that you are not sharing in it!" My advice is: "Go outside, to the fields, enjoy nature and the sunshine, go out and try to recapture happiness in yourself and in God. Think of all the beauty that's still left in and around you and be happy!"

I don't see how Mummy's idea can be right, because then

how are you supposed to behave if you go through the misery yourself? Then you are lost. On the contrary, I've found that there is always some beauty left—in nature, sunshine, freedom, in yourself; these can all help you. Look at these things, then you find yourself again, and God, and then you regain your balance.

And whoever is happy will make others happy too. He who has courage and faith will never perish in misery!

Yours, Anne

Sunday, 12 March, 1944

Dear Kitty,

I can't seem to sit still lately; I run upstairs and down and then back again. I love talking to Peter, but I'm always afraid of being a nuisance. He has told me a bit about the past, about his parents and about himself. It's not half enough though and I ask myself why it is that I always long for more. He used to think I was unbearable; and I returned the compliment; now I have changed my opinion, has he changed his too?

I think so; still it doesn't necessarily mean that we shall become great friends, although as far as I am concerned it would make the time here much more bearable. But still, I won't get myself upset about it—I see quite a lot of him and there's no need to make you unhappy about it too, Kitty, just because I feel so miserable.

On Saturday afternoon I felt in such a whirl, after hearing a whole lot of sad news, that I went and lay on my divan for a sleep. I only wanted to sleep to stop myself thinking. I slept till four o'clock, then I had to go into the living room. I found it difficult to answer all Mummy's questions and think of some little excuse to tell Daddy, as an explanation for my long sleep. I resorted to a "headache," which wasn't a lie, as I had one . . . but inside!

Ordinary people, ordinary girls, teen-agers like myself, will think I'm a bit cracked with all my self-pity. Yes, that's what it is, but I pour out my heart to you, then for the rest of the day I'm as impudent, gay, and self-confident as I can be, in order to avoid questions and getting on my own nerves.

Margot is very sweet and would like me to trust her, but

still, I can't tell her everything. She's a darling, she's good and pretty, but she lacks the nonchalance for conducting deep discussions; she takes me so seriously, much too seriously, and then thinks about her queer little sister for a long time afterwards, looks searchingly at me, at every word I say, and keeps on thinking: "Is this just a joke or does she really mean it?" I think that's because we are together the whole day long, and that if I trusted someone completely, then I shouldn't want them hanging around me all the time.

When shall I finally untangle my thoughts, when shall I find peace and rest within myself again?

Yours, Anne

Tuesday, 14 March, 1944

Dear Kitty,

Perhaps it would be entertaining for you—though not in the least for me—to hear what we are going to eat today. As the charwoman is at work downstairs, I'm sitting on the Van Daans' table at the moment. I have a handkerchief soaked in some good scent (bought before we came here) over my mouth and held against my nose. You won't gather much from this, so let's "begin at the beginning."

The people from whom we obtained food coupons have been caught, so we just have our five ration cards and no extra coupons, and no fats. As both Miep and Koophuis are ill, Elli hasn't time to do any shopping, so the atmosphere is dreary and dejected, and so is the food. From tomorrow we shall not have a scrap of fat, butter, or margarine left. We can't have fried potatoes (to save bread) for breakfast any longer, so we have porridge instead, and as Mrs. Van Daan thinks we're starving, we have bought some full cream milk "under the counter." Our supper today consists of a hash made from kale which has been preserved in a barrel. Hence the precautionary measure with the handkerchief! It's incredible how kale can stink when it's a year old! The smell in the room is a mixture of bad plums, strong preservatives, and rotten eggs. Ugh! the mere thought of eating that muck makes me feel sick.

Added to this, our potatoes are suffering from such peculiar diseases that out of two buckets of *pommes de terre,* one whole one ends up on the stove. We amuse ourselves by searching for all the different kinds of diseases, and have come to the conclusion that they range from cancer and smallpox to measles! Oh, no, it's no joke to be in hiding during the fourth year of the war. If only the whole rotten business was over!

Quite honestly, ı wouldn't care so much about the food, if only it were more pleasant here in other ways. There's the rub: this tedious existence is beginning to make us all touchy.

The following are the views of the five grownups on the present situation:

Mrs. Van Daan: "The job as queen of the kitchen lost its attraction a long time ago. It's dull to sit and do nothing, so I go back to my cooking again. Still, I have to complain that it's impossible to cook without any fats, and all these nasty smells make me feel sick. Nothing but ingratitude and rude remarks do I get in return for my services. I am always the black sheep, always the guilty one. Moreover, according to me, very little progress is being made in the war; in the end the Germans will still win. I'm afraid we're going to starve, and if I'm in a bad mood I scold everyone."

Mr. Van Daan: "I must smoke and smoke and smoke, and then the food, the political situation, and Kerli's moods don't seem so bad. Kerli is a darling wife."

But if he hasn't anything to smoke, then nothing is right, and this is what one hears: "I'm getting ill, we don't live well enough, I must have meat. Frightfully stupid person, my Kerli!" After this a terrific quarrel is sure to follow.

Mrs. Frank: "Food is not very important, but I would love a slice of rye bread now, I feel so terribly hungry. If I were Mrs. Van Daan I would have put a stop to Mr. Van Daan's everlasting smoking a long time ago. But now I must definitely have a cigarette, because my nerves are getting the better of me. The English make a lot of mistakes, but still the war is progressing. I must have a chat and be thankful I'm not in Poland."

Mr. Frank: "Everything's all right, I don't require anything. Take it easy, we've ample time. Give me my potatoes and then I will keep my mouth shut. Put some of my rations on one side for Elli. The political situation is very promising, I'm extremely optimistic!"

Mr. Dussel: "I must get my task for today, everything must
be finished on time. Political situation 'outschtänding' and it
is 'eempossible' that we'll be caught.

"I, I, I . . . !"

Yours, Anne

Wednesday, 15 March, 1944

Dear Kitty,

Phew! Oh dear, oh dear—released from the somber scenes
for a moment! Today I hear nothing but "if this or that should
happen, then we are going to be in difficulties . . . if he or she
should become ill, then we'll be completely isolated, and then
if . . ." *Enfin*, I expect you know the rest, at least I presume
you know the "Secret Annexers" well enough by this time to
be able to guess the trend of their conversations.

The reason for all this "if, if" is that Mr. Kraler has been
called up to go digging. Elli has a streaming cold and will probably have to stay at home tomorrow. Miep hasn't fully recovered from her flu yet, and Koophuis has had such bad
hemorrhage of the stomach that he lost consciousness. What a
tale of woe!

The warehouse people are getting a free day tomorrow; Elli
can stay at home, then the door will remain locked and we
shall have to be as quiet as mice, so that the neighbors don't
hear us. Henk is coming to visit the deserted ones at one o'clock
—playing the role of zoo-keeper, as it were. For the first time
in ages he told us something about the great wide world this
afternoon. You should have seen the eight of us sitting around
him; it looked exactly like a picture of grandmother telling a
story. He talked nineteen to the dozen to his grateful audience
about food, of course, and then Miep's doctor, and everything
that we asked about. "Doctor," he said, "don't talk to me about
the doctor! I rang him up this morning, had his assistant on the
phone and asked for a prescription for flu. The reply was that I
could come and get the prescription any time between eight
and nine in the morning. If you have a very bad attack of flu,
the doctor comes to the telephone himself and says 'Put out
your tongue, say Aah. I can hear all right that your throat is
inflamed. I'll write out a prescription for you to order from the

chemist. Good-by.' And that's that." A fine practice that, run by telephone only.

But I don't want to criticize the doctors; after all, a person has but two hands, and in these days there's an abundance of patients and very few doctors to cope with them. Still, we couldn't help laughing when Henk repeated the telephone conversation to us.

I can just imagine what a doctor's waiting room must look like nowadays. One doesn't look down on panel patients any more, but on the people with minor ailments, and thinks: "Hi, you, what are you doing here, end of the line, please; urgent cases have priority!"

Yours, Anne

Thursday, 16 March, 1944

Dear Kitty,

The weather is lovely, superb, I can't describe it; I'm going up to the attic in a minute.

Now I know why I'm so much more restless than Peter. He has his own room where he can work, dream, think, and sleep. I am shoved about from one corner to another. I hardly spend any time in my "double" room and yet it's something I long for so much. That is the reason too why I so frequently escape to the attic. There, and with you, I can be myself for a while, just a little while. Still, I don't want to moan about myself, on the contrary, I want to be brave. Thank goodness the others can't tell what my inward feelings are, except that I'm growing cooler towards Mummy daily, I'm not so affectionate to Daddy and don't tell Margot a single thing. I'm completely closed up. Above all, I must maintain my outward reserve, no one must know that war still reigns incessantly within. War between desire and common sense. The latter has won up till now; yet will the former prove to be the stronger of the two? Sometimes I fear that it will and sometimes I long for it to be!

Oh, it is so terribly difficult never to say anything to Peter, but I know that the first to begin must be he; there's so much I want to say and do, I've lived it all in my dreams, it is so hard to find that yet another day has gone by, and none of it comes true! Yes, Kitty, Anne is a crazy child, but I do live in crazy times and under still crazier circumstances.

But, still, the brightest spot of all is that at least I can write down my thoughts and feelings, otherwise I would be absolutely stifled! I wonder what Peter thinks about all these things? I keep hoping that I can talk about it to him one day. There must be something he has guessed about me, because he certainly can't love the outer Anne, which is the one he knows so far.

How can he, who loves peace and quiet, have any liking for all my bustle and din? Can he possibly be the first and only one to have looked through my concrete armor? And will it take him long to get there? Isn't there an old saying that love often springs from pity, or that the two go hand in hand? Is that the case with me too? Because I'm often just as sorry for him as I am for myself.

I really don't honestly know how to begin, and however would he be able to, when he finds talking so much more difficult than I do? If only I could write to him, then at least I would know that he would grasp what I want to say, because it's so terribly difficult to put it into words!

Yours, Anne

Friday, 17 March, 1944

Dear Kitty,

A sigh of relief has gone through the "Secret Annexe." Kraler has been exempted from digging by the Court. Elli has given her nose a talking to and strictly forbidden it to be a nuisance to her today. So everything is all right again, except that Margot and I are getting a bit tired of our parents. Don't misunderstand me, I can't get on well with Mummy at the moment, as you know. I still love Daddy just as much, and Margot loves Daddy and Mummy, but when you are as old as we are, you do want to decide just a few things for yourself, you want to be independent sometimes.

If I go upstairs, then I'm asked what I'm going to do, I'm not allowed salt with my food, every evening regularly at a quarter past eight Mummy asks whether I ought not to start undressing, every book I read must be inspected. I must admit that they are not at all strict, and I'm allowed to read nearly everything, and yet we are both sick of all the remarks plus all the questioning that go on the whole day long.

Something else, especially about me, that doesn't please them: I don't feel like giving lots of kisses any more and I think fancy nicknames are terribly affected. In short, I'd really like to be rid of them for a while. Margot said last evening, "I think it's awfully annoying, the way they ask if you've got a headache, or whether you don't feel well, if you happen to give a sigh and put your hand to your head!"

It is a great blow to us both, suddenly to realize how little remains of the confidence and harmony that we used to have at home. And it's largely due to the fact that we're all "skew-wiff" here. By this I mean that we are treated as children over outward things, and we are much older than most girls of our age inwardly.

Although I'm only fourteen, I know quite well what I want, I know who is right and who is wrong, I have my opinions, my own ideas and principles, and although it may sound pretty mad from an adolescent, I feel more of a person than a child, I feel quite independent of anyone.

I know that I can discuss things and argue better than Mummy, I know I'm not so prejudiced, I don't exaggerate so much, I am more precise and adroit and because of this— you may laugh—I feel superior to her over a great many things. If I love anyone, above all I must have admiration for them, admiration and respect. Everything would be all right if only I had Peter, for I do admire him in many ways. He is such a nice, good-looking boy!

Yours, Anne

Sunday, 19 March, 1944

Dear Kitty,

Yesterday was a great day for me. I had decided to talk things out with Peter. Just as we were going to sit down to supper I whispered to him, "Are you going to do shorthand this evening, Peter?" "No," was his reply. "Then I'd just like to talk to you later!" He agreed. After the dishes were done, I stood by the window in his parents' room awhile for the look of things, but it wasn't long before I went to Peter. He was standing on the left side of the open window, I went and stood on the right side, and we talked. It was much easier to talk beside the open window in semidarkness than in bright light, and I believe Peter felt the same.

We told each other so much, so very very much, that I can't repeat it all, but it was lovely; the most wonderful evening I have ever had in the "Secret Annexe." I will just tell you briefly the various things we talked about. First we talked about the quarrels and how I regard them quite differently now, and then about the estrangement between us and our parents.

I told Peter about Mummy and Daddy, and Margot, and about myself.

At one moment he asked, "I suppose you always give each other a good night kiss, don't you?"

"*One,* dozens, why, don't you?"

"No, I have hardly ever kissed anyone."

"Not even on your birthday?"

"Yes, I have then."

We talked about how we neither of us confide in our parents, and how his parents would have loved to have his confidence, but that he didn't wish it. How I cry my heart out in bed, and he goes up into the loft and swears. How Margot and I really only know each other well for a little while, but that, even so, we don't tell each other everything, because we are always together. Over every imaginable thing—oh, he was just as I thought!

Then we talked about 1942, how different we were then. We just don't recognize ourselves as the same people any more. How we simply couldn't bear each other in the beginning. He thought I was much too talkative and unruly, and I soon came to the conclusion that I'd no time for him. I couldn't understand why he didn't flirt with me, but now I'm glad. He also mentioned how much he isolated himself from us all. I said that there was not much difference between my noise and his silence. That I love peace and quiet too, and have nothing for myself alone, except my diary. How glad he is that my parents have children here, and that I'm glad he is here. That I understand his reserve now and his relationship with his parents, and how I would love to be able to help him.

"You always do help me," he said. "How?" I asked, very surprised. "By your cheerfulness." That was certainly the loveliest thing he said. It was wonderful, he must have grown to love me as a friend, and that is enough for the time being. I am so grateful and happy, I just can't find the words. I must apologize, Kitty, that my style is not up to standard today.

I have just written down what came into my head. I have the feeling now that Peter and I share a secret. If he looks at me with those eyes that laugh and wink, then it's just as if a little light goes on inside me. I hope it will remain like this and that we may have many, many more glorious times together!

Your grateful, happy Anne

Monday, 20 March, 1944

Dear Kitty,

This morning Peter asked me if I would come again one evening, and said that I really didn't disturb him, and if there's room for one there's room for two. I said that I couldn't come every evening, because they wouldn't like it downstairs, but he thought that I needn't let that bother me. Then I said that I would love to come one Saturday evening and especially asked him to warn me when there was a moon. "Then we'll go downstairs," he answered, "and look at the moon from there."

In the meantime a little shadow has fallen on my happiness. I've thought for a long time that Margot liked Peter quite a lot too. How much she loves him I don't know, but I think it's wretched. I must cause her terrible pain each time I'm with Peter, and the funny part of it is that she hardly shows it.

I know quite well that I'd be desperately jealous, but Margot only says that I needn't pity her.

"I think it's so rotten that you should be the odd one out," I added. "I'm used to that," she answered, somewhat bitterly.

I don't dare tell Peter this yet, perhaps later on, but we've got to talk about so many other things first.

I had a little ticking off yesterday evening from Mummy, which I certainly deserved. I mustn't overdo my indifference towards her. So in spite of everything, I must try once again to be friendly and keep my observations to myself.

Even Pim is different lately. He is trying not to treat me as such a child, and it makes him much too cool. See what comes of it!

Enough for now, I'm full to the brim with Peter and can do nothing but look at him!

Evidence of Margot's goodness: I received this today,

March 20th, 1944

Anne, when I said yesterday that I was not jealous of you I was only fifty per cent honest. It is like this; I'm jealous of neither you nor Peter. I only feel a bit sorry that I haven't found anyone yet, and am not likely to for the time being, with whom I can discuss my thoughts and feelings. But I should not grudge it to you for that reason. One misses enough here anyway, things that other people just take for granted.

On the other hand, I know for certain that I would never have got so far with Peter, anyway, because I have the feeling that if I wished to discuss a lot with anyone, I should want to be on rather intimate terms with him. I would want to have the feeling that he understood me through and through without my having to say much. But for that reason it would have to be someone whom I felt was my superior intellectually, and that is not the case with Peter. But I can imagine it being so with you and Peter.

You are not doing me out of anything which is my due; do not reproach yourself in the least on my account. You and Peter can only gain by the friendship.

My reply:

Dear Margot,

I thought your letter was exceptionally sweet, but I still don't feel quite happy about it and nor do I think that I shall.

At present there is no question of such confidence as you have in mind between Peter and myself, but in the twilight beside an open window you can say more to each other than in brilliant sunshine. Also it's easier to whisper your feelings than to trumpet them forth out loud. I believe that you are beginning to feel a kind of sisterly affection for Peter, and that you would love to help him, just as much as I. Perhaps you will still be able to do that sometime, although that is not the kind of confidence we have in mind. I think it must come from both sides, and I believe that's the reason why Daddy and I have never got so far.

Let's not talk about it any more; but if you still want anything please write to me about it, because I can say what I mean much better on paper.

You don't know how much I admire you, and I only hope that I may yet acquire some of the goodness that you and Daddy have, because now I don't see much difference between you and Daddy in that sense.

Yours, Anne

Wednesday, 22 March, 1944

Dear Kitty,
I received this from Margot last evening:

Dear Anne,
After your letter yesterday I have the unpleasant feeling that you will have prickings of conscience when you visit Peter; but really there is no reason for this. In my heart of hearts I feel that I have the right to share mutual confidence with someone, but I could not bear Peter in that role yet.

However, I do feel just as you say, that Peter is a bit like a brother, but—a younger brother; we have put out feelers towards each other, the affection of a brother and sister might grow if they touched, perhaps they will later—perhaps never; however, it has certainly not reached that stage yet.

Therefore you really needn't pity me. Now that you've found companionship, enjoy it as much as you can.

In the meantime it is getting more and more wonderful here. I believe, Kitty, that we may have a real great love in the "Secret Annexe." Don't worry, I'm not thinking of marrying him. I don't know what he will be like when he grows up, nor do I know whether we should ever love each other enough to marry. I know now that Peter loves me, but just how I myself don't know yet.

Whether he only wants a great friend, or whether I attract him as a girl or as a sister, I can't yet discover.

When he said that I always helped him over his parents'

quarrels, I was awfully glad; it was one step towards making me believe in his friendship. I asked him yesterday what he would do if there were a dozen Annes here who always kept coming to him. His reply was, "If they were all like you, it certainly wouldn't be too bad!" He's tremendously hospitable towards me and I really believe he likes to see me. Meanwhile he is working diligently at his French, even when he's in bed, going on until a quarter past ten. Oh, when I think about Saturday evening and recall it all, word for word, then for the first time I don't feel discontented about myself; I mean that I would still say exactly the same and wouldn't wish to change anything, as is usually the case.

He is so handsome, both when he laughs and when he looks quietly in front of him; he is such a darling and so good. I believe what surprised him most about me was when he discovered that I'm not a bit the superficial worldly Anne that I appear, but just as dreamy a specimen, with just as many difficulties as he himself.

Yours, Anne

Reply:

Dear Margot,

I think the best thing we can do is simply to wait and see what happens. It can't be very long before Peter and I come to a definite decision, either to go on as before or be different. Just which way it will go I don't know myself, and I don't bother to look beyond my own nose. But I shall certainly do *one* thing, if Peter and I decide to be friends, I shall tell him that you are very fond of him too and would always be prepared to help him should the need arise. The latter may not be what you wish, but I don't care now; I don't know what Peter thinks about you, but I shall ask him then.

I'm sure it's not bad—the opposite! You are always welcome to join us in the attic, or wherever we are; you honestly won't disturb us because I feel we have a silent agreement to talk only in the evenings when it's dark.

Keep your courage up! Like I do. Although it's not always easy; your time may come sooner than you think.

Yours, Anne

Thursday, 23 March, 1944

Dear Kitty,

Things are running more or less normally again now. Our coupon men are out of prison again, thank goodness!

Miep returned yesterday. Elli is better, although she still has a cough; Koophuis will have to stay at home for a long time still.

A plane crashed near here yesterday; the occupants were able to jump out in time by parachute. The machine crashed onto a school, but there were no children there at the time. The result was a small fire and two people killed. The Germans shot at the airmen terribly as they were coming down. The Amsterdammers who saw it nearly exploded with rage and indignation at the cowardliness of such a deed. We—I'm speaking of the ladies—nearly jumped out of our skins, I loathe the blasted shooting.

I often go upstairs after supper nowadays and take a breath of the fresh evening air. I like it up there, sitting on a chair beside him and looking outside.

Van Daan and Dussel make very feeble remarks when I disappear into his room; "Anne's second home," they call it, or "Is it suitable for young gentlemen to receive young girls in semidarkness?" Peter shows amazing wit in his replies to these so-called humorous sallies. For that matter, Mummy too is somewhat curious and would love to ask what we talk about, if she wasn't secretly afraid of being snubbed. Peter says it's nothing but envy on the part of the grownups, because we are young and we don't pay much attention to their spitefulness. Sometimes he comes and gets me from downstairs, but he turns simply scarlet in spite of all precautions, and can hardly get the words out of his mouth. How thankful I am that I don't blush, it must be a highly unpleasant sensation. Daddy always says I'm prudish and vain but that's not true, I'm just simply vain! I have not often had anyone tell me I was pretty. Except a boy at school, who said I looked so attractive when I laughed. Yesterday I received a genuine compliment from Peter, and just for fun I will tell you roughly how the conversation went:

Peter so often used to say, "Do laugh, Anne!" This struck me as odd, and I asked, "Why must I always laugh?"

"Because I like it; you get such dimples in your cheeks when you laugh; how do they come, actually?"

"I was born with them. I've got one in my chin too. That's my only beauty!"

"Of course not, that's not true."

"Yes, it is, I know quite well that I'm not a beauty; I never have been and never shall be."

"I don't agree at all, I think you're pretty."

"That's not true."

"If I say so, then you can take it from me it is!"

Then I naturally said the same of him.

I hear a lot from all sides about the sudden friendship. We don't take much notice of all this parental chatter, their remarks are so feeble. Have the two sets of parents forgotten their own youth? It seems like it, at least they seem to take us seriously, if we make a joke, and laugh at us when we are serious.

Yours, Anne

Monday, 27 March, 1944

Dear Kitty,

One very big chapter of our history in hiding should really be about politics, but as this subject doesn't interest me personally very much, I've rather let it go. So for once I will devote my whole letter to politics today.

It goes without saying that there are very many different opinions on this topic, and it's even more logical that it should be a favorite subject for discussion in such critical times, but— it's just simply stupid that there should be so many quarrels over it.

They may speculate, laugh, abuse, and grumble, let them do what they will, as long as they stew in their own juice and don't quarrel, because the consequences are usually unpleasant.

The people from outside bring with them a lot of news that is not true; however, up till now our radio set hasn't lied to us. Henk, Miep, Koophuis, Elli, and Kraler all show ups and downs in their political moods, Henk least of all.

Political feeling here in the "Secret Annexe" is always about the same. During the countless arguments over invasion, air raids, speeches, etc., etc., one also always hears the countless cries of "impossible," or *"Um Gottes Willen,* if they are going to start now however long is it going to last." "It's going splendidly, first class, good!" Optimists and pessimists, and, above all, don't let's forget the realists who give their opinions with untiring energy and, just as with everything else, each one thinking he is right. It annoys a certain lady that her spouse has such unparalleled faith in the British, and a certain gentleman attacks his lady because of her teasing and disparaging remarks about his beloved nation.

They never seem to tire of it. I have discovered something —the effects are stupendous, just like pricking someone with a pin and waiting to see how they jump. This is what I do: begin on politics. One question, one word, one sentence, and at once they're off!

Just as if the German Wehrmacht news bulletins and the English B.B.C. were not enough, they have now introduced "Special Air-Raid Announcements." In one word, magnificent; but on the other hand often disappointing too. The British are making a non-stop business of their air attacks, with the same zest as the Germans make a business of lying. The radio therefore goes on early in the morning and is listened to at all hours of the day, until nine, ten, and often eleven o'clock in the evening.

This is certainly a sign that the grownups have infinite patience, but it also means the power of absorption of their brains is pretty limited, with exceptions, of course—I don't want to hurt anyone's feelings. One or two news bulletins would be ample per day! But the old geese, well—I've said my piece!

Arbeiter-Programm, Radio "Oranje," Frank Phillips or Her Majesty Queen Wilhelmina, they each get their turn, and an ever attentive ear. And if they are not eating or sleeping, then they're sitting around the radio and discussing food, sleep, and politics.

Ugh! It gets so boring, and it's quite a job not to become a dull old stick oneself. Politics can't do much more harm to the parents!

I must mention one shining exception—a speech by our beloved Winston Churchill is quite perfect.

Nine o'clock on Sunday evening. The teapot stands, with the cozy over it, on the table, and the guests come in. Dussel next to the radio on the left, Mr. Van Daan in front of it, with Peter beside him. Mummy next to Mr. Van Daan and Mrs. Van Daan behind him, and Pim at the table, Margot and I beside. I see I haven't described very clearly how we sit. The gentlemen puff away at their pipes, Peter's eyes are popping out of his head with the strain of listening, Mummy wearing a long dark negligée, and Mrs. Van Daan trembling because of the planes, which take no notice of the speech but fly blithely on towards Essen, Daddy sipping tea, Margot and I united in a sisterly fashion by the sleeping Mouschi, who is monopolizing both our knees. Margot's hair is in curlers, I am wearing a nightdress, which is much too small, too narrow, and too short.

It all looks so intimate, snug, peaceful, and this time it is too; yet I await the consequences with horror. They can hardly wait till the end of the speech, stamping their feet, so impatient are they to get down to discussing it. Brr, brr, brr— they egg each other on until the arguments lead to discord and quarrels.

Yours, Anne

Tuesday, 28 March, 1944

Dearest Kitty,

I could write a lot more about politics, but I have heaps of other things to tell you today. First, Mummy has more or less forbidden me to go upstairs so often, because, according to her, Mrs. Van Daan is jealous. Secondly, Peter has invited Margot to join us upstairs; I don't know whether it's just out of politeness or whether he really means it. Thirdly, I went and asked Daddy if he thought I need pay any regard to Mrs. Van Daan's jealousy, and he didn't think so. What next? Mummy is cross, perhaps jealous too. Daddy doesn't grudge us these times together, and thinks it's nice that we get on so well. Margot is fond of Peter too, but feels that two's company and three's a crowd.

Mummy thinks that Peter is in love with me; quite frankly, I only wish he were, then we'd be quits and really be able to get to know each other. She also says that he keeps on looking at me. Now, I suppose that's true, but still I can't help it if he looks at my dimples and we wink at each other occasionally, can I?

I'm in a very difficult position. Mummy is against me and I'm against her, Daddy closes his eyes and tries not to see the silent battle between us. Mummy is sad, because she does really love me, while I'm not in the least bit sad, because I don't think she understands. And Peter—I don't want to give Peter up, he's such a darling. I admire him so; it can grow into something beautiful between us; why do the "old 'uns" have to poke their noses in all the time? Luckily I'm quite used to hiding my feelings and I manage extremely well not to let them see how mad I am about him. Will he ever say anything? Will I ever feel his cheek against mine, like I felt Petel's cheek in my dream? Oh, Peter and Petel, you are one and the same! They don't understand us; won't they ever grasp that we are happy, just sitting together and not saying a word. They don't understand what has driven us together like this. Oh, when will all these difficulties be overcome? And yet it is good to overcome them, because then the end will be all the more wonderful. When he lies with his head on his arm with his eyes closed, then he is still a child; when he plays with Boche, he is loving; when he carries potatoes or anything heavy, then he is strong; when he goes and watches the shooting, or looks for burglars in the darkness, then he is brave; and when he is so awkward and clumsy, then he is just a pet.

I like it much better if he explains something to me than when I have to teach him; I would really adore him to be my superior in almost everything.

What do we care about the two mothers? Oh, but if only he would speak!

Yours, Anne

Wednesday, 29 March, 1944

Dear Kitty,

Bolkestein, an M.P., was speaking on the Dutch News from London, and he said that they ought to make a collection of diaries and letters after the war. Of course, they all made a rush at my diary immediately. Just imagine how interesting it would be if I were to publish a romance of the "Secret

Annexe." The title[1] alone would be enough to make people think it was a detective story.

But, seriously, it would seem quite funny ten years after the war if we Jews were to tell how we lived and what we ate and talked about here. Although I tell you a lot, still, even so, you only know very little of our lives.

How scared the ladies are during the air raids. For instance, on Sunday, when 350 British planes dropped half a million kilos of bombs on Ijmuiden, how the houses trembled like a wisp of grass in the wind, and who knows how many epidemics now rage. You don't know anything about all these things, and I would need to keep on writing the whole day if I were to tell you everything in detail. People have to line up for vegetables and all kinds of other things; doctors are unable to visit the sick, because if they turn their backs on their cars for a moment, they are stolen; burglaries and thefts abound, so much so that you wonder what has taken hold of the Dutch for them suddenly to have become such thieves. Little children of eight and eleven years break the windows of people's homes and steal whatever they can lay their hands on. No one dares to leave his house unoccupied for five minutes, because if you go, your things go too. Every day there are announcements in the newspapers offering rewards for the return of lost property, typewriters, Persian rugs, electric clocks, cloth, etc., etc. Electric clocks in the streets are dismantled, public telephones are pulled to pieces—down to the last thread. Morale among the population can't be good, the weekly rations are not enough to last for two days except the coffee substitute. The invasion is a long time coming, and the men have to go to Germany. The children are ill or undernourished, everyone is wearing old clothes and old shoes. A new sole costs 7.50 florins in the black market; moreover, hardly any of the shoemakers will accept shoe repairs or, if they do, you have to wait months, during which time the shoes often disappear.

There's one good thing in the midst of it all, which is that as the food gets worse and the measures against the people more severe, so sabotage against the authorities steadily increases. The people in the food offices, the police, officials, they all either work with their fellow citizens and help them or they

---

[1]The original title of this diary was *Het Achterhuis*. There is no exact translation into English, the nearest being *The Secret Annexe*.

tell tales on them and have them sent to prison. Fortunately, only a small percentage of Dutch people are on the wrong side.

Yours, Anne

Friday, 31 March, 1944

Dear Kitty,

Think of it, it's still pretty cold, but most people have been without coal for about a month—pleasant, eh! In general public feeling over the Russian front is optimistic again, because that is terrific! You know I don't write much about politics, but I must just tell you where they are now; they are right by the Polish border and have reached the Pruth near Rumania. They are close to Odessa. Every evening here they expect an extra communiqué from Stalin.

They fire off so many salvos in Moscow to celebrate their victories that the city must rumble and shake just about every day—whether they think it's fun to pretend that the war is close at hand again or that they know of no other way of expressing their joy, I don't know!

Hungary is occupied by German troops. There are still a million Jews there, so they too will have had it now.

The chatter about Peter and me has calmed down a bit now. We are very good friends, are together a lot and discuss every imaginable subject. It is awfully nice never to have to keep a check on myself as I would have to with other boys, whenever we get on to precarious ground. We were talking, for instance, about blood and via that subject we began talking about menstruation. He thinks we women are pretty tough. Why on earth? My life here has improved, greatly improved. God has not left me alone and will not leave me alone.

Yours, Anne

Saturday, 1 April, 1944

Dear Kitty,

And yet everything is still so difficult; I expect you can guess what I mean, can't you? I am so longing for a kiss, the kiss that is so long in coming. I wonder if all the time he still regards me as a friend? Am I nothing more?

You know and I know that I am strong, that I can carry most

of my burdens alone. I have never been used to sharing my troubles with anyone, I have never clung to my mother, but now I would so love to lay my head on "his" shoulder just once and remain still.

I can't, I simply can't ever forget that dream of Peter's cheek, when it was all, all so good! Wouldn't he long for it too? Is it that he is just too shy to acknowledge his love? Why does he want me with him so often? Oh, why doesn't he speak?

I'd better stop, I must be quiet, I shall remain strong and with a bit of patience the other will come too, but—and that is the worst of it—it looks just as if I'm running after him; *I* am always the one who goes upstairs, *he* doesn't come to me.

But that is just because of the rooms, and he is sure to understand the difficulty.

Oh, yes, and there's more he'll understand.

Yours, Anne

Monday, 3 April, 1944

Dear Kitty,

Contrary to my usual custom, I will for once write more fully about food because it has become a very difficult and important matter, not only here in the "Secret Annexe" but in the whole of Holland, all Europe, and even beyond.

In the twenty-one months that we've spent here we have been through a good many "food cycles"—you'll understand what that means in a minute. When I talk of "food cycles" I mean periods in which one has nothing else to eat but one particular dish or kind of vegetable. We had nothing but endive for a long time, day in, day out, endive with sand, endive without sand, stew with endive, boiled or *en casserole;* then it was spinach, and after that followed kohlrabi, salsify, cucumbers, tomatoes, sauerkraut, etc., etc.

For instance, it's really disagreeable to eat a lot of sauerkraut for lunch and supper every day, but you do it if you're hungry. However, we have the most delightful period of all now, because we don't get any fresh vegetables at all. Our weekly menu for supper consists of kidney beans, pea soup, potatoes with dumplings, potato-chalet and, by the grace of God, occasionally turnip tops or rotten carrots, and then the kidney beans once again. We eat potatoes at every meal, beginning with breakfast, because of the bread shortage. We make our soup from kidney or haricot beans, potatoes, Julienne soup in packets, French beans in packets, kidney beans in packets. Everything contains beans, not to mention the bread!

In the evening we always have potatoes with gravy substitute and—thank goodness we've still got it—beetroot salad. I must still tell you about the dumplings, which we make out of government flour, water, and yeast. They are so sticky and tough, they lie like stones in one's stomach—ah, well!

The great attraction each week is a slice of liver sausage, and jam on dry bread. But we're still alive, and quite often we even enjoy our poor meals.

Yours, Anne

Tuesday, 4 April, 1944

Dear Kitty,

For a long time I haven't had any idea of what I was working for any more; the end of the war is so terribly far away, so unreal, like a fairy tale. If the war isn't over by September I shan't go to school any more, because I don't want to be two years behind. Peter filled my days—nothing but Peter, dreams and thoughts until Saturday, when I felt so utterly miserable; oh, it was terrible. I was holding back my tears all the while I was with Peter, then laughed with Van Daan over a lemon punch, was cheerful and excited, but the moment I was alone I knew that I would have to cry my heart out. So, clad in my nightdress, I let myself go and slipped down onto the floor. First I said my long prayer very earnestly, then I cried with my head on my arms, my knees bent up, on the bare floor, completely folded up. One large sob brought me back to earth again, and I quelled my tears because I didn't want them to hear anything in the next room. Then I began trying to talk some courage into myself. I could only say: "I must, I must, I must . . ." Completely stiff from the unnatural position, I fell against the side of the bed and fought on, until I climbed into bed again just before half past ten. It was over!

And now it's all over. I must work, so as not to be a fool, to get on, to become a journalist, because that's what I want! I know that I can write, a couple of my stories are good, my descriptions of the "Secret Annexe" are humorous, there's a lot in my diary that speaks, but—whether I have real talent remains to be seen.

"Eva's Dream" is my best fairy tale, and the queer thing about it is that I don't know where it comes from. Quite a lot of "Cady's Life" is good too, but on the whole, it's nothing.

I am the best and sharpest critic of my own work. I know myself what is and what is not well written. Anyone who doesn't write doesn't know how wonderful it is; I used to bemoan the fact that I couldn't draw at all, but now I am more than happy that I can at least write. And if I haven't any talent for writing books or newspaper articles, well, then I can always write for myself.

I want to get on; I can't imagine that I would have to lead the same sort of life as Mummy and Mrs. Van Daan and all the women who do their work and are then forgotten. I must have something besides a husband and children, something that I can devote myself to!

I want to go on living even after my death! And therefore I am grateful to God for giving me this gift, this possibility of developing myself and of writing, of expressing all that is in me.

I can shake off everything if I write; my sorrows disappear, my courage is reborn. But, and that is the great question, will I ever be able to write anything great, will I ever become a journalist or a writer? I hope so, oh, I hope so very much, for I can recapture everything when I write, my thoughts, my ideals and my fantasies.

I haven't done anything more to "Cady's Life" for ages; in my mind I know exactly how to go on, but somehow it doesn't flow from my pen. Perhaps I never shall finish it, it may land up in the wastepaper basket, or the fire . . . that's a horrible idea, but then I think to myself, "At the age of fourteen and with so little experience, how can you write about philosophy?"

So I go on again with fresh courage; I think I shall succeed, because I want to write!

Yours, Anne

Thursday, 6 April, 1944

Dear Kitty,

You asked me what my hobbies and interests were, so I want to reply. I warn you, however, that there are heaps of them, so don't get a shock!

First of all: writing, but that hardly counts as a hobby.

Number two: family trees. I've been searching for family trees of the French, German, Spanish, English, Austrian, Russian, Norwegian, and Dutch royal families in all the newspapers, books, and pamphlets I can find. I've made great progress with a lot of them, as, for a long time already, I've been taking down notes from all the biographies and history books that I read; I even copy out many passages of history.

My third hobby then is history, on which Daddy has already bought me a lot of books. I can hardly wait for the day that I shall be able to comb through the books in a public library.

Number four is Greek and Roman mythology. I have various books about this too.

Other hobbies are film stars and family photos. Mad on books and reading. Have a great liking for history of art, poets and painters. I may go in for music later on. I have a great loathing for algebra, geometry, and figures.

I enjoy all the other school subjects, but history above all!

Yours, Anne

Tuesday, 11 April, 1944

Dear Kitty,

My head throbs, I honestly don't know where to begin.

On Friday (Good Friday) we played Monopoly, Saturday afternoon too. These days passed quickly and uneventfully. On Sunday afternoon, on my invitation, Peter came to my room at half past four; at a quarter past five we went to the front attic, where we remained until six o'clock. There was a beautiful Mozart concert on the radio from six o'clock until a quarter past seven. I enjoyed it all very much, but especially the "Kleine Nachtmusik." I can hardly listen in the room because I'm always so inwardly stirred when I hear lovely music.

On Sunday evening Peter and I went to the front attic together and, in order to sit comfortably, we took with us a few divan cushions that we were able to lay our hands on. We seated ourselves on one packing case. Both the case and the cushions were very narrow, so we sat absolutely squashed together, leaning against other cases. Mouschi kept us company too, so we weren't unchaperoned.

Suddenly, at a quarter to nine, Mr. Van Daan whistled and asked if we had one of Dussel's cushions. We both jumped up and went downstairs with cushion, cat, and Van Daan.

A lot of trouble arose out of this cushion, because Dussel was annoyed that we had one of his cushions, one that he used as a pillow. He was afraid that there might be fleas in it and made a great commotion about his beloved cushion! Peter and I put two hard brushes in his bed as a revenge. We had a good laugh over this little interlude!

Our fun didn't last long. At half past nine Peter knocked softly on the door and asked Daddy if he would just help him upstairs over a difficult English sentence. "That's a blind," I said to Margot, "anyone could see through that one!" I was right. They were in the act of breaking into the warehouse. Daddy, Van Daan, Dussel, and Peter were downstairs in a flash. Margot, Mummy, Mrs. Van Daan, and I stayed upstairs and waited.

Four frightened women just have to talk, so talk we did, until we heard a bang downstairs. After that all was quiet, the clock struck a quarter to ten. The color had vanished from our faces, we were still quiet, although we were afraid. Where could the men be? What was that bang? Would they be fighting the burglars? Ten o'clock, footsteps on the stairs: Daddy, white and nervous, entered, followed by Mr. Van Daan. "Lights out, creep upstairs, we expect the police in the house!"

There was no time to be frightened: the lights went out, I quickly grabbed a jacket, and we were upstairs. "What has happened? Tell us quickly!" There was no one to tell us, the men having disappeared downstairs again. Only at ten past ten did they reappear; two kept watch at Peter's open window, the door to the landing was closed, the swinging cupboard shut. We hung a jersey round the night light, and after that they told us:

Peter heard two loud bangs on the landing, ran downstairs, and saw there was a large plank out of the left half of the door. He dashed upstairs, warned the "Home Guard" of the family, and the four of them proceeded downstairs. When they entered the warehouse, the burglars were in the act of enlarging the hole. Without further thought Van Daan shouted: "Police!"

A few hurried steps outside, and the burglars had fled. In order to avoid the hole being noticed by the police, a plank was put against it, but a good hard kick from outside sent it flying to the ground. The men were perplexed at such impudence, and both Van Daan and Peter felt murder welling up within them; Van Daan beat on the ground with a chopper, and all was quiet again. Once more they wanted to put the plank in front of the hole. Disturbance! A married couple outside shone a torch through the opening, lighting up the whole warehouse. "Hell!" muttered one of the men, and now they switched over from their role of police to that of burglars. The four of them sneaked upstairs, Peter quickly opened the doors and windows of the kitchen and private office, flung the telephone onto the floor, and finally the four of them landed behind the swinging cupboard.

END OF PART ONE

The married couple with the torch would probably have warned the police: it was Sunday evening, Easter Sunday, no one at the office on Easter Monday, so none of us could budge until Tuesday morning. Think of it, waiting in such fear for two nights and a day! No one had anything to suggest, so we simply sat there in pitch-darkness, because Mrs. Van Daan in her fright had unintentionally turned the lamp right out; talked in whispers, and at every creak one heard "Sh! sh!"

It turned half past ten, eleven, but not a sound; Daddy and Van Daan joined us in turns. Then a quarter past eleven, a bustle and noise downstairs. Everyone's breath was audible, otherwise no one moved. Footsteps in the house, in the private office, kitchen, then . . . on our staircase. No one breathed audibly now, footsteps on our staircase, then a rattling of the swinging cupboard. This moment is indescribable. "Now we are lost!" I said, and could see us all being taken away by the Gestapo that very night. Twice they rattled at the cupboard, then there was nothing, the footsteps withdrew, we were saved so far. A shiver seemed to pass from one to another, I heard someone's teeth chattering, no one said a word.

There was not another sound in the house, but a light was burning on our landing, right in front of the cupboard. Could that be because it was a secret cupboard? Perhaps the police had forgotten the light? Would someone come back to put it out? Tongues loosened, there was no one in the house any longer, perhaps there was someone on guard outside.

Next we did three things: we went over again what we supposed had happened, we trembled with fear, and we had to go to the lavatory. The buckets were in the attic, so all we had was Peter's tin wastepaper basket. Van Daan went first, then Daddy, but Mummy was too shy to face it. Daddy brought the wastepaper basket into the room, where Margot, Mrs. Van Daan, and I gladly made use of it. Finally Mummy decided to do so too. People kept on asking for paper—fortunately I had some in my pocket!

The tin smelled ghastly, everything went on in a whisper, we were tired, it was twelve o'clock. "Lie down on the floor then and sleep." Margot and I were each given a pillow and one blanket; Margot lying just near the store cupboard and I between the table legs. The smell wasn't quite so bad when one was on the floor, but still Mrs. Van Daan quietly brought some chlorine, a tea towel over the pot serving as a second expedient.

Talk, whispers, fear, stink, flatulation, and always someone on the pot; then try to go to sleep! However, by half past two I was so tired that I knew no more until half past three. I awoke when Mrs. Van Daan laid her head on my foot.

"For heaven's sake, give me something to put on!" I asked. I was given something, but don't ask what—a pair of woolen knickers over my pajamas, a red jumper, and a black skirt, white oversocks and a pair of sports stockings full of holes. Then Mrs. Van Daan sat in the chair and her husband came and lay on my feet. I lay thinking till half past three, shivering the whole time, which prevented Van Daan from sleeping. I prepared myself for the return of the police, then we'd have to say that we were in hiding; they would either be good Dutch people, then we'd be saved, or N.S.B.-ers,[1] then we'd have to bribe them!

"In that case, destroy the radio," sighed Mrs. Van Daan.

[1] The Dutch National Socialist Movement.

"Yes, in the stove!" replied her husband. "If they find us, then let them find the radio as well!"

"Then they will find Anne's diary," added Daddy. "Burn it then," suggested the most terrified member of the party. This, and when the police rattled the cupboard door, were my worst moments. "Not my diary; if my diary goes, I go with it!" But luckily Daddy didn't answer.

There is no object in recounting all the conversations that I can still remember; so much was said. I comforted Mrs. Van Daan, who was very scared. We talked about escaping and being questioned by the Gestapo, about ringing up, and being brave.

"We must behave like soldiers, Mrs. Van Daan. If all is up now, then let's go for Queen and Country, for freedom, truth, and right, as they always say on the Dutch News from England. The only thing that is really rotten is that we get a lot of other people into trouble too."

Mr. Van Daan changed places again with his wife after an hour, and Daddy came and sat beside me. The men smoked non-stop, now and then there was a deep sigh, then someone went on the pot and everything began all over again.

Four o'clock, five o'clock, half past five. Then I went and sat with Peter by his window and listened, so close together that we could feel each other's bodies quivering; we spoke a word or two now and then, and listened attentively. In the room next door they took down the blackout. They wanted to call up Koophuis at seven o'clock and get him to send some-one around. Then they wrote down everything they wanted to tell Koophuis over the phone. The risk that the police on guard at the door, or in the warehouse, might hear the tele-phone was very great, but the danger of the police returning was even greater.

The points were these:

Burglars broken in: police have been in the house, as far as the swinging cupboard, but no further.

Burglars apparently disturbed, forced open the door in the warehouse and escaped through the garden.

Main entrance bolted, Kraler must have used the second door when he left. The typewriters and adding machine are safe in the black case in the private office.

Try to warn Henk and fetch the key from Elli, then go and look round the office—on the pretext of feeding the cat.

Everything went according to plan. Koophuis was phoned, the typewriters which we had upstairs were put in the case. Then we sat around the table again and waited for Henk or the police.

Peter had fallen asleep and Van Daan and I were lying on the floor, when we heard loud footsteps downstairs. I got up quietly: "That's Henk."

"No, no, it's the police," some of the others said.

Someone knocked at the door, Miep whistled. This was too much for Mrs. Van Daan, she turned as white as a sheet and sank limply into a chair; had the tension lasted one minute longer she would have fainted.

Our room was a perfect picture when Miep and Henk entered, the table alone would have been worth photographing! A copy of *Cinema and Theater*, covered with jam and a remedy for diarrhea, opened at a page of dancing girls, two jam pots, two started loaves of bread, a mirror, comb, matches, ash, cigarettes, tobacco, ash tray, books, a pair of pants, a torch, toilet paper, etc., etc., lay jumbled together in variegated splendor.

Of course Henk and Miep were greeted with shouts and tears. Henk mended the hole in the door with some planks, and soon went off again to inform the police of the burglary. Miep had also found a letter under the warehouse door from the night watchman Slagter, who had noticed the hole and warned the police, whom he would also visit.

So we had half an hour to tidy ourselves. I've never seen such a change take place in half an hour. Margot and I took the bedclothes downstairs, went to the W.C., washed, and did our teeth and hair. After that I tidied the room a bit and went upstairs again. The table there was already cleared, so we ran off some water and made coffee and tea, boiled the milk, and laid the table for lunch. Daddy and Peter emptied the potties and cleaned them with warm water and chlorine.

At eleven o'clock we sat round the table with Henk, who was back by that time, and slowly things began to be more normal and cozy again. Henk's story was as follows:

Mr. Slagter was asleep, but his wife told Henk that her

husband had found the hole in our door when he was doing his tour round the canals, and that he had called a policeman, who had gone through the building with him. He would be coming to see Kraler on Tuesday and would tell him more then. At the police station they knew nothing of the burglary yet, but the policeman had made a note of it at once and would come and look round on Tuesday. On the way back Henk happened to meet our greengrocer at the corner, and told him that the house had been broken into. "I know that," he said quite coolly. "I was passing last evening with my wife and saw the hole in the door. My wife wanted to walk on, but I just had a look in with my torch; then the thieves cleared at once. To be on the safe side, I didn't ring up the police, as with you I didn't think it was the thing to do. I don't know anything, but I guess a lot."

Henk thanked him and went on. The man obviously guesses that we're here, because he always brings the potatoes during the lunch hour. Such a nice man!

It was one by the time Henk had gone and we'd finished doing the dishes. We all went for a sleep. I awoke at a quarter to three and saw that Dr. Dussel had already disappeared. Quite by chance, and with my sleepy eyes, I ran into Peter in the bathroom; he had just come down. We arranged to meet downstairs.

I tidied myself and went down. "Do you still dare to go to the front attic?" he asked. I nodded, fetched my pillow, and we went up to the attic. It was glorious weather, and soon the sirens were wailing; we stayed where we were. Peter put his arm around my shoulder, and I put mine around his and so we remained, our arms around each other, quietly waiting until Margot came to fetch us for coffee at four o'clock.

We finished our bread, drank lemonade and joked (we were able to again), otherwise everything went normally. In the evening I thanked Peter because he was the bravest of us all.

None of us has ever been in such danger as that night. God truly protected us; just think of it—the police at our secret cupboard, the light on right in front of it, and still we remained undiscovered.

If the invasion comes, and bombs with it, then it is each man for himself, but in this case the fear was also for our good, innocent protectors. "We are saved, go on saving us!" That is all we can say.

This affair has brought quite a number of changes with it. Mr. Dussel no longer sits downstairs in Kraler's office in the evenings, but in the bathroom instead. Peter goes round the house for a checkup at half past eight and half past nine. Peter isn't allowed to have his window open at nights any more. No one is allowed to pull the plug after half past nine. This evening there's a carpenter coming to make the warehouse doors even stronger.

Now there are debates going on all the time in the "Secret Annexe." Kraler reproached us for our carelessness. Henk, too, said that in a case like that we must never go downstairs. We have been pointedly reminded that we are in hiding, that we are Jews in chains, chained to one spot, without any rights, but with a thousand duties. We Jews mustn't show our feelings, must be brave and strong, must accept all inconveniences and not grumble, must do what is within our power and trust in God. Sometimes this terrible war will be over. Surely the time will come when we are people again, and not just Jews.

Who has inflicted this upon us? Who has made us Jews different from all other people? Who has allowed us to suffer so terribly up till now? It is God that has made us as we are, but it will be God, too, who will raise us up again. If we bear all this suffering and if there are still Jews left, when it is over, then Jews, instead of being doomed, will be held up as an example. Who knows, it might even be our religion from which the world and all peoples learn good, and for that reason and that reason only do we have to suffer now. We can never become just Netherlanders, or just English, or representatives of any country for that matter, we will always remain Jews, but we want to, too.

Be brave! Let us remain aware of our task and not grumble, a solution will come, God has never deserted our people. Right through the ages there have been Jews, through all the ages they have had to suffer, but it has made them strong too; the weak fall, but the strong will remain and never go under!

During that night I really felt that I had to die, I waited for the police, I was prepared, as the soldier is on the battlefield. I was eager to lay down my life for the country, but now, now I've been saved again, now my first wish after the war is that

I may become Dutch! I love the Dutch, I love this country, I love the language and want to work here. And even if I have to write to the Queen myself, I will not give up until I have reached my goal.

I am becoming still more independent of my parents, young as I am, I face life with more courage than Mummy; my feeling for justice is immovable, and truer than hers. I know what I want, I have a goal, an opinion, I have a religion and love. Let me be myself and then I am satisfied. I know that I'm a woman, a woman with inward strength and plenty of courage.

If God lets me live, I shall attain more than Mummy ever has done, I shall not remain insignificant, I shall work in the world and for mankind!

And now I know that first and foremost I shall require courage and cheerfulness!

Yours, Anne

Friday, 14 April, 1944

Dear Kitty,

The atmosphere here is still extremely strained. Pim has just about reached boiling point. Mrs. Van Daan is in bed with a cold and trumpeting away. Mr. Van Daan grows pale without his fags, Dussel, who is giving up a lot of his comfort, is full of observations, etc., etc.

There is no doubt that our luck's not in at the moment. The lavatory leaks and the washer of the tap has gone, but, thanks to our many connections, we shall soon be able to get these things put right.

I am sentimental sometimes, I know that, but there is occasion to be sentimental here at times, when Peter and I are sitting somewhere together on a hard, wooden crate in the midst of masses of rubbish and dust, our arms around each other's shoulders, and very close, he with one of my curls in his hand; when the birds sing outside and you see the trees changing to green, the sun invites one to be out in the open air, when the sky is so blue, then—oh, then, I wish for so much!

One sees nothing but dissatisfied, grumpy faces here, nothing but sighs and suppressed complaints; it really would seem as if suddenly we were very badly off here. If the truth is told, things are just as bad as you yourself care to make them. There's no one here that sets a good example; everyone should see that he gets the better of his own moods. Every day you hear, "If only it was all over."

My work, my hope, my love, my courage, all these things keep my head above water and keep me from complaining.

I really believe, Kits, that I'm slightly bats today, and yet I don't know why. Everything here is so mixed up, nothing's connected any more, and sometimes I very much doubt whether in the future anyone will be interested in all my tosh.

"The unbosomings of an ugly duckling" will be the title of all this nonsense. My diary really won't be much use to Messrs. Bolkestein or Gerbrandy.[1]

Yours, Anne

Saturday, 15 April, 1944

Dear Kitty,

"Shock upon shock. Will there ever be an end?" We honestly can ask ourselves that question now. Guess what's the latest. Peter forgot to unbolt the front door (which is bolted on the inside at night) and the lock of the other door doesn't work. The result was that Kraler and the men could not get into the house, so he went to the neighbors, forced open the kitchen window, and entered the building from the back. He is livid at us for being so stupid.

I can tell you, it's upset Peter frightfully. At one meal, when Mummy said she felt more sorry for Peter than anyone else, he almost started to cry. We're all just as much to blame as he is, because nearly every day the men ask whether the door's been unbolted and, just today, no one did.

Perhaps I shall be able to console him a bit later on; I would so love to help him.

Yours, Anne

[1]Two members of the wartime Dutch Cabinet-in-Exile in London.

Sunday morning, just before eleven o'clock,
16 April, 1944

Darlingest Kitty,

Remember yesterday's date, for it is a very important day in my life. Surely it is a great day for every girl when she receives her first kiss? Well, then, it is just as important for me too! Bram's kiss on my right cheek doesn't count any more, likewise the one from Mr. Walker on my right hand.

How did I suddenly come by this kiss? Well, I will tell you.

Yesterday evening at eight o'clock I was sitting with Peter on his divan, it wasn't long before his arm went round me. "Let's move up a bit," I said, "then I don't bump my head against the cupboard." He moved up, almost into the corner, I laid my arm under his and across his back, and he just about buried me, because his arm was hanging on my shoulder.

Now we've sat like this on other occasions, but never so close together as yesterday. He held me firmly against him, my left shoulder against his chest; already my heart began to beat faster, but we had not finished yet. He didn't rest until my head was on his shoulder and his against it. When I sat upright again after about five minutes, he soon took my head in his hands and laid it against him once more. Oh, it was so lovely, I couldn't talk much, the joy was too great. He stroked my cheek and arm a bit awkwardly, played with my curls and our heads lay touching most of the time. I can't tell you, Kitty, the feeling that ran through me all the while. I was too happy for words, and I believe he was as well.

We got up at half past eight. Peter put on his gym shoes, so that when he toured the house he wouldn't make a noise, and I stood beside him. How it came about so suddenly, I don't know, but before we went downstairs he kissed me, through my hair, half on my left cheek, half on my ear; I tore downstairs without looking round, and am simply longing for today!

Yours, Anne

Monday, 17 April, 1944

Dear Kitty,

Do you think that Daddy and Mummy would approve of my sitting and kissing a boy on a divan—a boy of seventeen and a half and a girl of just under fifteen? I don't really think they would, but I must rely on myself over this. It is so quiet and peaceful to lie in his arms and to dream, it is so thrilling to feel his cheek against mine, it is so lovely to know that there is someone waiting for me. But there is indeed a big "but," because will Peter be content to leave it at this? I haven't forgotten his promise already, but . . . he *is* a boy!

I know myself that I'm starting very soon, not even fifteen, and so independent already! It's certainly hard for other people to understand, I know almost for certain that Margot would never kiss a boy unless there had been some talk of an engagement or marriage, but neither Peter nor I have anything like that in mind. I'm sure too that Mummy never touched a man before Daddy. What would my girl friends say about it if they knew that I lay in Peter's arms, my heart against his chest, my head on his shoulder and with his head against mine!

Oh, Anne, how scandalous! But honestly, I don't think it is; we are shut up here, shut away from the world, in fear and anxiety, especially just lately. Why, then, should we who love each other remain apart? Why should we wait until we've reached a suitable age? Why should we bother?

I have taken it upon myself to look after myself; he would never want to cause me sorrow or pain. Why shouldn't I follow the way my heart leads me, if it makes us both happy? All the same, Kitty, I believe you can sense that I'm in doubt, I think it must be my honesty which rebels against doing anything on the sly! Do you think it's my duty to tell Daddy what I'm doing? Do you think we should share our secret with a third person? A lot of the beauty would be lost, but would my conscience feel happier? I will discuss it with "him."

Oh, yes, there's still so much I want to talk to him about, for I don't see the use of only just cuddling each other. To exchange our thoughts, that shows confidence and faith in each other, we would both be sure to profit by it!

Yours, Anne

Tuesday, 18 April, 1944

Dear Kitty,

Everything goes well here. Daddy's just said that he definitely expects large-scale operations to take place before the twentieth of May, both in Russia and Italy, and also in the West; I find it more and more difficult to imagine our liberation from here.

Yesterday Peter and I finally got down to our talk, which had already been put off for at least ten days. I explained everything about girls to him and didn't hesitate to discuss the most intimate things. The evening ended by each giving the other a kiss, just about beside my mouth, it's really a lovely feeling.

Perhaps I'll take my diary up there sometime, to go more deeply into things for once. I don't get any satisfaction out of lying in each other's arms day in, day out, and would so like to feel that he's the same.

We are having a superb spring after our long, lingering winter; April is really glorious, not too hot and not too cold, with little showers now and then. Our chestnut tree is already quite greenish and you can even see little blooms here and there.

Elli gave us a treat on Saturday, by bringing four bunches of flowers, three bunches of narcissus and one of grape hyacinths, the latter being for me.

I must do some algebra, Kitty—good-by.

Yours, Anne

Wednesday, 19 April, 1944

My darling,

Is there anything more beautiful in the world than to sit before an open window and enjoy nature, to listen to the birds singing, feel the sun on your cheeks and have a darling boy in your arms? It is so soothing and peaceful to feel his arms around me, to know that he is close by and yet to remain silent, it can't be bad, for this tranquillity is good. Oh, never to be disturbed again, not even by Mouschi.

Yours, Anne

Friday, 21 April, 1944

Dear Kitty,

Yesterday afternoon I was lying in bed with a sore throat, but since I was already bored on the first day and did not have a temperature, I got up again today. It's the eighteenth birthday of Her Royal Highness Princess Elizabeth of York. The B.B.C. has said that she will not be declared of age yet, though it's usually the case with royal children. We have been asking ourselves what prince this beauty is going to marry, but cannot think of anyone suitable. Perhaps her sister, Princess Margaret Rose, can have Prince Baudouin of Belgium one day.

Here we are having one misfortune after another. Scarcely had the outside doors been strengthened than the warehouse man appeared again. In all probability it was he who stole the potato meal and wants to put the blame on to Elli's shoulders. The whole "Secret Annexe" is understandably het up again. Elli is beside herself with anger.

I want to send in to some paper or other to see if they will take one of my stories, under a pseudonym, of course.

Till next time, darling!

Yours, Anne

Tuesday, 25 April, 1944

Dear Kitty,

Dussel has not been on speaking terms with Van Daan for ten days and just because, ever since the burglary, a whole lot of fresh security measures have been made that don't suit him. He maintains that Van Daan has been shouting at him. "Everything here happens upside down," he told me. "I am going to speak to your father about it." He is not supposed to sit in the office downstairs on Saturday afternoons and Sundays any more, but he goes on doing it just the same. Van Daan was furious and Father went downstairs to talk to him. Naturally, he kept on inventing excuses, but this time he could not get around even Father. Father now talks to him as little as possible, as Dussel has insulted him. None of us know in what way, but it must have been very bad.

I have written a lovely story called "Blurry, the Explorer," which pleased the three to whom I read it very much.

Yours, Anne

Thursday, 27 April, 1944

Dear Kitty,

Mrs. Van Daan was in such a bad mood this morning, nothing but complaints! First, there's her cold, and she can't get any lozenges, and so much nose-blowing is unendurable. Next, it's that the sun's not shining, that the invasion doesn't come, that we can't look out of the windows, etc., etc. We all had to laugh at her; and she was sporting enough to join in. At the moment I'm reading *The Emperor Charles V*, written by a professor at Göttingen University; he worked at the book for forty years. I read fifty pages in five days; it's impossible to do more. The book has 598 pages, so now you can work out how long it will take me—and there is a second volume to follow. But very interesting!

What doesn't a schoolgirl get to know in a single day! Take me, for example. First, I translated a piece from Dutch into English, about Nelson's last battle. After that, I went through some more of Peter the Great's war against Norway (1700–1721), Charles XII, Augustus the Strong, Stanislavs Leczinsky, Mazeppa, Von Görz, Brandenburg, Pomerania and Denmark, plus the usual dates.

After that I landed up in Brazil, read about Bahia tobacco, the abundance of coffee and the one and a half million inhabitants of Rio de Janeiro, of Pernambuco and Sao Paulo, not forgetting the river Amazon; about Negroes, Mulattos, Mestizos, Whites, more than fifty per cent of the population being illiterate, and the malaria. As there was still some time left, I quickly ran through a family tree. Jan the Elder, Willem Lodewijk, Ernst Casimir I, Hendrik Casimir I, right up to the little Margriet Franciska (born in 1943 in Ottawa).

Twelve o'clock: In the attic, I continued my program with the history of the Church—Phew! Till one o'clock.

Just after two, the poor child sat working ('hm, 'hm!) again, this time studying narrow- and broad-nosed monkeys. Kitty, tell me quickly how many toes a hippopotamus has!! Then followed the Bible, Noah and the Ark, Shem, Ham, and Japheth. After that Charles V. Then with Peter: *The Colonel*, in English, by Thackeray. Heard my French verbs and then compared the Mississippi with the Missouri.

I've still got a cold and have given it to Margot as well as to Mummy and Daddy. As long as Peter doesn't get it! He called me his "Eldorado" and wanted a kiss. Of course, I couldn't! Funny boy! But still, he's a darling.

Enough for today, good-by!

Yours, Anne

Friday, 28 April, 1944

Dear Kitty,

I have never forgotten my dream about Peter Wessel (see beginning of January). If I think of it, I can still feel his cheek against mine now, and recall that lovely feeling that made everything good.

Sometimes I have had the same feeling here with Peter, but never to such an extent, until yesterday, when we were, as usual, sitting on the divan, our arms around each other's waists. Then suddenly the ordinary Anne slipped away and a second Anne took her place, a second Anne who is not reckless and jocular, but one who just wants to love and be gentle.

I sat pressed closely against him and felt a wave of emotion come over me, tears sprang into my eyes, the left one trickled onto his dungarees, the right one ran down my nose and also fell onto his dungarees. Did he notice? He made no move or sign to show that he did. I wonder if he feels the same as I do? He hardly said a word. Does he know that he has two Annes before him? These questions must remain unanswered.

At half past eight I stood up and went to the window, where we always say good-by. I was still trembling, I was still Anne number two. He came towards me, I flung my arms around his neck and gave him a kiss on his left cheek, and was about to kiss the other cheek, when my lips met his and we pressed them together. In a whirl we were clasped in each other's arms, again and again, never to leave off. Oh, Peter does so need tenderness. For the first time in his life he has discovered a girl, has seen for the first time that even the most irritating girls have another side to them, that they have hearts and can be different when you are alone with them. For the first time in his life he has given of himself and, having never had a boy or girl friend in his life before, shown his real self. Now we have found each other. For that matter, I didn't know him

either, like him having never had a trusted friend, and this is
what it has come to. . . .

Once more there is a question which gives me no peace: "Is
it right? Is it right that I should have yielded so soon, that I
am so ardent, just as ardent and eager as Peter himself? May
I, a girl, let myself go to this extent?" There is but *one* answer:
"I have longed so much and for so long—I am so lonely—and
now I have found consolation."

In the mornings we just behave in an ordinary way, in the
afternoons more or less so (except just occasionally); but in
the evenings the suppressed longings of the whole day, the
happiness and the blissful memories of all the previous occasions
come to the surface and we only think of each other. Every
evening, after the last kiss, I would like to dash away, not to
look into his eyes any more—away, away, alone in the darkness.

And what do I have to face, when I reach the bottom of
the staircase? Bright lights, questions, and laughter; I have to
swallow it all and not show a thing. My heart still feels too
much; I can't get over a shock such as I received yesterday all
at once. The Anne who is gentle shows herself too little anyway and, therefore, will not allow herself to be suddenly driven
into the background. Peter has touched my emotions more
deeply than anyone has ever done before—except in my
dreams. Peter has taken possession of me and turned me inside out; surely it goes without saying that anyone would
require a rest and a little while to recover from such an up-
heaval?

Oh Peter, what have you done to me? What do you want
of me? Where will this lead us? Oh, now I understand Elli;
now, now that I am going through this myself, now I understand her doubt; if I were older and he should ask me to
marry him, what should I answer? Anne, be honest! You would
not be able to marry him, but yet, it would be hard to let him
go. Peter hasn't enough character yet, not enough will power,
too little courage and strength. He is still a child in his heart
of hearts, he is no older than I am; he is only searching for
tranquillity and happiness.

Am I only fourteen? Am I really still a silly little schoolgirl?
Am I really so inexperienced about everything? I have more
experience than most; I have been through things that hardly
anyone of my age has undergone. I am afraid of myself, I am

afraid that in my longing I am giving myself too quickly. How, later on, can it ever go right with other boys? Oh, it is so difficult, always battling with one's heart and reason; in its own time, each will speak, but do I know for certain that I have chosen the right time?

Yours, Anne

Tuesday, 2 May, 1944

Dear Kitty,

On Saturday evening I asked Peter whether he thought that I ought to tell Daddy a bit about us; when we'd discussed it a little, he came to the conclusion that I should. I was glad, for it shows that he's an honest boy. As soon as I got downstairs I went off with Daddy to get some water; and while we were on the stairs I said, "Daddy, I expect you've gathered that when we're together Peter and I don't sit miles apart. Do you think it's wrong?" Daddy didn't reply immediately, then said, "No, I don't think it's wrong, but you must be careful, Anne; you're in such a confined space here." When we went upstairs, he said something else on the same lines. On Sunday morning he called me to him and said, "Anne, I have thought more about what you said." I felt scared already. "It's not really very right—here in this house; I thought that you were just pals. Is Peter in love?"

"Oh, of course not," I replied.

"You know that I understand both of you, but you must be the one to hold back. Don't go upstairs so often, don't encourage him more than you can help. It is the man who is always the active one in these things; the woman can hold him back. It is quite different under normal circumstances, when you are free, you see other boys and girls, you can get away sometimes, play games and do all kinds of other things; but here, if you're together a lot, and you want to get away, you can't; you see each other every hour of the day—in fact, all the time. Be careful, Anne, and don't take it too seriously!"

"I don't, Daddy, but Peter is a decent boy, really a nice boy!"

"Yes, but he is not a strong character; he can be easily influenced, for good, but also for bad; I hope for his sake that his good side will remain uppermost, because, by nature, that is how he is."

We talked on for a bit and agreed that Daddy should talk to him too.

On Sunday morning in the attic he asked, "And have you talked to your father, Anne?"

"Yes," I replied, "I'll tell you about it. Daddy doesn't think it's bad, but he says that here, where we're so close together all the time, clashes may easily arise."

"But we agreed, didn't we, never to quarrel; and I'm determined to stick to it!"

"So will I, Peter, but Daddy didn't think that it was like this, he just thought we were pals; do you think that we still can be?"

"I can—what about you?"

"Me too, I told Daddy that I trusted you. I do trust you, Peter, just as much as I trust Daddy, and I believe you to be worthy of it. You are, aren't you, Peter?"

"I hope so." (He was very shy and rather red in the face.)

"I believe in you, Peter," I went on, "I believe that you have good qualities, and that you'll get on in the world."

After that, we talked about other things. Later I said, "If we come out of here, I know quite well that you won't bother about me any more!"

He flared right up. "That's not true, Anne, oh no, I won't let you think that of me!"

Then I was called away.

Daddy has talked to him; he told me about it today. "Your father thought that the friendship might develop into love sooner or later," he said. But I replied that we would keep a check on ourselves.

Daddy doesn't want me to go upstairs so much in the evenings now, but I don't want that. Not only because I like being with Peter; I have told him that I trust him. I do trust him and I want to show him that I do, which can't happen if I stay downstairs through lack of trust.

No, I'm going!

In the meantime the Dussel drama has righted itself again. At supper on Saturday evening he apologized in beautiful Dutch. Van Daan was nice about it straight away; it must have taken Dussel a whole day to learn that little lesson off by heart.

Sunday, his birthday, passed peacefully. We gave him a bottle of good 1919 wine, from the Van Daans (who could give their presents now after all), a bottle of piccalilli and a packet of razor blades, a jar of lemon jam from Kraler, a book, *Little Martin*, from Miep, and a plant from Elli. He treated each one of us to an egg.

Yours, Anne

Wednesday, 3 May, 1944

Dear Kitty,

First, just the news of the week. We're having a holiday from politics; there is nothing, absolutely nothing to announce. I too am gradually beginning to believe that the invasion will come. After all, they can't let the Russians clear up everything; for that matter, they're not doing anything either at the moment.

Mr. Koophuis comes to the office every morning again now. He's got a new spring for Peter's divan, so Peter will have to do some upholstering, about which, quite understandably, he doesn't feel a bit happy.

Have I told you that Boche has disappeared? Simply vanished—we haven't seen a sign of her since Thursday of last week. I expect she's already in the cats' heaven, while some animal lover is enjoying a succulent meal from her. Perhaps some little girl will be given a fur cap out of her skin. Peter is very sad about it.

Since Saturday we've changed over, and have lunch at half past eleven in the mornings, so we have to last out with one cupful of porridge; this saves us a meal. Vegetables are still very difficult to obtain: we had rotten boiled lettuce this afternoon. Ordinary lettuce, spinach and boiled lettuce, there's nothing else. With these we eat rotten potatoes, so it's a delicious combination!

As you can easily imagine we often ask ourselves here despairingly: "What, oh, what is the use of the war? Why can't people live peacefully together? Why all this destruction?"

The question is very understandable, but no one has found a satisfactory answer to it so far. Yes, why do they make still more gigantic planes, still heavier bombs and, at the same time, prefabricated houses for reconstruction? Why should millions be spent daily on the war and yet there's not a penny available for medical services, artists, or for poor people?

Why do some people have to starve, while there are surpluses rotting in other parts of the world? Oh, why are people so crazy?

I don't believe that the big men, the politicians and the capitalists alone, are guilty of the war. Oh no, the little man is just as guilty, otherwise the peoples of the world would have risen in revolt long ago! There's in people simply an urge to destroy, an urge to kill, to murder and rage, and until all mankind, without exception, undergoes a great change, wars will be waged, everything that has been built up, cultivated, and grown will be destroyed and disfigured, after which mankind will have to begin all over again.

I have often been downcast, but never in despair; I regard our hiding as a dangerous adventure, romantic and interesting at the same time. In my diary I treat all the privations as amusing. I have made up my mind now to lead a different life from other girls and, later on, different from ordinary housewives. My start has been so very full of interest, and that is the sole reason why I have to laugh at the humorous side of the most dangerous moments.

I am young and I possess many buried qualities; I am young and strong and am living a great adventure; I am still in the midst of it and can't grumble the whole day long. I have been given a lot, a happy nature, a great deal of cheerfulness and strength. Every day I feel that I am developing inwardly, that the liberation is drawing nearer and how beautiful nature is, how good the people are about me, how interesting this adventure is! Why, then, should I be in despair?

Yours, Anne

Friday, 5 May, 1944

Dear Kitty,

Daddy is not pleased with me; he thought that after our talk on Sunday I automatically wouldn't go upstairs every evening. He doesn't want any "necking," a word I can't bear. It was bad enough talking about it, why must he make it so unpleasant now? I shall talk to him today. Margot has given me some good advice, so listen; this is roughly what I want to say:

"I believe, Daddy, that you expect a declaration from me, so I will give it you. You are disappointed in me, as you had expected more reserve from me, and I suppose you want me to be just as a fourteen-year-old should be. But that's where you're mistaken!

"Since we've been here, from July 1942 until a few weeks ago, I can assure you that I haven't had any easy time. If you only knew how I cried in the evenings, how unhappy I was, how lonely I felt, then you would understand that I want to go upstairs!

"I have now reached the stage that I can live entirely on my own, without Mummy's support or anyone else's for that matter. But it hasn't just happened in a night; it's been a bitter, hard struggle and I've shed many a tear, before I became as independent as I am now. You can laugh at me and not believe me, but that can't harm me. I know that I'm a separate individual and I don't feel in the least bit responsible to any of you. I am only telling you this because I thought that otherwise you might think that I was underhand, but I don't have to give an account of my deeds to anyone but myself.

"When I was in difficulties you all closed your eyes and stopped up your ears and didn't help me; on the contrary, I received nothing but warnings not to be so boisterous. I was only boisterous so as not to be miserable all the time. I was reckless so as not to hear that persistent voice within me continually. I played a comedy for a year and a half, day in, day out, I never grumbled, never lost my cue, nothing like that—and now, now the battle is over. I have won! I am independent both in mind and body. I don't need a mother any more, for all this conflict has made me strong.

"And now, now that I'm on top of it, now that I know that I've fought the battle, now I want to be able to go on in my own way too, the way that I think is right. You can't and mustn't regard me as fourteen, for all these troubles have made me older; I shall not be sorry for what I have done, but shall act as I think I can. You can't coax me into not going upstairs; *either* you forbid it, *or* you trust me through thick and thin, but then leave me in peace as well!"

Yours, Anne

Saturday, 6 May, 1944

Dear Kitty,

I put a letter, in which I wrote what I explained to you yesterday, in Daddy's pocket before supper yesterday. After reading it, he was, according to Margot, very upset for the rest of the evening. (I was upstairs doing the dishes.) Poor Pim, I might have known what the effect of such an epistle would be. He is so sensitive! I immediately told Peter not to ask or say anything more. Pim hasn't said any more about it to me. Is that yet in store, I wonder?

Here everything is going on more or less normally again. What they tell us about the prices and the people outside is almost unbelievable, half a pound of tea costs 350 florins,[1] a pound of coffee 80 florins, butter 35 florins per pound, an egg 1.45 florin. People pay 14 florins for an ounce of Bulgarian tobacco! Everyone deals in the black market, every errand boy has something to offer. Our baker's boy got hold of some sewing silk, 0.9 florin for a thin little skein, the milkman manages to get clandestine ration cards, the undertaker delivers the cheese. Burglaries, murders, and theft go on daily. The police and night watchmen join in just as strenuously as the professionals, everyone wants something in their empty stomachs and because wage increases are forbidden the people simply have to swindle. The police are continually on the go, tracing girls of fifteen, sixteen, seventeen and older, who are reported missing every day.

Yours, Anne

Sunday morning, 7 May, 1944

Dear Kitty,

Daddy and I had a long talk yesterday afternoon, I cried terribly and he joined in. Do you know what he said to me, Kitty? "I have received many letters in my life, but this is certainly the most unpleasant! You, Anne, who have received such love from your parents, you, who have parents who are always ready to help you, who have always defended you whatever it might be, can you talk of feeling no responsibility towards us? You feel wronged and deserted; no, Anne, you have done us a great injustice!

[1]A florin is equal to approximately twenty-eight cents.

"Perhaps you didn't mean it like that, but it is what you wrote; no, Anne, we haven't deserved such a reproach as this!"

Oh, I have failed miserably; this is certainly the worst thing I've ever done in my life. I was only trying to show off with my crying and my tears, just trying to appear big, so that he would respect me. Certainly, I have had a lot of unhappiness, but to accuse the good Pim, who has done and still does do everything for me—no, that was too low for words.

It's right that for once I've been taken down from my inaccessible pedestal, that my pride has been shaken a bit, for I was becoming much too taken up with myself again. What Miss Anne does is by no means always right! Anyone who can cause such unhappiness to someone else, someone he professes to love, and on purpose, too, is low, very low!

And the way Daddy has forgiven me makes me feel more than ever ashamed of myself, he is going to throw the letter in the fire and is so sweet to me now, just as if he had done something wrong. No, Anne, you still have a tremendous lot to learn, begin by doing that first, instead of looking down on others and accusing them!

I have had a lot of sorrow, but who hasn't at my age? I have played the clown a lot too, but I was hardly conscious of it; I felt lonely, but hardly ever in despair! I ought to be deeply ashamed of myself, and indeed I am.

What is done cannot be undone, but one can prevent it happening again. I want to start from the beginning again and it can't be difficult, now that I have Peter. With him to support me, I can and will!

I'm not alone any more; he loves me. I love him, I have my books, my storybook and my diary, I'm not so frightfully ugly, not utterly stupid, have a cheerful temperament and want to have a good character!

Yes, Anne, you've felt deeply that your letter was too hard and that it was untrue. To think that you were even proud of it! I will take Daddy as my example, and I *will* improve.

Yours, Anne

Monday, 8 May, 1944

Dear Kitty,

Have I ever really told you anything about our family?

I don't think I have, so I will begin now. My father's parents were very rich. His father had worked himself right up and his mother came from a prominent family, who were also rich. So in his youth Daddy had a real little rich boy's upbringing, parties every week, balls, festivities, beautiful girls, dinners, a large home, etc., etc.

After Grandpa's death all the money was lost during the World War and the inflation that followed. Daddy was therefore extremely well brought up and he laughed very much yesterday when, for the first time in his fifty-five years, he scraped out the frying pan at table.

Mummy's parents were rich too and we often listen openmouthed to stories of engagement parties of two hundred and fifty people, private balls and dinners. One certainly could not call us rich now, but all my hopes are pinned on after the war.

I can assure you I'm not at all keen on a narrow, cramped existence like Mummy and Margot. I'd adore to go to Paris for a year and London for a year to learn the languages and study the history of art. Compare that with Margot, who wants to be a midwife in Palestine! I always long to see beautiful dresses and interesting people.

I want to see something of the world and do all kinds of exciting things. I've already told you this before. And a little money as well won't do any harm.

Miep told us this morning about a party she went to, to celebrate an engagement. Both the future bride and bridegroom came from rich families and everything was very grand. Miep made our mouths water telling us about the food they had: vegetable soup with minced meat balls in it, cheese, rolls, hors d'oeuvre with eggs and roast beef, fancy cakes, wine and cigarettes, as much as you wanted of everything (black market). Miep had ten drinks—can that be the woman who calls herself a teetotaler? If Miep had all those, I wonder however many her spouse managed to knock back? Naturally, everyone at the party was a bit tipsy. There were two policemen from the fighting squad, who took photos of the engaged couple. It seems as if we are never far from Miep's thoughts, because she took down the addresses of these men at once, in case anything should happen at some time or other, and good Dutchmen might come in useful.

She made our mouths water. We, who get nothing but two spoonfuls of porridge for our breakfast and whose tummies were so empty that they were positively rattling, we, who get nothing but half-cooked spinach (to preserve the vitamins) and rotten potatoes day after day, we, who get nothing but lettuce, cooked or raw, spinach and yet again spinach in our hollow stomachs. Perhaps we may yet grow to be as strong as Popeye, although I don't see much sign of it at present!

If Miep had taken us to the party we shouldn't have left any rolls for the other guests. I can tell you, we positively drew the words from Miep's lips, we gathered round her, as if we'd never heard about delicious food or smart people in our lives before!

And these are the granddaughters of a millionaire. The world is a queer place!

Yours, Anne

Tuesday, 9 May, 1944

Dear Kitty,

I've finished my story of Ellen the fairy. I have copied it out on nice note paper. It certainly looks very attractive, but is it really enough for Daddy's birthday? I don't know. Margot and Mummy have both written poems for him.

Mr. Kraler came upstairs this afternoon with the news that Mrs. B., who used to act as demonstrator for the business, wants to eat her box lunch in the office here at two o'clock every afternoon. Think of it! No one can come upstairs any more, the potatoes cannot be delivered, Elli can't have any lunch, we can't go to the W.C., we mustn't move, etc., etc. We thought up the wildest and most varied suggestions to wheedle her away. Van Daan thought that a good laxative in her coffee would be sufficient. "No," replied Koophuis, "I beg of you not, then we'd never get her off the box!" Resounding laughter. "Off the box," asked Mrs. Van Daan, "what does that mean?" An explanation followed. "Can I always use it?" she then asked stupidly. "Imagine it," Elli giggled, "if one asked for the box in Bijenkorf's[1] they wouldn't even understand what you mean!"

Oh, Kit, it's such wonderful weather, if only I could go out-doors!

Yours, Anne

Wednesday, 10 May, 1944

Dear Kitty,

We were sitting in the attic doing some French yesterday afternoon when I suddenly heard water pattering down be-hind me. I asked Peter what it could be, but he didn't even reply, simply tore up to the loft, where the source of the disaster was, and pushed Mouschi, who, because of the wet earth box, had sat down beside it, harshly back to the right place. A great din and disturbance followed, and Mouschi, who had finished by that time, dashed downstairs.

Mouschi, seeking the convenience of something similar to his box, had chosen some wood shavings. The pool had trickled down from the loft into the attic immediately and, unfortu-nately, landed just beside and in the barrel of potatoes. The ceiling was dripping, and as the attic floor is not free from holes either, several yellow drips came through the ceiling into the dining room between a pile of stockings and some books, which were lying on the table. I was doubled up with laughter, it really was a scream. There was Mouschi crouching under a chair, Peter with water, bleaching powder, and floor cloth, and Van Daan trying to soothe everyone. The calamity was soon over, but it's a well-known fact that cats' puddles positively stink. The potatoes proved this only too clearly and also the wood shavings, that Daddy collected in a bucket to be burned. Poor Mouschi! How were you to know that peat is unobtainable?

Yours, Anne

P.S. Our beloved Queen spoke to us yesterday and this eve-ning. She is taking a holiday in order to be strong for her return to Holland. She used words like "soon, when I am back, speedy liberation, heroism, and heavy burdens."

A speech by Gerbrandy followed. A clergyman concluded

[1]"Bijenkorf" is a large store in Amsterdam.

with a prayer to God to take care of the Jews, the people in concentration camps, in prisons, and in Germany.

                                                        Yours, Anne

                                        Thursday, 11 May, 1944

Dear Kitty,

I'm frightfully busy at the moment, and although it sounds mad, I haven't time to get through my pile of work. Shall I tell you briefly what I have got to do? Well, then, by tomorrow I must finish reading the first part of *Galileo Galilei*, as it has to be returned to the library. I only started it yesterday, but I shall manage it.

Next week I have got to read *Palestine at the Crossroads* and the second part of *Galilei*. Next I finished reading the first part of the biography of *The Emperor Charles V* yesterday, and it's essential that I work out all the diagrams and family trees that I have collected from it. After that I have three pages of foreign words gathered from various books, which have all got to be recited, written down, and learned. Number four is that my film stars are all mixed up together and are simply gasping to be tidied up; however, as such a clearance would take several days, and since Professor Anne, as she's already said, is choked with work, the chaos will have to remain a chaos.

Next Theseus, Oedipus, Peleus, Orpheus, Jason, and Hercules are all awaiting their turn to be arranged, as their different deeds lie crisscross in my mind like fancy threads in a dress; it's also high time Myron and Phidias had some treatment, if they wish to remain at all coherent. Likewise it's the same with the seven and nine years' war; I'm mixing everything up together at this rate. Yes, but what can one do with such a memory! Think how forgetful I shall be when I'm eighty!

Oh, something else, the Bible; how long is it still going to take before I meet the bathing Suzanna? And what do they mean by the guilt of Sodom and Gomorrah? Oh, there is still such a terrible lot to find out and to learn. And in the meantime I've left Lisolette of the Pfalz completely in the lurch.

Kitty, can you see that I'm just about bursting?

Now, about something else: you've known for a long time that my greatest wish is to become a journalist someday and later on a famous writer. Whether these leanings towards greatness (or insanity?) will ever materialize remains to be seen, but I certainly have the subjects in my mind. In any case, I want to publish a book entitled *Het Achterhuis* after the war. Whether I shall succeed or not, I cannot say, but my diary will be a great help. I have other ideas as well, besides *Het Achterhuis*. But I will write more fully about them some other time, when they have taken a clearer form in my mind.

Yours, Anne

Saturday, 13 May, 1944

Dearest Kitty,

It was Daddy's birthday yesterday. Mummy and Daddy have been married nineteen years. The charwoman wasn't below and the sun shone as it has never shone before in 1944. Our horse chestnut is in full bloom, thickly covered with leaves and much more beautiful than last year.

Daddy received a biography of the life of Linnaeus from Koophuis, a book on nature from Kraler, *Amsterdam by the Water* from Dussel, a gigantic box from Van Daan, beautifully done up and almost professionally decorated, containing three eggs, a bottle of beer, a bottle of yoghourt, and a green tie. It made our pot of syrup seem rather small. My roses smelled lovely compared with Miep's and Elli's carnations, which had no smell, but were very pretty too. He was certainly spoiled. Fifty fancy pastries have arrived, heavenly! Daddy himself treated us to spiced gingerbread, beer for the gentlemen, and yoghourt for the ladies. Enjoyment all around!

Yours, Anne

Tuesday, 16 May, 1944

Dearest Kitty,

Just for a change, as we haven't talked about them for so long, I want to tell you a little discussion that went on between Mr. and Mrs. Van Daan yesterday.

Mrs. Van Daan: "The Germans are sure to have made the Atlantic Wall very strong indeed, they will certainly do all in their power to hold back the English. It's amazing how strong the Germans are!"

Mr. Van Daan: "Oh yes, incredibly."

Mrs. Van Daan: "Ye-es."

Mr. Van Daan: "The Germans are so strong they're sure to win the war in the end, in spite of everything!"

Mrs. Van Daan: "It's quite possible, I'm not convinced of the opposite yet."

Mr. Van Daan: "I won't bother to reply any more."

Mrs. Van Daan: "Still you always do answer me, you can't resist capping me every time."

Mr. Van Daan: "Of course not, but my replies are the bare minimum."

Mrs. Van Daan: "But still you do reply, and you always have to be in the right! Your prophecies don't always come true by a long shot."

Mr. Van Daan: "They have up till now."

Mrs. Van Daan: "That's not true. The invasion was to have come last year, and the Finns were to have been out of the war by now. Italy was finished in the winter, but the Russians would already have Lemberg; oh, no, I don't think much of your prophecies."

Mr. Van Daan (standing up): "It's about time you shut your mouth. One day I'll show you that I'm right; sooner or later you'll get enough of it. I can't bear any more of your grousing. You're so infuriating but you'll stew in your own juice one day."

End of Part I.

I really couldn't help laughing. Mummy too, while Peter sat biting his lip. Oh, those stupid grownups, they'd do better to start learning themselves, before they have so much to say to the younger generation!

Yours, Anne

Friday, 19 May, 1944

Dear Kitty,

I felt rotten yesterday, really out of sorts (unusual for Anne!), with tummy-ache and every other imaginable misery. I'm much better again today, feel very hungry, but I'd better not touch the kidney beans we're having today.

All goes well with Peter and me. The poor boy seems to need a little love even more than I do. He blushes every evening when he gets his good-night kiss and simply begs for another.

I wonder if I'm a good substitute for Boche? I don't mind, he is so happy now that he knows that someone loves him.

After my laborious conquest I've got the situation a bit more in hand now, but I don't think my love has cooled off. He's a darling, but I soon closed up my inner self from him. If he wants to force the lock again he'll have to work a good deal harder than before!

Yours, Anne

Saturday, 20 May, 1944

Dear Kitty,

Last evening I came downstairs from the attic and as I entered the room saw at once the lovely vase of carnations lying on the floor, Mummy down on hands and knees mopping up and Margot fishing up some papers from the floor.

"What's happened here?" I asked, full of misgivings and, not even waiting for their answer, tried to sum up the damage from a distance. My whole portfolio of family trees, writing books, textbooks, everything was soaked. I nearly wept and was so worked up that I can hardly remember what I said, but Margot said that I let fly something about "incalculable loss, frightful, terrible, can never be repaired," and still more. Daddy burst out laughing, Mummy and Margot joined in, but I could have cried over all the toil that was wasted, and the diagrams I'd so carefully worked out.

On closer inspection the "incalculable loss" didn't turn out to be as bad as I'd thought. I carefully sorted out all the papers that were stuck together and separated them in the attic. After that I hung them all up on the clothes lines to dry. It was a funny sight and I couldn't help laughing myself. Maria de Medici beside Charles V, William of Orange and Marie Antoinette; it's a "racial outrage," was Mr. Van Daan's joke on the subject. After I'd entrusted my papers into Peter's care I went downstairs again.

"Which books are spoiled?" I asked Margot, who was checking up on them. "Algebra," she said. I hurried to her side, but unfortunately not even the algebra book was spoiled. I wish it had fallen right in the vase; I've never loathed *any* other book so much as that one. There are the names of at least twenty girls in the front, all previous owners; it is old, yellow, full of scribbles and improvements. If I'm ever in a really very wicked mood, I'll tear the blasted thing to pieces!

Yours, Anne

Monday, 22 May, 1944

Dear Kitty,

On May 20th Daddy lost five bottles of yoghourt on a bet with Mrs. Van Daan. The invasion still hasn't come yet; it's no exaggeration to say that all Amsterdam, all Holland, yes, the whole west coast of Europe, right down to Spain, talks about the invasion day and night, debates about it, and makes bets on it and . . . hopes.

The suspense is rising to a climax. By no means everyone we had regarded as "good" Dutch have stuck to their faith in the English; by no means everyone thinks the English bluff a masterly piece of strategy, oh no, the people want to see deeds at last, great, heroic deeds. Nobody sees beyond his own nose, no one thinks that the English are fighting for their own land and their own people, everyone thinks that it's their duty to save Holland, as quickly and as well as they can.

What obligations have the English towards us? How have the Dutch earned the generous help that they seem so explicitly to expect? Oh no, the Dutch will have made a big mistake, the English, in spite of all their bluff, are certainly no more to blame than all the other countries, great and small, which are not under occupation. The English really won't offer us their apologies, for even if we do reproach them for being asleep during the years when Germany was rearming, we cannot deny that all the other countries, especially those bordering Germany, also slept. We shan't get anywhere by following an ostrich policy. England and the whole world have seen that only too well now, and that is why, one by one, England, no less than the rest, will have to make heavy sacrifices.

No country is going to sacrifice its men for nothing and certainly not in the interests of another. England is not going to do that either. The invasion, with liberation and freedom, will come sometime, but England and America will appoint the day, not all the occupied countries put together.

To our great horror and regret we hear that the attitude of a great many people towards us Jews has changed. We hear that there is anti-Semitism now in circles that never thought of it before. This news has affected us all very, very deeply. The cause of this hatred of the Jews is understandable, even human sometimes, but not good. The Christians blame the Jews for giving secrets away to the Germans, for betraying their helpers and for the fact that, through the Jews, a great many Christians have gone the way of so many others before them, and suffered terrible punishments and a dreadful fate.

This is all true, but one must always look at these things from both sides. Would Christians behave differently in our place? The Germans have a means of making people talk. Can a person, entirely at their mercy, whether Jew or Christian, always remain silent? Everyone knows that is practically impossible. Why, then, should people demand the impossible of the Jews?

It's being murmured in underground circles that the German Jews who emigrated to Holland and who are now in Poland may not be allowed to return here; they once had the right of asylum in Holland, but when Hitler has gone they will have to go back to Germany again.

When one hears this one naturally wonders why we are carrying on with this long and difficult war. We always hear that we're all fighting together for freedom, truth, and right! Is discord going to show itself while we are still fighting, is the Jew once again worth less than another? Oh, it is sad, very sad, that once more, for the umpteenth time, the old truth is confirmed: "What *one* Christian does is his own responsibility, what *one* Jew does is thrown back at all Jews."

Quite honestly, I can't understand that the Dutch, who are such a good, honest, upright people, should judge us like this, we, the most oppressed, the unhappiest, perhaps the most pitiful of all peoples of the whole world.

I hope *one* thing only, and that is that this hatred of the Jews will be a passing thing, that the Dutch will show what they are after all, and that they will never totter and lose their sense of right. For anti-Semitism is unjust!

And if this terrible threat should actually come true, then the pitiful little collection of Jews that remain will have to leave Holland. We, too, shall have to move on again with our little bundles, and leave this beautiful country, which offered us such a warm welcome and which now turns its back on us.

I love Holland. I who, having no native country, had hoped
that it might become my fatherland, and I still hope it will!

Yours, Anne

Thursday, 25 May, 1944

Dear Kitty,

There's something fresh every day. This morning our vegetable man was picked up for having two Jews in his house.
It's a great blow to us, not only that those poor Jews are balancing on the edge of an abyss, but it's terrible for the man himself.

The world has turned topsy-turvy, respectable people are
being sent off to concentration camps, prisons, and lonely cells,
and the dregs that remain govern young and old, rich and poor.
One person walks into the trap through the black market, a
second through helping the Jews or other people who've had to
go "underground"; anyone who isn't a member of the N.S.B.
doesn't know what may happen to him from one day to another.

This man is a great loss to us too. The girls can't and aren't
allowed to haul along our share of potatoes, so the only thing to
do is to eat less. I will tell you how we shall do that; it's certainly not going to make things any pleasanter. Mummy says
we shall cut out breakfast altogether, have porridge and bread
for lunch, and for supper fried potatoes and possibly once or
twice per week vegetables or lettuce, nothing more. We're going
to be hungry, but anything is better than being discovered.

Yours, Anne

Friday, 26 May, 1944

Dear Kitty,

At last, at last I can sit quietly at my table in front of a
crack of window and write you everything.

I feel so miserable, I haven't felt like this for months; even
after the burglary I didn't feel so utterly broken. On the one
hand, the vegetable man, the Jewish question, which is being
discussed minutely over the whole house, the invasion delay,
the bad food, the strain, the miserable atmosphere, my disappointment in Peter; and on the other hand, Elli's engagement,

Whitsun reception, flowers, Kraler's birthday, fancy cakes, and stories about cabarets, films, and concerts. That difference, that huge difference, it's always there; one day we laugh and see the funny side of the situation, but the next we are afraid, fear, suspense, and despair staring from our faces. Miep and Kraler carry the heaviest burden of the eight in hiding, Miep in all she does, and Kraler through the enormous responsibility, which is sometimes so much for him that he can hardly talk from pent-up nerves and strain. Koophuis and Elli look after us well too, but they can forget us at times, even if it's only for a few hours, or a day, or even two days. They have their own worries, Koophuis over his health, Elli over her engagement, which is not altogether rosy, but they also have their little outings, visits to friends, and the whole life of ordinary people. For them the suspense is sometimes lifted, even if it is only for a short time, but for us it never lifts for a moment. We've been here for two years now; how long have we still to put up with this almost unbearable, ever increasing pressure?

The sewer is blocked, so we mustn't run water, or rather only a trickle; when we go to the W.C. we have to take a lavatory brush with us, and we keep dirty water in a large Cologne pot. We can manage for today, but what do we do if the plumber can't do the job alone? The municipal scavenging service doesn't come until Tuesday.

Miep sent us a currant cake, made up in the shape of a doll, with the words "Happy Whitsun" on the note attached to it. It's almost as if she's ridiculing us; our present frame of mind and our uneasiness could hardly be called "happy." The affair of the vegetable man has made us more nervous, you hear "shh, shh" from all sides again, and we're being quieter over everything. The police forced the door there, so they could do it to us too! If one day we too should . . . no, I mustn't write it, but I can't put the question out of my mind today. On the contrary, all the fear I've already been through seems to face me again in all its frightfulness.

This evening at eight o'clock I had to go to the downstairs lavatory all alone; there was no one down there, as everyone was listening to the radio; I wanted to be brave, but it was difficult. I always feel much safer here upstairs than alone downstairs in that large, silent house; alone with the mysterious muffled noises from upstairs and the tooting of motor horns in

the street. I have to hurry for I start to quiver if I begin thinking about the situation.

Again and again I ask myself, would it not have been better
for us all if we had not gone into hiding, and if we were dead
now and not going through all this misery, especially as we
shouldn't be running our protectors into danger any more. But
we all recoil from these thoughts too, for we still love life; we
haven't yet forgotten the voice of nature, we still hope, hope
about everything. I hope something will happen soon now,
shooting if need be—nothing can crush us *more* than this rest-
lessness. Let the end come, even if it is hard; then at least we
shall know whether we are finally going to win through or go
under.

Yours, Anne

Wednesday, 31 May, 1944

Dear Kitty,

It was so frightfully hot on Saturday, Sunday, Monday, and
Tuesday that I simply couldn't hold a fountain pen in my
hand. That's why it was impossible to write to you. The drains
went phut again on Friday, were mended again on Saturday;
Mr. Koophuis came to see us in the afternoon and told us
masses about Corry and her being in the same hockey club as
Jopie.

On Sunday Elli came to make sure no one had broken in and
stayed for breakfast, on Whit Monday Mr. Van Santen acted
as the hide-out watchman, and, finally, on Tuesday the windows could be opened again at last.

There's seldom been such a beautiful, warm, one can even
say hot, Whitsun. The heat here in the "Secret Annexe" is terrible; I will briefly describe these warm days by giving you a
sample of the sort of complaints that arise:

Saturday: "Lovely, what perfect weather," we all said in the
morning. "If only it wasn't quite so warm," in the afternoon
when the windows had to be closed.

Sunday: "It's positively unbearable, this heat. The butter's
melting, there's not a cool spot anywhere in the house, the
bread's getting so dry, the milk's going sour, windows can't be
opened, and we, wretched outcasts, sit here suffocating while
other people enjoy their Whitsun holiday."

Monday: "My feet hurt me, I haven't got any thin clothes. I can't wash the dishes in this heat," all this from Mrs. Van Daan. It was extremely unpleasant.

I still can't put up with heat and am glad that there's a stiff breeze today, and yet the sun still shines.

Yours, Anne

Monday, 5 June, 1944

Dear Kitty,

Fresh "Secret Annexe" troubles, a quarrel between Dussel and the Franks over something very trivial: the sharing out of the butter. Dussel's capitulation. Mrs. Van Daan and the latter very thick, flirtations, kisses and friendly little laughs. Dussel is beginning to get longings for women. The Fifth Army has taken Rome. The city has been spared devastation by both armies and air forces, and is undamaged. Very few vegetables and potatoes. Bad weather. Heavey bombardments against the French coast and Pas de Calais continue.

Yours, Anne

Tuesday, 6 June, 1944

Dear Kitty,

"This is D-day," came the announcement over the English news and quite rightly, "this is *the* day."[1] The invasion has begun!

The English gave the news at eight o'clock this morning: Calais, Boulogne, Le Havre, and Cherbourg, also the Pas de Calais (as usual), were heavily bombarded. Moreover, as a safety measure for all occupied territories, all people who live within a radius of thirty-five kilometers from the coast are warned to be prepared for bombardments. If possible, the English will drop pamphlets one hour before hand.

According to German news, English parachute troops have landed on the French coast, English landing craft are in battle with the German Navy, says the B.B.C.

We discussed it over the "Annexe" breakfast at nine o'clock: Is this just a trial landing like Dieppe two years ago?

[1]Original English.

English broadcast in German, Dutch, French, and other languages at ten o'clock: "The invasion has begun!"—that means the "real" invasion. English broadcast in German at eleven o'clock, speech by the Supreme Commander, General Dwight Eisenhower.

The English news at twelve o'clock in English: "This is D-day." General Eisenhower said to the French people: "Stiff fighting will come now, but after this the victory. The year 1944 is the year of complete victory; good luck."[1]

English news in English at one o'clock (translated): 11,000 planes stand ready, and are flying to and fro non-stop, landing troops and attacking behind the lines; 4000 landing boats, plus small craft, are landing troops and matériel between Cherbourg and Le Havre incessantly. English and American troops are already engaged in hard fighting. Speeches by Gerbrandy, by the Prime Minister of Belgium, King Haakon of Norway, De Gaulle of France, the King of England, and last, but not least, Churchill.

Great commotion in the "Secret Annexe"! Would the long-awaited liberation that has been talked of so much, but which still seems *too* wonderful, *too* much like a fairy tale, ever come true? Could we be granted victory this year, 1944? We don't know yet, but hope is revived within us; it gives us fresh courage, and makes us strong again. Since we must put up bravely with all the fears, privations, and sufferings, the great thing now is to remain calm and steadfast. Now more than ever we must clench our teeth and not cry out. France, Russia, Italy, and Germany, too, can all cry out and give vent to their misery, but we haven't the right to do that yet!

Oh, Kitty, the best part of the invasion is that I have the feeling that friends are approaching. We have been oppressed by those terrible Germans for so long, they have had their knives so at our throats, that the thought of friends and delivery fills us with confidence!

Now it doesn't concern the Jews any more; no, it concerns Holland and all occupied Europe. Perhaps, Margot says, I may yet be able to go back to school in September or October.

Yours, Anne

P.S. I'll keep you up to date with all the latest news!

[1]Original English.

Friday, 9 June, 1944

Dear Kitty,

Super news of the invasion. The Allies have taken Bayeux, a small village on the French coast, and are now fighting for Caen. It's obvious that they intend to cut off the peninsula where Cherbourg lies. Every evening war correspondents give news from the battle front, telling us of the difficulties, courage, and enthusiasm of the army; they manage to get hold of the most incredible stories. Also some of the wounded who are already back in England again came to the microphone. The air force are up all the time in spite of the miserable weather. We heard over the B.B.C. that Churchill wanted to land with the troops on D-day, however, Eisenhower and the other generals managed to get him out of the idea. Just think of it, what pluck he has for such an old man—he must be seventy at least.

The excitement here has worn off a bit; still, we're hoping that the war will be over at the end of this year. It'll be about time too! Mrs. Van Daan's grizzling is absolutely unbearable; now she can't any longer drive us crazy over the invasion, she nags us the whole day long about the bad weather. It really would be nice to dump her in a bucket of cold water and put her up in the loft.

The whole of the "Secret Annexe" except Van Daan and Peter have read the trilogy *Hungarian Rhapsody*. This book deals with the life history of the composer, virtuoso, and child prodigy, Franz Liszt. It is a very interesting book, but in my opinion there is a bit too much about women in it. In his time Liszt was not only the greatest and most famous pianist, but also the greatest ladies' man—right up to the age of seventy. He lived with the Duchess Marie d'Agould, Princess Caroline Sayn-Wittgenstein, the dancer Lola Montez, the pianist Agnes Kingworth, the pianist Sophie Menter, Princess Olga Janina, Baroness Olga Meyendorff, the actress Lilla what's-her-name, etc., etc.; it is just endless. The parts of the book that deal with music and art are much more interesting. Among those mentioned are Schumann, Clara Wieck, Hector Berlioz, Johannes Brahms, Beethoven, Joachim, Richard Wagner, Hans von Bülow, Anton Rubinstein, Frédéric Chopin, Victor Hugo, Honoré de Balzac, Hiller, Hummel, Czerny, Rossini, Cherubini, Paganini, Mendelssohn, etc., etc.

Liszt was personally a fine man, very generous, and modest about himself though exceptionally vain. He helped everyone, his art was everything to him, he was mad about cognac and about women, could not bear to see tears, was a gentleman, would never refuse to do anyone a favor, didn't care about money, loved religious liberty and world freedom.

Yours, Anne

Tuesday, 13 June, 1944

Dear Kitty,

Another birthday has gone by, so now I'm fifteen. I received quite a lot of presents.

All five parts of Sprenger's *History of Art*, a set of underwear, a handkerchief, two bottles of yoghourt, a pot of jam, a spiced gingerbread cake, and a book on botany from Mummy and Daddy, a double bracelet from Margot, a book from the Van Daans, sweet peas from Dussel, sweets and exercise books from Miep and Elli and, the high spot of all, the book *Maria Theresa* and three slices of full-cream cheese from Kraler. A lovely bunch of peonies from Peter; the poor boy took a lot of trouble to try and find something, but didn't have any luck.

There's still excellent news of the invasion, in spite of the wretched weather, countless gales, heavy rains, and high seas.

Yesterday Churchill, Smuts, Eisenhower, and Arnold visited French villages which have been conquered and liberated. The torpedo boat that Churchill was in shelled the coast. He appears, like so many men, not to know what fear is—makes me envious!

It's difficult for us to judge from our secret redoubt how people outside have reacted to the news. Undoubtedly people are pleased that the idle (?) English have rolled up their sleeves and are doing something at last. Any Dutch people who still look down on the English, scoff at England and her government of old gentlemen, call the English cowards, and yet hate the Germans deserve a good shaking. Perhaps it would put some sense into their woolly brains.

I hadn't had a period for over two months, but it finally started again on Saturday. Still, in spite of all the unpleasantness and bother, I'm glad it hasn't failed me any longer.

Yours, Anne

Wednesday, 14 June, 1944

Dear Kitty,

My head is haunted by so many wishes and thoughts, accusations and reproaches. I'm really not as conceited as so many people seem to think, I know my own faults and shortcomings better than anyone, but the difference is that I also know that I want to improve, shall improve, and have already improved a great deal.

Why is it then, I so often ask myself, that everyone still thinks I'm so terribly knowing and forward? Am I so knowing? Is it that I really am, or that maybe the others aren't? That sounds queer, I realize now, but I shan't cross out the last sentence, because it really isn't so crazy. Everyone knows that Mrs. Van Daan, one of my chief accusers, is unintelligent. I might as well put it plainly and say "stupid." Stupid people usually can't take it if others do better than they do.

Mrs. Van Daan thinks I'm stupid because I'm not quite so lacking in intelligence as she is; she thinks I'm forward because she's even more so; she thinks my dresses are too short, because hers are even shorter. And that's also the reason that she thinks I'm knowing, because she's twice as bad about joining in over subjects she knows absolutely nothing about. But one of my favorite sayings is "There's no smoke without fire," and I readily admit that I'm knowing.

Now the trying part about me is that I criticize and scold myself far more than anyone else does. Then if Mummy adds her bit of advice the pile of sermons becomes so insurmountable that in my despair I become rude and start contradicting and then, of course, the old well-known Anne watchword comes back: "No one understands me!" This phrase sticks in my mind; I know it sounds silly, yet there is some truth in it. I often accuse myself to such an extent that I simply long for a word of comfort, for someone who could give me sound advice and also draw out some of my real self; but, alas, I keep on looking, but I haven't found anyone yet.

I know that you'll immediately think of Peter, won't you, Kit? It's like this: Peter loves me not as a lover but as a friend and grows more affectionate every day. But what is the mysterious something that holds us both back? I don't understand it myself. Sometimes I think that my terrible longing for him was exaggerated, yet that's really not it, because if I don't go up to see him for two days, then I long for him more desperately than ever before. Peter is good and he's a darling, but still there's no denying that there's a lot about him that disappoints me. Especially his dislike of religion and all his talk about food and various other things don't appeal to me. Yet I feel quite convinced that we shall never quarrel now that we've made that straightforward agreement together. Pete is a peace-loving person; he's tolerant and gives in very easily. He lets me say a lot of things to him that he would never accept from his mother, he tried most persistently to keep his things in order. And yet why should he keep his innermost self to himself and why am I never allowed there? By nature he is more closed-up than I am, I agree, but I know—and from my own experience—that at some time or other even the most uncommunicative people long just as much, if not more, to find someone in whom they can confide.

Both Peter and I have spent our most meditative years in the "Secret Annexe." We often discuss the future, the past, and the present, but, as I've already said, I still seem to miss the real thing and yet I know that it's there.

Yours, Anne

Thursday, 15 June, 1944

Dear Kitty,

I wonder if it's because I haven't been able to poke my nose outdoors for so long that I've grown so crazy about everything to do with nature? I can perfectly well remember that there was a time when a deep blue sky, the song of the birds, moonlight and flowers could never have kept me spellbound. That's changed since I've been here.

At Whitsun, for instance, when it was so warm, I stayed awake on purpose until half past eleven one evening in order to have a good look at the moon for once by myself. Alas, the sacrifice was all in vain, as the moon gave far too much light and I didn't dare risk opening a window. Another time, some months ago now, I happened to be upstairs one evening when the window was open. I didn't go downstairs until the window had to be shut. The dark, rainy evening, the gale, the scudding clouds held me entirely in their power; it was the first time in a year and a half that I'd seen the night face to face. After that evening my longing to see it again was greater than my fear of burglars, rats, and raids on the house. I went downstairs all by myself and looked outside through the windows in the kitchen and the private office. A lot of people are fond of nature, many sleep outdoors occasionally, and people in prisons and hospitals long for the day when they will be free to enjoy the beauties of nature, but few are so shut away and isolated from that which can be shared alike by rich and poor. It's not imagination on my part when I say that to look up at the sky, the clouds, the moon, and the stars makes me calm and patient. It's a better medicine than either valerian or bromine; Mother Nature makes me humble and prepared to face every blow courageously.

Alas, it has had to be that I am only able—except on a few rare occasions—to look at nature through dirty net curtains hanging before very dusty windows. And it's no pleasure looking through these any longer, because nature is just the one thing that really must be unadulterated.

Yours, Anne

Friday, 16 June, 1944

Dear Kitty,

New problems: Mrs. Van Daan is desperate, talks about a bullet through her head, prison, hanging, and suicide. She's jealous that Peter confides in me and not her. She's offended that Dussel doesn't enter into her flirtations with him, as she'd hoped, afraid that her husband is smoking all the fur-coat money away, she quarrels, uses abusive language, cries, pities herself, laughs, and then starts a fresh quarrel again. What on earth can one do with such a foolish, blubbering specimen? No one takes her seriously, she hasn't any character, and she grumbles to everyone. The worst of it is that it makes Peter rude, Mr. Van Daan irritable, and Mummy cynical. Yes, it's a frightful situation! There's *one* golden rule to keep before you: laugh about everything and don't bother yourself about the others! It sounds selfish, but it's honestly the only cure for anyone who has to seek consolation in himself.

Kraler has received another call-up to go digging for four weeks. He's trying to get out of it with a doctor's certificate and a letter from the business. Koophuis wants to have an operation on his stomach. All private telephones were cut off at eleven o'clock yesterday.

Yours, Anne

Friday, 23 June, 1944

Dear Kitty,

Nothing special going on here. The English have begun their big attack on Cherbourg; according to Pim and Van Daan, we're sure to be free by October 10. The Russians are taking part in the campaign, and yesterday began their offensive near Vitebsk; it's exactly three years to a day since the Germans attacked. We've hardly got any potatoes; from now on we're going to count them out for each person, then everyone knows what he's getting.

Yours, Anne

Tuesday, 27 June, 1944

Dearest Kitty,

The mood has changed, everything's going wonderfully. Cherbourg, Vitebsk, and Sloben fell today. Lots of prisoners and booty. Now the English can land what they want now they've got a harbor, the whole Cotentin Peninsular three weeks after the English invasion! A tremendous achievement! In the three weeks since D-day not a day has gone by without rain and gales, both here and in France, but a bit of bad luck didn't prevent the English and Americans from showing their enormous strength, and how! Certainly the "wonder weapon" is in full swing, but of what consequence are a few squibs apart from a bit of damage in England and pages full of it in the Boche newspapers? For that matter, when they really realize in "Bocheland" that the Bolshevists really are on the way, they'll get even more jittery.

All German women not in military service are being evacuated to Groningen, Friesland, and Gelderland with their children. Mussert[1] has announced that if they get as far as here with the invasion he'll put on a uniform. Does the old fatty

[1]Mussert was the Dutch National Socialist leader.

want to do some fighting? He could have done so in Russia before now. Some time ago Finland turned down a peace offer, now the negotiations have just been broken off again, they'll be sorry for it later, the silly fools!

How far do you think we'll be on July 27?

Yours, Anne

Friday, 30 June, 1944

Dear Kitty,

Bad weather, or *bad weather at a stretch to the thirtieth of June*.[1] Isn't that well said! Oh yes, I have a smattering of English already; just to show that I can, I'm reading *An Ideal Husband* with the aid of a dictionary. War going wonderfully! Bobroisk, Mogilef, and Orsa have fallen, lots of prisoners.

Everything's all right here and tempers are improving. The superoptimists are triumphing. Elli has changed her hair style, Miep has the week off. That's the latest news.

Yours, Anne

Thursday, 6 July, 1944

Dear Kitty,

It strikes fear to my heart when Peter talks of later being a criminal, or of gambling; although it's meant as a joke, of course, it gives me the feeling that he's afraid of his own weakness. Again and again I hear from both Margot and Peter: "Yes, if I was as strong and plucky as you are, if I always stuck to what I wanted, if I had such persistent energy, yes then . . . !"

I wonder if it's really a good quality not to let myself be influenced. Is it really good to follow almost entirely my own conscience?

Quite honestly, I can't imagine how anyone can say: "I'm weak," and then remain so. After all, if you know it, why not fight against it, why not try to train your character? The answer was: "Because it's so much easier not to!" This reply rather discouraged me. Easy? Does that mean that a lazy, deceitful life is an easy life? Oh no, that can't be true, it mustn't

[1] In English in the original.

be true, people can so easily be tempted by slackness . . . and by money.

I thought for a long time about the best answer to give Peter, how to get him to believe in himself and, above all, to try and improve himself; I don't know whether my line of thought is right though, or not.

I've so often thought how lovely it would be to have some-one's complete confidence, but now, now that I'm that far, I realize how difficult it is to think what the other person is thinking and then to find the *right* answer. More especially be-cause the very ideas of "easy" and "money" are something en-tirely foreign and new to me. Peter's beginning to lean on me a bit and that mustn't happen under any circumstances. A type like Peter finds it difficult to stand on his own feet, but it's even harder to stand on your own feet as a conscious, living being. Because if you do, then it's twice as difficult to steer a right path through the sea of problems and still remain constant through it all. I'm just drifting around, have been searching for days, searching for a good argument against that terrible word "easy," something to settle it once and for all.

How can I make it clear to him that what appears easy and attractive will drag him down into the depths, depths where there is no comfort to be found, no friends and no beauty, depths from which it is almost impossible to raise oneself?

We all live, but we don't know the why or the wherefore. We all live with the object of being happy; our lives are all different and yet the same. We three have been brought up in good circles, we have the chance to learn, the possibility of attaining something, we have all reason to hope for much hap-piness, but . . . we must earn it for ourselves. And that is never easy. You must work and do good, not be lazy and gamble, if you wish to earn happiness. Laziness may *appear* attractive, but work *gives* satisfaction.

I can't understand people who don't like work, yet that isn't the case with Peter; he just hasn't got a fixed goal to aim at, and he thinks he's too stupid and too inferior to achieve anything. Poor boy, he's never known what it feels like to make other people happy, and I can't teach him that either. He has no religion, scoffs at Jesus Christ, and swears, using the name of God; although I'm not orthodox either, it hurts me every time I see how deserted, how scornful, and how poor he really is.

People who have a religion should be glad, for not everyone has the gift of believing in heavenly things. You don't necessarily even have to be afraid of punishment after death; purgatory, hell, and heaven are things that a lot of people can't accept, but still a religion, it doesn't matter which, keeps a person on the right path. It isn't the fear of God but the upholding of one's own honor and conscience. How noble and good everyone could be if, every evening before falling asleep, they were to recall to their minds the events of the whole day and consider exactly what has been good and bad. Then, without realizing it, you try to improve yourself at the start of each new day; of course, you achieve quite a lot in the course of time. Anyone can do this, it costs nothing and is certainly very helpful. Whoever doesn't know it must learn and find by experience that: "A quiet conscience makes one strong!"

Yours, Anne

Saturday, 8 July, 1944

Dear Kitty,

The chief representative of the business, Mr. B., has been in Beverwijk and managed, just like that, to get strawberries at the auction sale.[1] They arrived here dusty, covered with sand, but in large quantities. No less than twenty-four trays for the office people and us. That very same evening we bottled six jars and made eight pots of jam. The next morning Miep wanted to make jam for the office people.

At half past twelve, no strangers in the house, front door bolted, trays fetched, Peter, Daddy, Van Daan clattering on the stairs: Anne, get hot water; Margot, bring a bucket; all hands on deck! I went into the kitchen, which was chock-full, with a queer feeling in my tummy, Miep, Elli, Koophuis, Henk, Daddy, Peter: the families in hiding and their supply column, all mingling together, and in the middle of the day too!

People can't see in from outside because of the net curtains, but, even so, the loud voices and banging doors positively gave

[1] It is compulsory in Holland for all growers to sell their produce at public auction.

me the jitters. Are we really supposed to be in hiding? That's
what flashed through my mind, and it gives one a very queer
feeling to be able to appear in the world again. The pan was
full, and I dashed upstairs again. The rest of the family was
seated round our table in the kitchen busy stalk-picking—at
least that's what they were supposed to be doing; more went
into mouths than into buckets. Another bucket would soon be
required. Peter went to the downstairs kitchen again—the bell
rang twice; the bucket stayed where it was, Peter tore upstairs,
locked the cupboard door! We were kicking our heels impatiently, couldn't turn on a tap, even though the strawberries
were only half washed; the rule is: "If anyone in the house,
use no water, because of the noise," was strictly maintained.

At one o'clock Henk came down and told us that it was the
postman. Peter hurried downstairs again. Ting-a-ling . . . the
bell, right about turn. I go and listen to see if I can hear anyone
coming, first at our cupboard door and then creep to the top of
the stairs. Finally Peter and I both lean over the banisters like a
couple of thieves, listening to the din downstairs. No strange
voices, Peter sneaks down, stops halfway, and calls out: "Elli!"
No answer, one more: "Elli!" Peter's voice is drowned by the
din in the kitchen. He goes right down and into the kitchen.
I stand looking down tensely. "Get upstairs at once, Peter, the
accountant is here, clear out!" It was Koophuis speaking. Peter
comes upstairs sighing, the cupboard door closes. Finally Kraler
arrives at half past one. "Oh, dearie me, I see nothing but strawberries, strawberries at breakfast, strawberries stewed by Miep,
I smell strawberries, must have a rest from them and go upstairs—what is being washed up here . . . strawberries."

The remainder are being bottled. In the evening: two jars
unsealed. Daddy quickly makes them into jam. The next
morning: two more unsealed and four in the afternoon. Van
Daan hadn't brought them to the right temperature for steriliz-
ing. Now Daddy makes jam every evening.

We eat strawberries with our porridge, skimmed milk with
strawberries, bread and butter with strawberries, strawberries
for dessert, strawberries with sugar, strawberries with sand.
For two whole days strawberries and nothing but strawberries,
then the supply was finished or in bottles and under lock and
key.

"I say, Anne," Margot calls out, "the greengrocer on the corner has let us have some green peas, nineteen pounds." "That's nice of him," I replied. And it certainly is, but oh, the work . . . ugh!

"You've all got to help shelling peas on Saturday morning," Mummy announced when we were at table. And, sure enough, the big enamel pan duly appeared this morning, filled to the brim. Shelling peas is a boring job, but you ought to try "skinning" the pods. I don't think many people realize how soft and tasty the pod is when the skin on the inside has been removed. However, an even greater advantage is that the quantity which can be eaten is about triple the amount of when one only eats the peas. It's an exceptionally precise, finicky job, pulling out this skin; perhaps it's all right for pedantic dentists or precise office workers, but for an impatient teen-ager like me, it's frightful. We began at half past nine, I got up at half past ten, at half past eleven I sat down again. This refrain hummed in my ears: bend the top, pull the skin, remove the string, throw out the pod, etc., etc., they dance before my eyes, green, green, green maggots, strings, rotten pods, green, green, green. Just for the sake of doing something, I chatter the whole morning, any nonsense that comes into my head, make everyone laugh, and bore them stiff. But every string that I pull makes me feel more certain that I never, never want to be just a housewife only!

We finally have breakfast at twelve o'clock, but from half past twelve until quarter past one we've got to go skinning pods again. I'm just about seasick when I stop, the others a bit too. I go and sleep till four o'clock, but I'm still upset by those wretched peas.

Yours, Anne

Saturday, 15 July, 1944

Dear Kitty,

We have had a book from the library with the challenging title of: *What Do You Think of the Modern Young Girl?* I want to talk about this subject today.

The author of this book criticizes "the youth of today" from top to toe, without, however, condemning the whole of the young brigade as "incapable of anything good." On the contrary, she is rather of the opinion that if young people wished, they have it in their hands to make a bigger, more beautiful and better world, but that they occupy themselves with superficial things, without giving a thought to real beauty.

In some passages the writer gave me very much the feeling she was directing her criticisms at me, and that's why I want to lay myself completely bare to you for once and defend myself against this attack.

I have one outstanding trait in my character, which must strike anyone who knows me for any length of time, and that is my knowledge of myself. I can watch myself and my actions, just like an outsider. The Anne of every day I can face entirely without prejudice, without making excuses for her and watch what's good and what's bad about her. This "self-consciousness" haunts me, and every time I open my mouth I know as soon as I've spoken whether "that ought to have been different" or "that was right as it was." There are so many things about myself that I condemn; I couldn't begin to name them all. I understand more and more how true Daddy's words were when he said: "All children must look after their own upbringing." Parents can only give good advice or put them on the right paths, but the final forming of a person's character lies in their own hands.

In addition to this, I have lots of courage, I always feel so strong and as if I can bear a great deal, I feel so free and so young! I was glad when I first realized it, because I don't think I shall easily bow down before the blows that inevitably come to everyone.

But I've talked about these things so often before. Now I want to come to the chapter of "Daddy and Mummy don't understand me." Daddy and Mummy have always thoroughly spoiled me, were sweet to me, defended me, and have done all that parents could do. And yet I've felt so terribly lonely for a long time, so left out, neglected, and misunderstood. Daddy tried all he could to check my rebellious spirit, but it was no use, I have cured myself, by seeing for myself what was wrong in my behavior and keeping it before my eyes.

How is it that Daddy was never any support to me in my struggle, why did he completely miss the mark when he wanted to offer me a helping hand? Daddy tried the wrong methods, he always talked to me as a child who was going through difficult phases. It sounds crazy, because Daddy's the only one who has always taken me into his confidence, and no one but Daddy has given me the feeling that I'm sensible. But there's one thing he's omitted: you see, he hasn't realized that for me the fight to get on top was more important than all else. I didn't want to hear about "symptoms of your age," or "other girls," or "it wears off by itself"; I didn't want to be treated as a girl-like-all-others, but as Anne-on-her-own-merits. Pim didn't understand that. For that matter, I can't confide in anyone, unless they tell me a lot about themselves, and as I know very little about Pim, I don't feel that I can tread upon more intimate ground with him. Pim always takes up the older, fatherly attitude, tells me that he too has had similar passing tendencies. But still he's not able to feel with me like a friend, however hard he tries. These things have made me never mention my views on life nor my well-considered theories to anyone but my diary and, occasionally, to Margot. I concealed from Daddy everything that perturbed me; I never shared my ideals with him. I was aware of the fact that I was pushing him away from me.

I couldn't do anything else. I have acted entirely according to my feelings, but I have acted in the way that was best for my peace of mind. Because I should completely lose my repose and self-confidence, which I have built up so shakily, if, at this stage, I were to accept criticisms of my half-completed task. And I can't do that even from Pim, although it sounds very hard, for not only have I not shared my secret thoughts with Pim but I have often pushed him even further from me, by my irritability.

This is a point that I think a lot about: why is it that Pim annoys me? So much so that I can hardly bear him teaching me, that his affectionate ways strike me as being put on, that I want to be left in peace and would really prefer it if he dropped me a bit, until I felt more certain in my attitude towards him? Because I still have a gnawing feeling of guilt over that horrible letter that I dared to write him when I was so wound up. Oh, how hard it is to be really strong and brave in every way!

Yet this was not my greatest disappointment; no, I ponder far more over Peter than Daddy. I know very well that I conquered him instead of he conquering me. I created an image of him in my mind, pictured him as a quiet, sensitive, lovable boy, who needed affection and friendship. I needed a living person to whom I could pour out my heart; I wanted a friend who'd help to put me on the right road. I achieved what I wanted, and, slowly but surely, I drew him towards me. Finally, when I had made him feel friendly, it automatically developed into an intimacy which, on second thought, I don't think I ought to have allowed.

We talked about the most private things, and yet up till now we have never touched on those things that filled, and still fill, my heart and soul. I still don't know quite what to make of Peter, is he superficial, or does he still feel shy, even of me? But dropping that, I committed one error in my desire to make a real friendship: I switched over and tried to get at him by developing it into a more intimate relation, whereas I should have explored all other possibilities. He longs to be loved and I can see that he's beginning to be more and more in love with me. He gets satisfaction out of our meetings, whereas they just have the effect of making me want to try it out with him again. And yet I don't seem able to touch on the subjects that I'm so longing to bring out into the daylight. I drew Peter towards me, far more than he realizes. Now he clings to me, and for the time being, I don't see any way of shaking him off and putting him on his own feet. When I realized that he could not be a friend for my understanding, I thought I would at least try to lift him up out of his narrow-mindedness and make him do something with his youth.

"For in its innermost depths youth is lonelier than old age." I read this saying in some book and I've always remembered it, and found it to be true. Is it true then that grownups have a more difficult time here than we do? No. I know it isn't. Older people have formed their opinions about everything, and don't waver before they act. It's twice as hard for us young ones to hold our ground, and maintain our opinions, in a time when all ideals are being shattered and destroyed, when people are showing their worst side, and do not know whether to believe in truth and right and God.

Anyone who claims that the older ones have a more difficult time here certainly doesn't realize to what extent our problems weigh down on us, problems for which we are probably much too young, but which thrust themselves upon us continually, until, after a long time, we think we've found a solution, but the solution doesn't seem able to resist the facts which reduce it to nothing again. That's the difficulty in these times: ideals, dreams, and cherished hopes rise within us, only to meet the horrible truth and be shattered.

It's really a wonder that I haven't dropped all my ideals, because they seem so absurd and impossible to carry out. Yet I keep them, because in spite of everything I still believe that people are really good at heart. I simply can't build up my hopes on a foundation consisting of confusion, misery, and death. I see the world gradually being turned into a wilderness, I hear the ever approaching thunder, which will destroy us too, I can feel the sufferings of millions and yet, if I look up into the heavens, I think that it will all come right, that this cruelty too will end, and that peace and tranquillity will return again.

In the meantime, I must uphold my ideals, for perhaps the time will come when I shall be able to carry them out.

Yours, Anne

Friday, 21 July, 1944

Dear Kitty,

Now I am getting really hopeful, now things are going well at last. Yes, really, they're going well! Super news! An attempt has been made on Hitler's life and not even by Jewish communists or English capitalists this time, but by a proud German general, and what's more, he's a count, and still quite young. The Führer's life was saved by Divine Providence and, unfortunately, he managed to get off with just a few scratches and burns. A few officers and generals who were with him have been killed and wounded. The chief culprit was shot.

Anyway, it certainly shows that there are lots of officers and generals who are sick of the war and would like to see Hitler descend into a bottomless pit. When they've disposed of Hitler, their aim is to establish a military dictator, who will make peace with the Allies, then they intend to rearm and start another war in about twenty years' time. Perhaps the Divine Power tarried on purpose in getting him out of the way, because it would be much easier and more advantageous to the Allies if the impeccable Germans kill each other off; it'll make less work for the Russians and the English and they'll be able to begin rebuilding their own towns all the sooner.

But still, we're not that far yet, and I don't want to antici-
pate the glorious events too soon. Still, you must have noticed,
this is all sober reality and that I'm in quite a matter-of-fact
mood today; for once, I'm not jabbering about high ideals.
And what's more, Hitler has even been so kind as to announce
to his faithful, devoted people that from now on everyone in
the armed forces must obey the Gestapo, and that any soldier
who knows that one of his superiors was involved in this low,
cowardly attempt upon his life may shoot the same on the spot,
without court-martial.

What a perfect shambles it's going to be. Little Johnnie's
feet begin hurting him during a long march, he's snapped at
by his boss, the officer, Johnnie grabs his rifle and cries out:
"You wanted to murder the Führer, so there's your reward."
One bang and the proud chief who dared to tick off little
Johnnie has passed into eternal life (or is it eternal death?).
In the end, whenever an officer finds himself up against a
soldier, or having to take the lead, he'll be wetting his pants
from anxiety, because the soldiers will dare to say more than
they do. Do you gather a bit what I mean, or have I been
skipping too much from one subject to another? I can't help it;
the prospect that I may be sitting on school benches next October makes me feel far too cheerful to be logical! Oh, dearie me,
hadn't I just told you that I didn't want to be too hopeful?
Forgive me, they haven't given me the name "little bundle of
contradictions" all for nothing!

Yours, Anne

Tuesday, 1 August, 1944

Dear Kitty,

"Little bundle of contradictions." That's how I ended my
last letter and that's how I'm going to begin this one. "A little
bundle of contradictions," can you tell me exactly what it is?
What does contradiction mean? Like so many words, it can
mean two things, contradiction from without and contradiction
from within.

The first is the ordinary "not giving in easily, always knowing best, getting in the last word," *enfin*, all the unpleasant
qualities for which I'm renowned. The second nobody knows
about, that's my own secret.

I've already told you before that I have, as it were, a dual personality. One half embodies my exuberant cheerfulness, making fun of everything, my high-spiritedness, and above all, the way I take everything lightly. This includes not taking offense at a flirtation, a kiss, an embrace, a dirty joke. This side is usually lying in wait and pushes away the other, which is much better, deeper and purer. You must realize that no one knows Anne's better side and that's why most people find me so insufferable.

Certainly I'm a giddy clown for one afternoon, but then everyone's had enough of me for another month. Really, it's just the same as a love film is for deep-thinking people, simply a diversion, amusing just for once, something which is soon forgotten, not bad, but certainly not good. I loathe having to tell you this, but why shouldn't I, if I know it's true anyway? My lighter superficial side will always be too quick for the deeper side of me and that's why it will always win. You can't imagine how often I've already tried to push this Anne away, to cripple her, to hide her, because after all, she's only half of what's called Anne: but it doesn't work and I know, too, why it doesn't work.

I'm awfully scared that everyone who knows me as I always am will discover that I have another side, a finer and better side. I'm afraid they'll laugh at me, think I'm ridiculous and sentimental, not take me seriously. I'm used to not being taken seriously but it's only the "lighthearted" Anne that's used to it and can bear it; the "deeper" Anne is too frail for it. Sometimes, if I really compel the good Anne to take the stage for a quarter of an hour, she simply shrivels up as soon as she has to speak, and lets Anne number one take over, and before I realize it, she has disappeared.

Therefore, the nice Anne is never present in company, has not appeared one single time so far, but almost always predominates when we're alone. I know exactly how I'd like to be, how I am too . . . inside. But, alas, I'm only like that for myself. And perhaps that's why, no, I'm sure it's the reason why I say I've got a happy nature within and why other people think I've got a happy nature without. I am guided by the pure Anne within, but outside I'm nothing but a frolicsome little goat who's broken loose.

As I've already said, I never utter my real feelings about

anything and that's how I've acquired the name of chaser-after-boys, flirt, know-all, reader of love stories. The cheerful Anne laughs about it, gives cheeky answers, shrugs her shoulders indifferently, behaves as if she doesn't care, but, oh dearie me, the quiet Anne's reactions are just the opposite. If I'm to be quite honest, then I must admit that it does hurt me, that I try terribly hard to change myself, but that I'm always fighting against a more powerful enemy.

A voice sobs within me: "There you are, that's what's become of you: you're uncharitable, you look supercilious and peevish, people dislike you and all because you won't listen to the advice given you by your own better half." Oh, I would like to listen, but it doesn't work; if I'm quiet and serious, everyone thinks it's a new comedy and then I have to get out of it by turning it into a joke, not to mention my own family, who are sure to think I'm ill, make me swallow pills for headaches and nerves, feel my neck and my head to see whether I'm running a temperature, ask if I'm constipated and criticize me for being in a bad mood. I can't keep that up: if I'm watched to that extent, I start by getting snappy, then unhappy, and finally I twist my heart round again, so that the bad is on the outside and the good is on the inside and keep on trying to find a way of becoming what I would so like to be, and what I could be, if . . . there weren't any other people living in the world.

Yours, Anne

FABLES

Kitty

Kitty is the girl next door. In fair weather, I can watch her playing in the yard through our window. Kitty has a wine-red velvet frock for Sundays and a cotton one for every day; she has pale-blond hair with tiny braids, and clear blue eyes.

Kitty has a sweet mother, but her father is dead. The mother is a laundress; sometimes she is gone during the day, cleaning other people's houses, and at night she does the wash for her customers.

Often she shakes out carpets late at night and hangs wash on the line. Kitty has six brothers and sisters. The smallest screams a lot and hangs onto the skirts of his eleven-year-old sister when mother says, "Children, it's bedtime!"

Kitty has a small cat which is so black that it looks like a Moor. She takes good care of the kitten, and every evening, before bedtime, you can hear her call, "Kitty, kitty, kitty!" That's how she came to be called Kitty, which may not be her name at all. She also has two rabbits, a white one and a brown one, that hop up and down in the grass.

Sometimes Kitty is naughty, just like other children. This happens mostly when she quarrels with her brothers. It's a sight to see her fight with them—she beats, kicks, and even bites them, and the little boys respect their sturdy sister.

"There are errands to be done!" Mother calls. Quickly Kitty sticks her fingers in her ears, so that she'll be able to say that she didn't hear her mother. Kitty hates running errands, but she wouldn't lie to escape it; Kitty doesn't lie; you need only to look into her blue eyes to know that.

One of Kitty's brothers is sixteen and works as an office boy. This brother sometimes bosses the other children as if he were their father. Kitty doesn't dare to contradict him, for she knows from experience that he is quick with his fists and also that he doesn't mind standing treat if one obeys him. Peter is generous and Kitty loves sweets.

Sundays, when the bell tolls, Kitty's mother and all the children go to church. Kitty prays for her dear father, who is in heaven, and also for her mother, that she may have a long, long life. After church they all go for a walk. Kitty enjoys this a lot; she is fond of wandering through the park, or, better still, through the zoo. But that happens only in September, when it costs a quarter.[1] Kitty's birthday is in September, and sometimes she asks for a trip to the zoo as a birthday gift. Other gifts her mother cannot afford.

Often Kitty comforts her mother who, after a day's hard work, weeps in the night. Then Kitty promises her all the things she, herself, would like to have when she is grown up.

[1]The Amsterdam Zoological Society is a membership organization. In the month of September, the public is admitted to the park for 25 Dutch cents—Transl.

Kitty wants so badly to be grown up, to earn money, buy pretty clothes, and treat her sisters to sweets, as Peter does. But before she can do all that, Kitty has to learn a lot and go to school for a long time.

Mother wants Kitty to go to Domestic Science School, but the girl doesn't care for that idea at all. She doesn't want a job in the house of some stuck-up lady. She wants to work in a factory, like those jolly chattering girls she sees passing by the window. In a factory you're never alone, you have company to gossip with. And Kitty loves gossiping. Once in a while she has to stand in the corner in school, because she talks too much.

Just the same, Kitty is fond of her teacher, who is sweet and terribly clever. How difficult it must be to study and get to know so much! But one can get along with less. Kitty's mother always says that a girl doesn't get a husband if she is too clever, and that, Kitty thinks, would be just awful. Later she should like to have dear little children, but not such children as her brothers and sisters. Kitty's children are going to be much prettier and sweeter. They will have curly brown hair instead of that straight flaxen stuff, and they will have no freckles, which Kitty has by the hundreds. Kitty doesn't want as many children as her mother has. Two or three would be enough, but, oh, it is so far, far off . . .

"Kitty!" her mother calls. "Come here. Where have you been, naughty girl? Just sitting there dreaming, I guess. Quick, to bed with you!"

Kitty sighs. To be interrupted just as you are thinking of a glorious future!

Eve's Dream

October 6, 1943

"Good night, Eve, sleep well."

"Same to you, Mum."

Click went the light and Eve lay in the dark, but only for a few moments, because when she got used to the darkness, she saw that her mother had closed the curtains in such a way that an opening was left through which she could look straight into the face of the moon. The moon stood so quietly in the sky; he didn't move, smiled, and was friendly to everyone.

"If I could only be like that," Eve said softly to herself, "always quiet and kind so that everybody would like me. That would be wonderful."

Eve thought and thought about the difference between the moon and herself, who was still so very small. She finally dozed off, and her thoughts seemed to be transformed into a dream, which Eve remembered so keenly next day that she afterward sometimes wondered whether it had not actually happened.

She stood at the entrance of a big park, looking through the fence and not quite daring to go in. Just as she was about to turn back, a little girl with wings came up to her and said, "Go right ahead, Eve, or don't you know the way?"

"No, I don't," said Eve shyly.

"Well, then I will guide you." And with those words, the smart little elf took Eve's hand.

Eve had walked in several parks with her mother and her grandmother, but a park like this one she had never seen.

She saw a wealth of flowers, trees, fields, every imaginable kind of insect, and small animals such as squirrels and turtles. The elf chatted gaily with her, and Eve had got over her fear enough to ask a question. But the elf stopped her by putting a finger to Eve's lips.

"I will show you and explain everything. After each explanation you may ask questions about things you don't understand, but otherwise you must be silent and not interrupt me. If you do, I shall take you home at once, and then you will know just as little as all the other stupid people.

"Well, now I begin: First of all, here is the rose, the queen of flowers. She is so beautiful and smells so wonderful that it goes to everybody's head, and most of all to her own.

"The rose is lovely, elegant, and fragrant, but if something doesn't please her, she immediately turns her thorns in your direction. She is like a spoiled little girl—very pretty and apparently quite sweet, too, but either touch her, or pay a little attention to somebody else, so that she is no longer the center of interest, and she shows her sharp nails. Her tone of voice becomes catty; she is offended but doesn't want to show it, and so her manners turn stilted and she puts on airs."

"But if all this is so, little elf, how is it that everybody considers the rose the queen of flowers?"

"It is because nearly all people are blinded by surface glitter; there are only a few who would not have voted for the rose if there had been an election. The rose is good-looking and dignified, and, just as in the rest of the world, scarcely anyone asks if there might not be another, outwardly a little plainer, perhaps, but inwardly more noble and gifted, for the role of ruler."

"But you yourself think the rose lovely, don't you, little elf?"

"Indeed, I do, and if she wouldn't always push herself into the foreground, she might be lovable as well. But since, by common consent, she is the flower of flowers, she will always regard herself as more beautiful than she really is, and so long as that is so, she will be full of false pride. I don't care for such creatures."

"Do you think that Lena, too, is full of false pride? She is also beautiful and, because she is rich, she is the head of the class."

"Think for a moment, Eve, and you will have to admit that, if little Marie, for example, had some complaint against Lena, Lena would turn the entire class against Marie. The reason? Simply that Marie is plain and poor. And you, all of you, would accept that false reason, because you know that if you did not, you would fall from Lena's good graces. And that, you think, is as bad as having the headmaster angry at you. You wouldn't be permitted to come to her beautiful home, and so you let her boss you. Later in life, such girls as Lena will stand alone, for the others, as they grow older, will understand how wrong she was. Rather than be lonely forever, girls like Lena should change their ways."

"Do you think, then, elf, that I should try to convince the other girls not to listen to Lena?"

"Yes. First she will be furious at you. But later, as she gets more sense and realizes how badly she has acted, she will be grateful and have friends who are more sincere than those she has had until now . . ."

"I understand. But tell me, little elf, am I as full of false pride as the rose?"

"Listen, Eve: people and children who ask themselves such questions prove by that very act that they are free from false pride. You can best answer the question yourself, and I advise you to do so . . . Now let us go on. Look at this: don't you think it is attractive?"

The elf knelt down by a small, blue, bell-shaped flower that waved back and forth in the grass to the rhythm of the wind.

"This little bell is kind, sweet, and simple. It brings joy to the world; it tolls for the other flowers just as a church bell tolls for people. It helps many flowers and comforts them. The little bell is never lonesome; it has music in its small heart.

This flower is much happier than the rose. It doesn't care about the praise of others. The rose lives only for and by admiration: if she doesn't get this, she has no other reason to be glad. Her outward splendor is for others; inside she is empty and, therefore, without happiness.

"The little bell, on the other hand, is not exactly beautiful, but it has genuine friends, who value its melodies; those friends live in its flower-heart."

"But the little bell is a pretty flower, too, isn't it?"

"Yes, but not as obviously as the rose. Unfortunately, it is this kind of 'show' that attracts most people."

"But I, too, often feel quite alone and like to have people about me. Is that not good?"

"That has nothing to do with it, Eve. Later, when you grow up, you, too, will hear the song in your heart; I am sure of it."

"Please, dear elf, go on with your story."

"All right, I will go on." The elf pointed upward with her small fingers. Eve looked at a huge, stately chestnut tree.

"This tree is impressive, isn't it?" asked the elf.

"Yes, it is grand; how old do you think it is?"

"It is surely more than a hundred and fifty years old, but it is still straight and doesn't feel old at all. Everybody admires this chestnut for its strength, and he proves that he knows his strength with his indifference about all this admiration. He doesn't tolerate anyone above himself and is egotistical in everything. So long as he lives, nothing else is of any importance. He looks as though he were generous and a support to others. But if you think that, you are mistaken. The chestnut is pleased when no one comes to him with troubles or complaints. He has a good life, but he begrudges it to everyone else. The trees and flowers know this. When they are in trouble, they go to the sympathetic pine and forget about the chestnut.

"Still, the chestnut, too, has a very small song in that big heart of his; you can tell that by his liking for the birds. For them he always has a little spot, and he often gives them a little something, though not much."

"Can the chestnut tree also be compared to some kind of person?"

"That, too, you need not ask, Eve. All living beings can be compared with each other, and the chestnut is no exception. He is not bad, you know, but neither is he good. He doesn't do anyone harm, lives his own life, and is satisfied. Any other questions, Eve?"

"No, I understand everything, and I am very grateful to you for your explanations, dear elf. Now I am going home. Will you come again some time to tell me more?"

"That is not possible. Sleep well, Eve."

The elf was gone. Eve woke up; the sun had replaced the moon, and a cuckoo clock at the neighbors' called out seven.

The dream had made a big impression on Eve. Nearly every day she caught herself doing or saying little unpleasant things, which she then corrected at once according to the elf's good advice. She also tried hard not always to give in to Lena. But girls like that feel at once that some one is making an effort to "take them down a peg or two." She defended herself vigorously, especially when Eve proposed some game in which another girl would be the leader. Then Lena did everything she could to turn her faithful following against Eve.

Eve noticed with pleasure that Lena wasn't quite as smart in her dealings with her as she was with little Marie. As Marie was a small, slight, and shy girl, it amazed Eve that she dared to stand up against Lena. As she got to know her better, it became very clear to Eve that Marie, as a friend, was to be valued much above Lena.

Eve had told her Mother nothing about the elf. She hardly knew why. Until now, she had confided in her mother, but for the first time she felt the need to keep something to herself. She didn't understand it, but she had a feeling that Mummy wouldn't be quite "with her" in this.

The little elf was so lovely, and Mummy had not been in the big park and hadn't seen the elf. Eve couldn't describe the elf's appearance. It wasn't long before the dream had such an influence on Eve that her mother noticed the change in her daughter. She talked about more interesting things than before and didn't get excited about trifles. But since Eve didn't speak of what had brought about the change, the mother didn't want to force herself into the child's confidence.

And so Eve lived on, thinking always of the elf's good counsel. She never saw the elf again. Lena no longer was the head of the class. The other girls now led the group by turns. At first, this had made Lena very cross, but when she found that angry words didn't help, she began to behave in a more friendly manner. Finally, her class mates, finding that she had outgrown her old faults, treated her like everyone else.

Eve decided to tell her mother of her experience. To her surprise, Mummy didn't laugh, but said: "That was a great privilege the elf gave you, Eve. I don't believe that she would think many children fit to receive it. Think always of the elf's trust in you, and don't talk about it to anyone. Do always what the elf told you, and don't get away from the path she showed you."

As Eve grew older, she became known for her good deeds. When she was sixteen, everyone in the community prized her as a kind, gentle, and helpful girl. Every time she did something good she felt warm and glad inside, and slowly she began to understand what the elf had meant by "the song in her heart."

When she was grown up, the solution of the dream and who and what the little elf had been suddenly came to her one day. She knew, as if in a flash, that it had been her own conscience which, in her dream, had shown her what was right. She was deeply thankful that, in her childhood, she had had the little elf as a guide and example.

Kathy

February 11, 1944

Kathy sat on the big boulder that lay in the sun in front of the farm. She was thinking, thinking very hard. Kathy was one of those quiet girls. What the youngster in the dirndl apron was thinking about, she alone knew; she never told her thoughts to anyone—she was much too withdrawn for that. She had no friends and probably would have found it hard to get any. Her mother found her a strange child, and the pity of it was that Kathy felt that. Her father, the farmer, was much too busy to concern himself with his only little daughter. And so Kathy was always by herself. It didn't disturb her; she didn't know any better and was soon satisfied.

But on this warm summer evening she sighed deeply as she looked up and glanced at the cornfields. How jolly it would be to play with those girls over there. Look, they ran about, and laughed; what fun they were having! Now the children came closer, and still closer—would they come to her? Oh, how awful, they came—but to laugh at her. She clearly heard them mention her name, not her real name, but the nickname that she hated so much and that she often heard the children whisper—Crazykate!

Oh, how miserable she felt; if she could only run into the house, but if she did, the children would laugh at her all the more. Poor girl, it surely isn't the first time that you have felt so forsaken and envied the other youngsters . . .

"Kathy! Kathy, come home! We are having supper!" Another sigh, and the child slowly rose to obey her mother.

"My, what a cheerful face! We surely have a happy daughter!" the farmer's wife cried when the child, more slowly and more depressed than ever, entered the room. "Can't you say something for yourself?" scolded the woman. Her tone was more unfriendly than she herself knew; her daughter never had been the bright, lively girl she had always wanted.

"Yes, Mother," whispered the child.

"You're a fine one, staying away all morning and not doing a stroke of work. Where have you been?"

"Outside." Kathy felt as though she had a gag in her throat, but the mother misunderstood the girl's embarrassment and now really became curious where the child had been all morning. Again she asked:

"Answer me properly; I want to know where you have been, do you understand? I can't stand that everlasting, slow-witted, crazy behavior!"

At the word that reminded her of the detested nickname, Kathy lost control of herself and burst into tears.

"What is the matter now? You're a real coward! Can't you tell me where you've been hanging out? Or is that perhaps a big secret?"

The child could not possibly answer; violent sobs kept her from speaking. Suddenly, she upset a chair, ran weeping out of the room and up to the attic, where she sank down on some bags in a corner, sobbing as if her heart would break.

The mother shrugged her shoulders as she cleared the table downstairs; she wasn't surprised at her child's conduct. Such "crazy" moods were not unusual; she decided to let the girl alone—there was nothing to be gained, and the everlasting tears were always on the point of coming. A fine specimen of a twelve-year-old farmer's daughter!

In the attic, Kathy had calmed down somewhat and was collecting her thoughts. She would presently go downstairs, tell her mother that she had simply been sitting on the boulder by the door and thinking about things, and offer to finish all of the work that afternoon. Her mother then would surely understand that she did not mind the work, and should she be asked why she had been sitting still all morning, she would answer that there was something important she HAD to figure out. Then, in the evening, when she had to deliver the eggs, she would buy a pretty, silver, glittering thimble for her mother; she had just enough money to buy one in the village.

Mother would realize that she wasn't so slow-witted and crazy, after all. Oh, if she could only get rid of that dreadful nickname! Here was a thought: If she had any money left over after buying the thimble, she'd get a bag of sweets and, on her way to school, divide them among the girls. Then they'd like her and ask her to play with them. They would soon see that she was as good at games as anyone, and nobody would ever call her anything but Kathy after that.

Softly she descended the stairs. When she met her mother in the passage, all courage to talk and explain the morning's absence left her, and she quickly started cleaning the windows, one of her regular tasks.

It was almost sundown when Kathy took the basket of eggs and began her rounds. After a half hour's walk she reached the first customer, who stood in her doorway, dish in hand.

"I'll take ten tonight, my child," said the friendly woman.

She counted off ten and, with a greeting, continued on her way.

In three quarters of an hour the basket was empty, and Kathy stepped into the small general store. A pretty thimble and a bagful of sweets were soon put into the basket, and now Kathy turned back toward home. About halfway, she saw two of the girls who had teased her in the morning coming toward her. She bravely suppressed a longing to hide, and, her heart beating wildly, she went on.

"Look! Here comes Crazykate!"

At her wits' end, Kathy took the bag of sweets from her basket and politely held it out to the children. They quickly grabbed it from her and ran away with it. One of them stuck out her tongue at Kathy.

Lonesome and heartbroken, Kathy sat down in the grass at

the edge of the road, and wept, wept, and wept. Finally, in the dark, she dried her tears, picked up the basket, and slowly set off in the direction of home.

Somewhere in the grass, the thimble glittered . . .

The Flower Girl

February 20, 1944

Every morning at seven-thirty the door of a little house at the edge of the village opens, and out steps a rather small girl, carrying a basket heaped with flowers on each arm. After shutting the door, she switches her burdens and starts the day's work. The people of the village, who answer her smiling nod as she passes, feel sorry for her. "That road is much too long and the job too hard," they think, "for a child of twelve."

But the little girl, herself, naturally doesn't know the thoughts of her fellow villagers. Merrily, and as quickly as her short legs will take her, she walks on and on and on. The road to the town is really very long; it takes her at least two and a half hours of steady walking to reach it and, with two heavy baskets, that's not easy.

When she finally trudges through the streets of the town she is exhausted, and it's only the prospect of soon being able to sit down and rest that sustains her. But the little one is brave and doesn't slow down her gait until she gets to her spot in the market. Then she sits down and waits and waits . . .

Sometimes she sits and waits all day because there are not enough people who want to buy something from the poor flower girl. Quite often Krista has to carry her baskets, still half full, back to the village in the evening.

But today things are different. It is Wednesday, and the market is unusually crowded and busy. Beside her, market women cry their wares, and all about her the little girl hears scolding and angry voices.

Passers-by can scarcely hear Krista, for her high little voice is almost drowned out in the market hubbub. But all day long, Krista doesn't stop calling, "Pretty flowers, a dime a bunch! Buy my pretty flowers!" Some people who, finished with their errands, take time to look into the baskets, gladly pay a dime for one of the lovely small bouquets.

At twelve o'clock, Krista walks to the opposite side of the market square, where the owner of the coffee stand is in the habit of giving her, free of charge, a cupful with plenty of sugar. For this kind man Krista keeps her prettiest flowers.

Then she takes her seat again and once more starts crying her wares. At last, about three-thirty, she picks up her baskets and returns to the village. Now she walks much more slowly than she did in the morning. Krista is tired, terribly tired.

The trip back takes her a full three hours, and it is six-thirty when she reaches the door of the little old house. Inside everything is still the way she left it—cold, lonesome, and untidy. Her sister, with whom she shares the place, works in the village from early morning to late at night. Krista can't afford to rest; she is no sooner home than she begins to peel potatoes and clean vegetables. Her sister gets back from work at seven-thirty, and they finally sit down and have something to eat.

At eight in the evening the door of the cottage opens again, and once more the little girl comes out with the two big baskets on her arms. Now she walks into the fields that surround the little house. She doesn't have to go far; soon she bends down in the grass and picks flowers, all kinds of them, big ones and little ones, and all of them go into the baskets. The sun has almost set, and the child still sits in the grass, collecting her next day's supply.

The task is finished at last; the baskets are full. The sun has set, and Krista lies down in the grass, her hands folded under her head, and looks up into the sky.

This is her favorite quarter hour, and nobody need think that the hard-working little flower girl is dissatisfied. She never is and never will be so long as, every day, she may have this wonderful short rest.

In the field, amid the flowers, beneath the darkening sky, Krista is content. Gone is fatigue, gone is the market, gone are the people. The little girl dreams and thinks only of the bliss of having, each day, this short while alone with God and nature.

The Guardian Angel

February 22, 1944

Once upon a time, an old lady and her young granddaughter lived for many years on the very edge of a large forest. The girl's parents had died when she was still quite small, and the grandmother had always taken good care of her. The little house in which they lived was a lonesome place, but they didn't seem to realize it and were happy together.

One morning the old lady couldn't get up, because she was in great pain. Her granddaughter was now fourteen years old, and she looked after her grandma as well as she could. It lasted five days; then the grandmother died and the girl was all alone in that lonesome cottage. As she knew hardly anyone and did not want to call in strangers to bury her grandmother, she dug a grave under an old tree in the woods, and there laid her grandma to rest.

When the poor girl came back to the house, she felt utterly forsaken and very sad. She lay down on her bed and cried her heart out. She lay there all day and didn't get up until evening, to get a bite to eat. So it went, day after day. The poor child no longer took pleasure in anything and only mourned and mourned for her dear old granny.

Then something happened that changed her entirely in just one day. It was night, and the girl was asleep when, suddenly, her grandmother stood before her. She was dressed in white from head to foot; her white hair hung down her shoulders, and she carried a small lamp.

From her bed, the girl watched her and waited for the grandmother to speak. "My dear little girl," the grandma began, "I have been watching you now every day for four weeks, and you never do anything but weep and sleep. That is not good, and I have come to tell you that you must work and spin; that you must take care of our little house and also dress prettily again.

"You mustn't think that, now I am dead, I no longer look after you; I am in heaven and always watch you from above. I have become your guardian angel, and I am always with you, just as before. Take up your work again, darling, and never forget that your granny is with you!"

Then granny disappeared, and the girl slept on.

Next morning when she awoke, she remembered what her grandmother had said, and she was filled with joy and no longer felt forsaken. She started working again, sold her spinning in the market, and followed her granny's advice at all times.

Later, much later, she also wasn't alone in the outside world. She was married to a fine man, a miller. She thanked her granny for not having left her alone, and she well knew that, though she now always had good company, her guardian angel would not leave her until the end of her days.

Fear

It was a terrible time through which I was living. The war raged about us, and nobody knew whether or not he would be alive the next hour. My parents, brothers, sisters, and I made our home in the city, but we expected that we either would be evacuated or have to escape in some other way. By day the sound of cannon and rifle shots was almost continuous, and the nights were mysteriously filled with sparks and sudden explosions that seemed to come from some unknown depth.

I cannot describe it; I don't remember that tumult quite clearly, but I do know that all day long I was in the grip of fear. My parents tried everything to calm me, but it didn't help. I felt nothing, nothing but fear; I could neither eat nor sleep—fear clawed at my mind and body and shook me. That lasted for about a week; then came an evening and a night which I recall as though it had been yesterday.

At half past eight, when the shooting had somewhat died down, I lay in a sort of half doze on a sofa. Suddenly all of us were startled by two violent explosions. As though stuck with knives, we all jumped up and ran into the hall. Even Mother,

usually so calm, looked pale. The explosions repeated themselves at pretty regular intervals. Then: a tremendous crash,
the noise of much breaking glass, and an ear-splitting chorus
of yelling and screaming. I put on what heavy clothes I could
find in a hurry, threw some things into a rucksack, and ran. I
ran as fast as I could, ran on and on to get away from the
fiercely burning mass about me. Everywhere shouting people
darted to and fro; the street was alight with a fearsome red
glow.

I didn't think of my parents or of my brothers and sisters.
I had thoughts only for myself and knew that I must rush,
rush, rush! I didn't feel any fatigue; my fear was too strong.
I didn't know that I had lost my rucksack. All I felt and knew
was that I had to run.

I couldn't possibly say how long I ran on with the image of
the burning houses, the desperate people and their distorted
faces before me. Then I sensed that it had got more quiet. I
looked around and, as if waking up from a nightmare, I saw
that there was nothing or no one behind me. No fire, no bombs,
no people. I looked a little more closely and found that I stood
in a meadow. Above me the stars glistened and the moon
shone; it was brilliant weather, crisp but not cold.

I didn't hear a sound. Exhausted, I sat down on the grass,
then spread the blanket I had been carrying on my arm, and
stretched out on it.

I looked up into the sky and realized that I was no longer
afraid; on the contrary, I felt very peaceful inside. The funny
thing was that I didn't think of my family, nor yearn for them;
I yearned only for rest, and it wasn't long before I fell asleep
there in the grass, under the sky.

When I woke up the sun was just rising. I immediately knew
where I was; in the daylight I recognized the houses at the
outskirts of our city. I rubbed my eyes and had a good look
around. There was no one to be seen; the dandelions and the
clover-leaves in the grass were my only company. Lying back
on the blanket for a while, I mused about what to do next. But
my thoughts wandered off from the subject and returned to
the wonderful feeling of the night before, when I sat in the
grass and was no longer afraid.

Later I found my parents, and together we moved to another town. Now that the war is over, I know why my fear

disappeared under the wide, wide heavens. When I was alone with nature, I realized—realized without actually knowing it—that fear is a sickness for which there is only one remedy. Anyone who is as afraid, as I was then, should look at nature and see that God is much closer than most people think.

Since that time I have never been afraid again, no matter how many bombs fell near me.

The Wise Old Dwarf

April 18, 1944

There once was a little elf called Dora. She was pretty and rich, and her parents spoiled her terribly. She was always laughing. She laughed from early morning until late at night; she was happy about everything and never gave sadness or sorrow a thought.

In the same forest where Dora made her home, there lived a dwarf by the name of Peldron. He was, in everything, the exact opposite of Dora. While Dora was forever smiling at all the beauty and goodness about her, Peldron worried because there was so much misery in the world, and especially in the world of elves and dwarves.

One day Dora had to do an errand at the shoemaker's in elves' village. And what do you think happened? She met that boring and long-faced Peldron. Dora was sweet but, because everyone liked her, she was a bit conceited, too. Boldly, she ran toward Peldron, grabbed his pretty dwarf's hat and, from a distance, laughed with the hat in her hands.

Peldron was really cross; he stamped on the ground and called, "Give me back my hat, give it back immediately!"

But Dora did no such thing, ran farther away, and finally hid the hat in a hollow tree. Then she quickly continued on her way to the shoemaker.

After looking for it a long time, Peldron did find his hat. He couldn't take a joke, and especially not from Dora, whom he didn't like at all. Listlessly, he went on his way. Suddenly, a deep voice roused him from his brooding:

"Peldron, I am the oldest dwarf in the world, and also the poorest. Please, give me something, so that I may buy some food."

Peldron shook his head, no. "I won't give you anything," he said. "You had better die, so you needn't endure the misery of this world." And he hurried on without looking back.

Meanwhile, Dora, on her way back from the shoemaker, also met the old dwarf, and she, too, was asked for alms. Like Peldron, she refused, but for a different reason.

"I won't give you any money," she said. "If you are poor, it's your own fault. The world is so wonderful that I can't be bothered with poor people." And she skipped along.

With a sigh, the old dwarf sat down on a mossy spot, wondering what he should do with those two children. One was too sad, the other too gay, and both wouldn't get very far in life that way.

Now, this ancient dwarf was no ordinary, everyday dwarf; he was a sorcerer, but not an evil one. On the contrary, he wanted people, and elves and dwarves to improve and the world to progress.

He sat there, thinking, for an hour. Then he rose and slowly walked to the house of Dora's parents.

The day after their meeting in the forest, Dora and Peldron found themselves locked up together in a small cabin. The old dwarf had taken them away to give them a proper training. The great sorcerer's wish was the same as a command, and even parents dared not disobey it.

What were those two to do in that hut? They weren't allowed to go out, nor were they permitted to quarrel. They had to work the whole day long! Those had been the old dwarf's orders. And so Dora worked, made jokes and laughed; and Peldron worked, looked gloomy and felt sad.

Every evening at seven, the old dwarf came to check on their work and then left again. They wondered how they could possibly get free. There was only one way, and that was to obey the old dwarf in everything.

You can't imagine how difficult it was for Dora to have to look at that long-jawed Peldron all day long; Peldron, Peldron, early and late, and never anybody else. But she hadn't much time to talk to him, anyway, even if she had wanted to, because she had to cook (she had learned that from her mother), keep the house clean and in order, and in her "spare time," if you please, get some spinning done.

Peldron, for his part, must chop wood in the enclosed garden, cultivate the grounds, and cobble shoes in the bargain. At seven in the evening, Dora called him to supper, and by that time they were both so tired that they could hardly talk to the old dwarf when he arrived on his nightly visit.

They kept this up for a week. Dora still laughed often, and yet she began to understand that there was a serious side to life. She realized that there were people who had a difficult time and that it was not asking too much to help such folk when they were in distress, instead of sending them away with some rude words. And Peldron lost a little of his gloom; it even happened, from time to time, that he whistled softly at his work, or grinned when he saw Dora laughing.

On Sunday they were both allowed to come with the old dwarf to chapel in elves' village. They paid more attention to the words of the dwarf-preacher than they had before, and they felt quite content as they walked back through the shady woods.

"Because you have been so good," said the old dwarf, "you may spend the day in the open, just as you used to do. But, mind you, tomorrow you go back to work. You can't go home, and you can't visit your friends."

Neither thought of running away; they were very glad to be permitted the freedom of the forest, even for one day. All that Sunday they played and had fun, watched the birds, the flowers and the blue sky, and enjoyed the warm sunshine.

Happily, they returned to their cabin in the evening, slept until morning, and then went back to work.

The old dwarf made them lead this kind of life for four long months. Every Sunday morning they went to church, spent the rest of the day in the open, and worked hard the remainder of the week.

When the four months were up, the old dwarf one evening took both of them by the hand and walked into the woods with them.

"Look here, children," he said, "I am sure that you often have been angry with me. I also think that you both must be longing to go home."

"Yes," said Dora. And "Yes," echoed Peldron.

"But do you understand that this has been good for you?"

No, sir, they didn't understand that so well.

"Well, I will explain it," said the old dwarf. "I took you here and left you together to teach you that there are other things in this world beside YOUR fun and YOUR gloom. You both will get along in life much better than before you came here. Little Dora has become somewhat more serious, and Peldron has cheered up a bit, because you were obliged to make the best of having to live together. I also believe that you like each other better than before. Don't you agree, Peldron?"

"Yes," said Peldron, "I like Dora much better now."

"Well," said the old dwarf, "you may go back to your parents. But think often about your stay in the little cabin. Enjoy all the fine things life will bring you, but don't forget the sorrows of others and try to comfort them. All people, children, dwarves and elves can help one another.

"So, on your way, and don't be cross with me any more. I have done for you what I could, and it was for your own good. Good day, children, till we meet again!"

"Bye-bye," said Dora and Peldron, and off they went to their homes.

Once more the old dwarf sat down in a shady spot. He had but one wish—that he might guide all the children of men into the right path, as he had guided those two.

And, truly, Dora and Peldron lived happily ever after! Once and for all they had learned the great lesson that people must laugh and weep, each at the right time. Later, much later, when they were grown up, they went to live together in a small house of their own free will, and Dora did the work inside and Peldron outside, just as they had when they were very young.

Blurry, the Explorer

April 23, 1944

Once, when he was still very small, Blurry felt a great desire to escape from the fussing care of his mother bear and see something of the wide, wide world for himself. For days he was much less playful than usual, so busy was he thinking over his plans. But on the evening of the fourth day, his mind was made up. His plan was ready and only awaited execution. Early in the morning he would go into the garden—very softly, of course, so that Mimi, his little mistress, wouldn't notice— then he would creep through a hole in the hedge, and after that, well, after that, he would discover the world! He did all this, and so quietly that nobody knew he had escaped before he had been gone several hours.

As he crept out from under the hedge, his fur was smeared with earth and mud, but a bear who wants to make a voyage of discovery mustn't mind a little thing like a few spots of dirt on his skin. So, looking straight ahead, so as not to stumble over the uneven cobblestones, Blurry stepped smartly in the direction of the street, which could be reached through the alley between the garden.

In the street he was a little frightened by the many grown-up people between whose legs he disappeared completely. "I must stay near the edge of the sidewalk," he told himself; "otherwise they'll run over me." And this was, indeed, the most sensible thing to do. Yes, Blurry was intelligent, which was self-evident because, tiny as he was, he wanted to see the world.

He kept close to the edge and saw to it that he wasn't caught between a pair of big, fast-moving feet. But suddenly his heart started pounding as if he had sledgehammers inside his chest . . . What was that? A big black abyss lay before his feet. It was an open cellar, but Blurry didn't know that, and he got dizzy. Must he go down in there? Terrified, he looked about, but the trousered men's legs and the skirted ladies' legs calmly walked around the gaping hole and acted as if nothing were amiss. Not quite recovered from the shock, step by little step, he followed their example, and it wasn't long before he could continue.

"Now I'm walking in the big world," thought Blurry, "but where IS the world? Because of all those trousers, skirts, and stockings, I cannot see the world at all. Perhaps I am too small to discover the world, but that doesn't matter. If I eat my porridge and swallow my cod-liver oil every day (he shuddered at the idea), I will get just as big as those people. Let's go on; sooner or later, in one way or another, I'll see the world."

He walked further and paid as little attention as possible to the many fat and thin, long and short legs around him. But must he just walk and walk and walk? He was getting hungry and it was also beginning to grow a bit dark. Blurry had not given eating and sleeping any thought. He had been too much occupied with his plans of discovery to think of such ordinary and unheroic things as eating and sleeping.

Sighing, he walked on for a while until he discovered an

open door. He hesitated on the threshold and then quietly went in. He was in luck, for, after passing through another door, he saw two saucers standing on the floor between some wooden legs. One of the saucers was filled with milk; the other with some sort of food. Starving, Blurry drank every drop of the milk. Then he ate the delicious food in the other saucer and felt entirely satisfied.

But, oh, what was THAT? Something white with green eyes approached slowly, staring at him. Directly in front of him, it stopped and asked in a strange small voice:

"Who are you, and why have you eaten all my food?"

"I am Blurry, and, on a voyage of discovery, a fellow needs something to eat. But I really didn't know that it belonged to you."

"So, you are on a voyage of discovery. But how is it that you had to discover just MY saucer?"

"Because I didn't see any other," Blurry answered in an unfriendly tone. Then he thought better of it, and asked in a kindlier manner:

"But what is your name, and what kind of strange creature are you?"

"I am Muriel and I belong to the family of Angora cats. I am very valuable, at least my mistress always says so. But you know, Blurry, I am forever alone and am often bored. Won't you stay with me for a while?"

"I will stay and sleep here," said Blurry as though he were doing Muriel a favor. "But tomorrow, I must go on and discover the world."

As a beginning, this seemed fair enough to Muriel.

"Come along," she said, and Blurry followed her to another

room where he again saw nothing but wooden legs. Still there was something else. In a corner stood a big wicker basket in which lay a pillow covered with green silk. Muriel stepped onto the pillow with her dirty feet, but Blurry thought it a pity to soil things that way. "Shan't I first wash up a bit?" he asked. "I'll wash you, just as I wash myself," replied Muriel. Blurry was not acquainted with that method, and that was a good thing, for had he known he wouldn't have permitted Muriel to start.

Now the cat told him to stand up straight and calmly ran her tongue over his feet. It made Blurry shiver and he asked if that was her usual way of taking and giving baths.

"Yes, it is," she said. "You will see how clean you'll get; you will shine, and a shiny bear has entree everywhere and so finds it much easier to discover the world." Blurry controlled his shivers and uttered no complaint, brave bear. Muriel's bath seemed to take hours; Blurry was getting a little impatient, and his feet hurt from standing so long, but finally he did shine. Muriel again stepped into the basket and Blurry, who was exhausted, lay down. In less than five minutes they were both asleep.

Next morning Blurry awoke, and it took him a while to realize where he was. Muriel snored a little, and Blurry badly wanted his breakfast. Without considering the comfort of his hostess, he shook her and started to give her orders:

"Give me my breakfast, please, Muriel; I am awfully hungry."

The pretty Angora puss first had a good yawn, stretched to twice her usual length, and answered:

"No, no, you get nothing more. My lady mustn't notice that you are here; you must leave, as quickly as possible, through the garden."

Muriel jumped out of the basket, took Blurry along through the room, out of the door, into another door, and then again out of a door, this time a glass one, and they were outside. "Bon voyage, Blurry," she said. "Till we meet again!" And she was gone.

Lonesome and no longer convinced of his cleverness, Blurry walked through the garden and then, through the hole in the hedge, into the street. Where should he go, and how long would it take to discover the world? Blurry didn't know. Very slowly he walked along when, suddenly, a big four-legged thing ran toward him at full speed. It made tremendous noises so that Blurry, almost deafened and shaking with fear, clung to the side of a house. The gigantic thing halted, and Blurry began to cry from fear. The monster, not a bit disturbed by this, sat down and did nothing but stare at the poor little bear with his big eyes. Blurry pulled himself together. "What do you want of me?" he asked.

"I only want to take a look at you, because I've never seen anything like you."

Blurry breathed a sigh of relief. After all, one could talk, even with this ogre. Here was a curious thing, Blurry thought; why couldn't his own little mistress ever understand him? But he didn't have much time to consider this weighty question, for the big beast opened his mouth wide, showing all his huge cruel teeth. This made Blurry shiver worse than he had during Muriel's washing session. What would the monster do to him? He soon found out, for the beast, without a by-your-leave or with-your-leave, grabbed him by the neck and dragged him through the street.

Blurry couldn't cry, for he would have choked to death if he had; shouting was also out of the question. All that was left him was to shudder, and that didn't give a fellow any courage. He didn't have to walk now; if his neck hadn't hurt so, it wouldn't have been too bad; it was like a ride.

After all, it could be worse. But you did get woozy in the head from that continuous pushing. Where, where, is he taking me? Where? . . . Blurry, held fast by the animal, had dozed off. But the nap didn't last long. The beast suddenly was at a loss to know why he carried this thing in his teeth. Carelessly, he dropped him and ran off. And there lay the helpless little bear who wanted to discover the world, all alone with his pain. Bravely, he rose in order not to be trampled upon, rubbed his eyes, and looked around.

Far fewer legs, far fewer people, much more sun, and fewer cobbles under his feet. Could this be the world? There was no room in his poor head for thoughts; everything hurt and hammered in there. He didn't want to walk any more. Why should he? Muriel was far away, his mother still further, and his little mistress . . . No! He was on his way, and he must persist until he had discovered the world.

A sound behind him startled him, and he turned around,

hoping that no other beast was going to bite him. No, it was a little girl.

"Look, Mama, a little bear! May I take him along?"

"No, my dear, he is sick. Look, he is bleeding."

"That doesn't matter, Mama; we can wash it off when we get home. Then I'll have something to play with."

Blurry didn't understand a word of this conversation; little bears know only animal talk. But the little blonde girl looked so sweet that he didn't resist when he was wrapped in a scarf and put into a bag.

So, swaying to and fro, Blurry continued his voyage through the world. After they had walked for a time, Blurry, with the scarf still around him, was taken out of the bag, and the girl carried him on her arm. That was a piece of luck, for now he could see the road from above. What big piles of stones, very high, with here and there a white opening! And, way on top, almost to the sky, there was a swirl of smoke. That must be for decoration, just like the feather on his little mistress' hat. Wasn't that funny?

Below, on the road, something said "toot-toot" and ran very fast, though it had no legs, only some round, blown-up things. Say what you like, it was worth the trouble to go discover the world! What was the use of always staying home? Why were you born? Surely not to stick forever with your mother. No, see and experience things, that was the way to grow up! Yes, Blurry knew what he wanted.

At long last the girl stopped at a door. She went in, and the first thing Blurry saw was something on the order of Muriel. This one was called Puss, if Blurry remembered right. This Puss stroked the legs of the blonde girl, but she pushed him away and took Blurry to a white thing. It was high above the ground, wide and smooth. At the side, there was something of shiny metal which could be turned. This the blonde girl did, and she set him down on a hard, cold place. Then the girl began to wash him, especially that part of his fur where that nasty beast had bitten him. It hurt a lot and Blurry cried, but no one seemed to mind.

Fortunately, this wash didn't last as long as the one Muriel had given him, but it was colder and much wetter. The girl finished her task pretty quickly, dried him, wrapped him in a fresh scarf, and put him in a down bed, just like the one his little mistress had for him. But why go to bed? Blurry wasn't the least bit tired and didn't want to go to sleep. The girl was no sooner out the room than he slid out of bed and, by way of a large number of doors and holes, landed once more in the street.

"I must get something to eat," thought Blurry. He sniffed; "Yes, there ought to be something good around here, for you can smell it."

He followed his nose and soon stood at the door from which the fine aroma came. He slipped into the big store between the stockinged legs of a lady. Behind a big high something stood two girls. They quickly caught sight of him. They must have worked hard all day long and could use a little help, for they picked him up at once and placed him in a rather dark space where it was very, very hot.

That wasn't so bad; the main thing was that you could eat there as much as you pleased. On the floor and on low shelves, there lay rows of buns, rolls, and pastries, prettier than any Blurry had ever seen. What, after all, HAD Blurry seen? Not so much, come to think of it. Hungrily, he attacked the good things and ate so much that he almost got sick.

Then he took another thorough look around. There was really much to be seen here, it looked like a sweet-tooth's paradise. Everywhere loaves of bread, rolls, tarts, cookies, just for the taking!

And it was very busy here. Blurry saw many white legs, very different from those in the street. But there wasn't much time for dreaming; the girls, who had been standing at a little distance, pushed a broom into his hands and showed him how to use it. Sweep the floor—Blurry knew all about it—he had seen his mother do it. But it wasn't as easy as it looked. He tried bravely, but the broom was big and heavy, and the dust tickled his nose so that he had to sneeze.

And it was so hot; he felt more and more uncomfortable from the work he wasn't used to and the heat, but each time he stopped to rest for a minute, somebody put him back to work and gave him a slap besides.

"If only I hadn't walked in here so hastily," he thought, "then I would have been spared all this heavy work." But there was nothing he could do about it. He had to sweep, and sweep he did. When he had swept a long time, so long that the dirt lay in a big heap in a corner, one of the girls took him by the hand and led him to a spot where some hard yellow shavings lay on the floor. They told him to lie down, and Blurry understood that he was allowed to sleep.

He stretched out as if the shavings were a comfortable bed, and he slept until the next morning. At seven o'clock he had to get up, was again permitted to eat all he wanted, and once more was put to work. Poor Blurry, he wasn't even rested. He wasn't used to working and the heat bothered him terribly. His little head, arms, and legs ached, and he felt as if every part of him was swollen.

Now for the first time, he began to long for home, for his mother, his little mistress, his soft bed, and the nice lazy life; but how would he ever get there? Escape was out of the question; they kept a sharp eye on him and, besides, the only door to the street was in the room where the two girls worked all day long. No, Blurry simply had to bide his time. His thoughts were confused, he felt dizzy and weak. Everything about him started to turn; he sat down—nobody told him not to. When he felt a little better, he went back to work.

After a week of sweeping from morning until evening, he scarcely knew anything else. Little bears forget quickly, and that is a good thing. But he had not forgotten his mother and his home; only they seemed so unreal and so very far away!

One evening the two girls who had caught Blurry read this advertisement in the newspaper:

REWARD FOR THE RETURN OF A SMALL BROWN BEAR
WHO ANSWERS TO THE NAME OF BLURRY.

"Do you think that could be our little bear?" they asked each other. "He doesn't work very hard; in fact, you can't expect it from such a small creature. If we get a reward for returning him, we will be better off than we are now."

They ran to the back of the store and yelled, "Blurry!"

Blurry looked up from his work; had anyone called him? The big broom fell from his hands; how did they know his name? The girls came closer, and once more they called, "Blurry!"

He ran toward them. "Yes, his name is Blurry, all right," one of the girls said to the other. "Let us take him back tonight."

Agreed. That same evening, Blurry was delivered to the home of his little mistress, and the girls got their reward.

Blurry's little mistress gave him a spanking for his disobedience, and then a kiss because he was safely home again. His mother only asked:

"Blurry, why did you run away?"

"I wanted to discover the world," was his answer.

"And did you discover it?"

"Oh, I have seen very, very much. I have become a very experienced bear."

"Yes, I know all that; but I asked you if you had discovered the world."

"No, no . . . not really; you see, I couldn't find it!"

The Fairy

May 12, 1944

That fairy I am talking about was no ordinary fairy of whom you find so many in fairyland. Oh, no, my fairy was a very special fairy, special in her appearance and special in her way of doing things. Why, everybody is sure to ask, was that fairy so special?

Well, because she didn't just help somebody here, and make some fun there, but because she had set herself the task of bringing happiness to the world and to all people.

This special fairy was called Ellen. Her parents had died when she was still quite little and had left her money. So Ellen could do as she chose and buy everything she wanted, even as a small girl. Other children, fairies and elves would get spoiled in that way, but not Ellen. As she grew older, she spent her money only to buy pretty clothes and delicious things to eat.

One morning Ellen lay awake in her soft bed, wondering what to do with all her money. "I can't use it all myself," she thought, "and I can't take it with me into the grave. Why shouldn't I use it to make others happy?"

That was a good plan, and Ellen wanted to carry it out at

once. She rose, dressed, took a small wicker basket, put into it part of one of her bundles of money, and went out.

"Where shall I begin?" she asked herself. "I know. The widow of the wood chopper is sure to be pleased with a visit of mine. Her husband has just died, and the poor lady must be having a difficult time."

Singing, Ellen walked through the grass and knocked at the door of the wood chopper's cottage. "Enter!" came a voice from the inside. Ellen softly opened the door and looked into a darkened room. In a far corner a little old woman sat knitting in a shabby armchair.

She was surprised as Ellen entered and immediately laid a handful of money on the table. Like everybody else, the woman knew that one must not refuse the gifts of fairies and elves.

"That is very sweet of you, little one," she said. "There are not many people who make gifts without expecting something in return, but happily the folk of fairyland are an exception."

Ellen looked at her in amazement. "What did you mean by that?" she asked.

"I simply meant that there are few who give and not want something back."

"Is that so? But why should I want something from you? I am glad that my basket is a little lighter."

"Good!" said the old lady. "Thank you very much."

Ellen bade her good-by and left. In ten minutes, she had reached the next cottage. Here she also knocked, though she didn't know the people. She hadn't been there long before she understood that money was not a problem here. The people did not lack *things*—they were poor in happiness. The lady of the house received her kindly, but she seemed to have no sparkle; her eyes were dull and she looked sad. Ellen decided to remain here a little longer.

"Perhaps I can help this lady in some other way," she thought, and really, when the sweet little fairy had seated herself upon a cushion, the woman began to talk about her troubles without being asked.

She spoke of her wicked husband, of her naughty children, and all her other misfortunes. Ellen listened, put in a question now and then, and became much concerned about the woman's sorrow.

When the woman had finished her story, Ellen spoke.

"Dear lady," she said, "I don't know about such things from experience, and I know even less how to help you. But, just the same, I'd like to give you some advice, which I, myself, always follow when I feel lonesome and sad.

"One fine morning, take a walk through the big forest until you reach the moor. Then, after walking a while in the heather, sit down somewhere and do nothing. Only look at the blue sky and the trees, and you will gradually feel peaceful inside and realize that nothing is so hopelessly bad that something can't be done to improve it—even a little."

"No," said the lady. "That remedy will help just as much as all the other pills I have swallowed."

"Try it, anyway," urged the fairy. "Alone with nature, all worries leave one. You grow first quiet, and then glad, and feel that God has not deserted you."

"If it will please you," said the woman, "I will try it one day."

"Fine. If I may, I will drop in again next week at this time."

And so Ellen went from house to house, cheering and comforting people, and at the end of the long day her basket was empty and her heart full; she knew that she had put her money to better use than by buying clothes. From that day on, Ellen often went on her rounds. She wore her yellow flowered frock, her hair was tied with a big bow, and she carried her basket on her arm. That's how she looked when she made her visits.

Even the woman who had enough money but too much trouble was beginning to feel happier. Ellen knew it; her remedy always worked.

The fairy gained many friends—not other fairies and elves, but people and children. The children told her everything, and this gave her much insight and the ability to have the right word of comfort on every occasion.

But so far as her money was concerned, she had miscalculated. After about a year, she had just enough left to live on.

Now, whoever thinks that this made Ellen sad and kept her from offering gifts is mistaken. She continued to give much, not money, but good advice and loving, healing words. She had learned that, even if one is all alone, he can still make his life beautiful; and no matter how poor one is, he can still give others riches.

When Ellen died, a very old fairy, there was more mourning

in the land than there had ever been before. But Ellen's spirit was not gone. When people slept, she returned to give them blissful dreams; even in their slumber they received the gift of wise counsel from this very special fairy.

Rita

It was a quarter past four, and I was walking through a rather quiet street. I had just decided to drop in at the nearest pastry shop when, from a sidestreet, there came a couple of teen-aged girls who, chatting busily, walked arm-in-arm in the direction I had chosen.

From time to time it is interesting and refreshing to listen to the conversation of teen-aged girls, not only because they laugh at the merest trifle, but also because their laughter is so infectious that everyone in their vicinity must involuntarily laugh with them.

So I walked stealthily behind the pair and eavesdropped on their talk, which had to do with the buying of sweets for ten cents. They consulted each other seriously on what to get for their money, and one could tell that their mouths watered at the thought of it. At the pastry shop, they continued their chat while looking at the wares in the show window.

As I, too, was fairly eating the delicious things with my eyes, I knew what their choice would be before they stepped into the shop. Inside it wasn't busy, and the girls were served at once. They had picked two fruit tarts which, wonder above wonder, they managed to take, untouched, out of the store.

A minute later I also was ready, and once more the two walked, talking loudly, ahead of me. On the next corner there was another pastry shop, in front of whose window there stood a little girl, taking in the display with greedy eyes. Soon the three were talking together, and I reached the corner in time to hear one of the teen-agers ask:

"Are you hungry, little one? Would you like a fruit tart?"

The tiny one, of course, said, "Yes."

"Don't be foolish, Rita," said the other teen-ager. "Put your tart quickly into your mouth, as I did, for if you give it to this kid, you'll have nothing."

Rita didn't answer but stood there undecided for a moment, looking from the tart to the little girl and back again. Then she suddenly gave the child the pastry and said:

"Please, eat this, my dear; I'm going home to dinner, anyway."

And before the little one could thank her, Rita and her friend had disappeared. As I passed the youngster, who had taken a big bite from the tart with obvious relish, she offered it to me.

"Have a taste, miss; I got this for a present."

I thanked her and, smiling, I walked on. Who do you think got the most pleasure from the fruit tart—Rita, her friend, or the little girl?

I think it was Rita.

PERSONAL REMINISCENCES AND SHORT STORIES

Do You Remember?

REMINISCENCES OF MY SCHOOL DAYS

July 7, 1943

Do you remember? I spend happy hours talking about school, the instructors, our adventures, and—boys. When we still were part of ordinary, everyday life, everything was just marvelous. That one year in the Lyceum was sheer bliss for me; the teachers, all that they taught me, the jokes, the prestige, the romances, and the adoring boys.

Do you remember the day I came home from midtown, and there was a package in the mailbox, marked "D'un ami—R.?" It couldn't have come from anyone but Rob. Wrapped in the little parcel was a breastpin worth at least two-and-one-half guilders, and ultramodern. Rob's father dealt in such things. I wore it two days, and then it broke.

Do you remember how Lies and I betrayed the class? We had a French test. I was pretty well prepared, but not Lies. She copied everything from me and I peeked at her work—to improve it! Though Lies' paper was a trifle better than mine, probably through the help I had given her, the teacher decided to give us both a big fat zero. Great indignation! We went to the headmaster to complain and set things straight. At the end of the conference, Lies blurted out, "But, mind you, Sir, the entire class had open books under the desks!" The head promised not to punish the class, provided that all who had copied their work would raise their hands when asked about it.

Ten hands, not even half the true number, went up. A day or two later, we were unexpectedly given the French test all over again. Lies and I were "cut dead" as traitors. Pretty soon I found myself unable to endure this treatment, and I wrote a long, pleading letter to Class 16 II, begging forgiveness. In two weeks, the whole thing was forgotten.

The letter was about as follows:

To the pupils of Class 16 II,

Anne Frank and Lies Goosens herewith offer the pupils of Class 16 II their sincere apologies for the cowardly betrayal in connection with the French test.

It was an unpremeditated, thoughtless act, and we admit without hesitation that we are the only ones who should have been punished. We think that anyone, in anger, might let a word or sentence slip that carries unpleasant consequences, but that was never intended to cause any harm. We hope that 16 II will regard the incident in that light and repay evil with good. Nothing can be done about it, and the two guilty ones can't undo their misdeed.

We wouldn't write this letter if we were not genuinely sorry. We ask those who have "cut" us until now to reconsider, for, after all, our act was not so heinous that we have to be looked upon as criminals for all eternity. We beg those who cannot get over our mistake to give us a thorough scolding or, if they prefer, ask us to perform some service which, if at all possible, we shall carry out.

We trust that all of the pupils in Class 16 II will forget the affair.

Anne Frank and
Lies Goosens

Do you remember how Pim told Rob in the tram that Anne was much prettier than Denise, especially when she smiled, and how Sanne, who was also a passenger, overheard this and repeated it to me? And that Rob answered, "Your nostrils are much too wide, Pim!"

Do you remember that Maurice wanted to call on Father to ask him if he could keep company with his daughter?

Do you remember that Rob and Anne Frank carried on a busy correspondence while Rob was sick in the hospital?

Do you remember how Sam pursued me on his bike and wanted to ride hand-in-hand with me?

Do you remember how Bram kissed me on the cheek when I gave him my solemn promise not to tell a soul about the goings on between him and Suzy?

Oh how I wish that those happy, carefree days could come again!

My First Day at the Lyceum

With a lot of fuss, talk, and planning, things were finally fixed so that I could register at the Lyceum and—without an entrance exam! I was a poor student in every subject, but particularly in math, and I trembled as I thought of the geometry course that stared me in the face.

At the end of September, the mail brought the long-awaited letter announcing the date in October on which I was to report at the Lyceum. That day it rained cats and dogs, and it was impossible to go by bike. So I used the tram, together with plenty of others.

There was a big crowd at the school; groups of boys and girls stood about, chatting; some walked from one group to another, recognizing friends and acquaintances, and asking, "What class are you in?"

Aside from Lies Goosens, I hadn't discovered a single person I knew who would become a classmate, and that situation didn't strike me as very pleasant. The school doors opened, and in our classroom we were welcomed by a gray teacher with a mouse-face, who wore a long dress and flat-heeled shoes.

She stood there rubbing her hands as she watched the hubbub in front of her and made the usual announcements. The teacher called and checked the names of the students, told us what books had to be ordered, and discussed some other details. Then we were dismissed and could go home again.

To tell the truth, I was deeply disappointed; I had expected at least to see the schedule and—to meet the director. I did see, in one of the halls, a jolly, fat little man with red cheeks, who, smiling at everyone who passed, stood talking with another chap of the same height, who was thin, had a dignified face and silky hair, and wore spectacles. But I had no idea that the fat man was the building superintendent, and the thin one the director.

Back home I gave an excited report of my experiences, but, to be honest, I knew as much of the school, the instructors, the children, and the schedule as I did before I left.

School started a week later. Again the rain came down in buckets, but I insisted on going by bike. Mother packed a cover-all in my schoolbag so that, in heaven's name, I shouldn't get drenched, and off I went.

Margot rides her bike at a furious clip, and in a couple of minutes I was so out of breath that I begged her to slow down a little. Another few minutes and the heavy rain changed into a regular cloudburst. Mindful of Mother's cover-all, I stopped and, with much difficulty, put on that unflattering garment. I remounted my bike, but soon the pace proved too fast for me again, and once more I asked Margot to take it easy. Very much out of sorts, she said that in the future she'd prefer to ride by herself; no doubt she was afraid of being late. But we reached the school with time to spare and, after parking the bikes, we stood chatting for a while in the shelter of the arcade that leads to the Amstel River.

We entered school on the dot of eight-thirty. Just inside the entrance there was a big sign announcing that about twenty students had to change classrooms. I was included, and I was told to move to Class 16 II. This meant that I would belong to a group in which I knew a few boys and girls, but Lies was to remain in 12 I.

When I was given the desk at the very bottom of the class, behind girls much bigger than myself, I felt lonely and forsaken. In the second hour I raised my hand and asked to be moved to another spot, as I could see very little unless I fairly hung into the aisle.

My request was granted immediately, and I picked up my things and moved. The third hour was gym, and the teacher seemed so nice that I asked her to try to have Lies transferred to my room. How the dear lady did it I will never know, but the next hour, in walked Lies and was given the desk beside mine.

Now I was reconciled to the school—the school where I was to have so much fun and learn such a lot. Full of courage, I paid close attention to what the geography man was telling us.

A Lecture in Biology

August 11, 1943

Rubbing her hands, she walks into the room; rubbing her hands, she sits down; rubbing her hands, rubbing her hands, rubbing her hands.

Miss Riegel of Biology—small, gray, with gray-blue eyes, a big nose and a mouse face. In her wake, someone carries a map and the skeleton.

She takes her place behind the stove, still rubbing her hands, and begins the lesson. First she questions the students on their homework, then she lectures. Oh, she knows a lot, does Miss Riegel, and she is a clever lecturer, starting with fish and ending with reindeer. Her favorite topic, according to Margot, is propagation, which surely must be so because she is an old maid.

Suddenly she is interrupted; a small wad of paper flies through the air and lands on my desk.

"What have you there?" she asks in an accent that shows she hails from The Hague.[1]

"I don't know, Miss Riegel."

"Come here, and bring that piece of paper with you."

I rise timidly and take the note to the front.

"Who is that from?"

"I don't know, Miss Riegel; I haven't read it."

"Ah, so we'll first attend to that."

[1] The setting of Anne's tales is, of course, Amsterdam. To the inhabitants of that city, the manner of speech of the people from The Hague sounds affected—Translator.

She unfolds the note and shows me its content—the single word "traitor." I turn red. She looks at me.

"Now do you know who sent it?"

"No, Miss Riegel."

"You are lying."

I feel myself getting flaming red and stare at the teacher with what I know are flashing eyes, but I don't say a word.

"Tell me who wrote that note!" says Miss Riegel, addressing the class. "Whoever did it, raise your hand!"

Way back in the room a hand is raised. Just as I thought— it was Rob.

"Rob, come here!"

Rob now faces the teacher.

"Why did you write that note?"

Silence.

"Do you know, Anne, what it means?"

"Yes, Miss Riegel."

"Explain!"

"Can't I do it some other time? It is a long story."

"No. Explain!"

I tell her about the French test and the zeros Lies and I got for cheating, and the way we betrayed the class.

"A pretty story! And Rob, did you think it necessary to give Anne your opinion during a lecture? And Anne—I simply don't believe that you didn't know where that note came from. Sit down, both of you!"

I was furious. At home I told the whole miserable story in detail. Some weeks later, I thought I had a justified complaint about the grade Miss Riegel had given me on my report card, and I asked Father to talk to her about it. He came back without an improved mark, but with the information that, by mistake, he had called the teacher Miss Riggle throughout the interview. He further reported that she thought Anne Frank a very sweet girl, and had no recollection of the dear child ever having lied to her!

A Geometry Lesson

August 12, 1943

He's impressive as he stands before the class—a big, strong old man, his bald dome ringed with a wreath of gray. He always wears a gray suit and an old-fashioned high collar, its tips bent outward. He speaks with a peculiar accent; he often mutters and as often smiles. He is quite patient with those who do their best, but loses his temper in dealing with the lazy ones.

Of the ten children questioned, nine give unsatisfactory answers. He takes endless trouble in explaining, clarifying the problems; he reasons with the pupils so that they, themselves, may find the answers. He is fond of posing riddles and, after class, likes to talk of the days when he was president of one of the biggest soccer clubs in the country.

But Mijnheer Heesing and I were often at loggerheads, and always because—yes, because of my talking habit. In three lessons I got six reprimands. This was too much for the instructor, who, by way of remedy, prescribed an essay of two pages. It was handed in at the next lesson, and Mijnheer Heesing, who could take a joke, laughed as he read it and seemed particularly amused by this paragraph:

"I must, indeed, try hard to control the talking habit, but I'm afraid that little can be done, as my case is hereditary. My mother, too, is fond of chatting, and has handed this weakness down to me. Until now, she hasn't succeeded in getting it under control."

I had been told to write my essay under the title, "A Chatterbox."

But at the next lesson, I again was tempted to whisper a few remarks to my neighbor, and—Mijnheer Heesing took his little notebook and jotted down, "Miss Anne Frank: An essay entitled, 'An Incorrigible Chatterbox.'"

This piece of prose, too, was duly delivered. In Mijnheer Heesing's next lecture, however, I repeated my misdeed, and the instructor wrote in his little book, "Miss Anne Frank: An essay of two pages, entitled, '"Quack, quack," said Mrs. Quackenbush.'"

What would you have thought in my place? It was pretty clear to me that Mijnheer Heesing was having a little joke; otherwise, he would surely have given me some stiff geometry problems to do. So I decided to answer his joke with a joke of my own and, with the help of Sanne Houtman, I wrote the "essay" in rhyme. Here is a part of it:

"Quack, quack," said Mrs. Quackenbush,
As she called her big, big brood;
They waddled as fast as ever they could
And gave each other many a push
In their rush to reach their mother's wings.
"Oh, Mama, we hope you have some bread,
For all of us are nearly dead!"
They were very hungry, the poor things.
"Yes, sure," said Mama, "I have your lunch,
Eat this, and I will give you more;
To get it, I had to go ashore,
But, as you see, it was quite a hunch.
I had to steal it, but you be fair,
And each take his honest part."
The little ducklings were pretty smart,
And obeyed the mother then and there.
In doing it, they made a rumpus;
They cried, "Peep-peep" and "Quack-quack-quack."
But who was that with a ruffled back?
An angry swan! Oh, Heaven, help us!

—Etc., etc.

Heesing read it; read it aloud to the class, also read it to some other student groups, and gave in. From then on, we were good friends; he paid no further attention to my chatter-ing, and never punished me again.

P.S. The long and short of it is that my math teacher was a very decent sort. The nickname "Mrs. Quackenbush" has stuck to me, and I have Mijnheer Heesing to thank for it.

Paying Guests

October 15, 1943

When hard necessity forced us to rent our big rear bedroom, we had to swallow our pride; none of us was used to having strangers around the house. The room was cleaned out and refurnished with whatever pieces we happened to have, but these were insufficient for an attractive bed-sitting room. And so Father made the rounds of the auction rooms and slowly picked up a few articles.

In three weeks we had become the owners of a pretty waste-basket and a tea table everybody liked, but what we badly needed were a decent wardrobe and a couple of comfortable armchairs.

Once more Father went out hunting, and this time he took me along. At the auction we sat down on a wooden bench, which was almost entirely occupied by hard-bitten buyers and other unwashed fellows, and waited, waited, waited . . . We could have waited until the next day, for that afternoon they sold nothing but china!

Disappointed, we left. Not very hopeful, we went back the next day for another try. This time we were luckier; Father bid on a good-looking oak wardrobe and a pair of leather-covered armchairs.

To celebrate our acquisitions, we stopped at a tearoom and each had a cup of tea and a piece of pastry. Then, quite gaily, we went home.

But, when the wardrobe and armchairs were delivered, Mother discovered some strange ridges in the wood of the wardrobe. Father, too, took a sharp look and, yes, the thing was full of termites. They don't hand out little leaflets announcing such things at auctions, and the salesrooms are generally so dark that you can't see them yourself.

Naturally, the chairs also were given a close examination. It was as we had feared—they, too, had fallen victim to the same sort of vermin.

We called the auction place and urged them to haul away the stuff as soon as possible. This done, Mother heaved a sigh of relief. Father also sighed, but for another reason; he had been told that his poor guilders would not be returned.

A few days later, Father met a friend who had some furniture he didn't use and was willing to lend us until we got something better. So now our problem was solved.

(Here, dumbbell that I am, I had to stop, since, as everyone knows, I dropped my fountain pen in the stove. I shall, however, continue with a poor old one.)

Now we stuck our heads together to think up and paint a smart little advertising poster to put in the window of the corner bookshop, for a consideration we had to pay the following week.

Soon people came to look at the room. The first was an elderly gentleman, who wanted a room for his bachelor son. The deal was almost made when the son, who was with him, put in his two cents' worth. What he said was so silly that Mother seriously doubted his sanity. She wasn't far off, for the old man shyly admitted that his son was sometimes given to "wandering."

Mother didn't know how to get those two out of the house quickly enough—but she did. Dozens of people came and went, until one day there arrived a stout, middle-aged chap. As he was willing to pay a good price and seemed to have few needs, he was accepted.

This man was lots of fun and little trouble. Sundays he brought chocolates for us children and cigarettes for the grownups, and more than once he took us all to the movies. He was with us for a year and a half, and then rented an apartment for his old mother, his sister, and himself. Later, when he came to call, he assured us that the time he had lived with us had been one of the nicest periods in his life.

Another ad was put in the bookshop window. Again the bell

was rung by small and large, young and old applicants. One
of them was a fairly young woman in a poke bonnet, and we
immediately nicknamed her "Salvation Nell." We rented her
the room, but she didn't prove as pleasant a guest as the fat
man.

First of all, she was very careless and left her room in a mess.
Secondly, and this was the worst, she had a fiancé who often
got drunk. Once, for example, we were startled by the bell in
the middle of the night. Father went to answer, and there
stood the fellow, dead drunk. He patted Father on the shoulder
and thickly repeated, over and over, "We are good friends,
aren't we? Yesh, yesh, we are good friends!" Bang! The door
was slammed in his face.

When, in May 1940, Holland was invaded, we asked Salvation Nell to leave and rented the room to an acquaintance
of ours, a young man of about thirty. This chap wasn't bad,
but he had one weakness—he was thoroughly spoiled. Once,
in the heart of winter, when we all saved as much electricity as
we could, he complained bitterly of the cold. It was badly
exaggerated, for the heat in his room was going full blast.

But one has to be indulgent with lodgers, and we gave him
permission to use the electric stove once in a while. What was
the result? He used it all day long! We begged and pleaded
with him to be a little less extravagant, but it did no good. The
electric bills went up scandalously, and one fine morning,
Mother took her courage in both hands, shut off the electricity,
and was not to be found for the rest of the day. Eventually
the electric stove was blamed, "It had overloaded the fuse,"
and the young man had to stand the cold as best he could.
Just the same, he, too, lived with us a year and half, and then
he got married.

Again the room was vacant, and Mother was about to dust
off our advertising sign, when a friend called and recommended a divorced man who urgently needed a room. He was
a tall fellow of around thirty-five, with glasses and an un-
sympathetic face. Mother didn't want to disappoint her friend,
and she took him in. He, too, was engaged, and his girl visited
us often. The wedding day was not far off when the pair got
into a terrific fight, and he suddenly married someone else.

About the same time we moved ourselves, and we hoped to
be rid of paying guests forever!

Dreams of Movie Stardom

December 24, 1943

(This was written as a "secret" answer to the questions of Mrs. Van Daan, who never tired of asking me why I didn't want to become a movie star.)

I was seventeen, an attractive girl with flirtatious eyes and a wealth of dark curls—a teen-ager filled with ideals, illusions, and daydreams. In one way or another, the day would come when my name would be a household word and my picture would occupy a place of honor in the memory book of every damp-eyed bobby-soxer.

The questions of how I was to achieve fame and in what field bothered me very little. When I was fourteen I used to think, "That will come in good time," and when I was seventeen I thought so still. My parents were not aware of my grandiose plans, and I was foxy enough to keep them to myself. It seemed to me that I'd be better off, should I ever become a celebrity, to experience things in private before sharing my adventures with Father and Mother. I suspected that they might not be overly enthusiastic about such a turn of events.

Let no one think that I took those daydreams of mine very seriously, or that I had thoughts for nothing else. On the contrary, I was always industrious in school and, besides, did much reading for pleasure. At fifteen I had finished one of our three-year high schools. Now, mornings, I attended a school that specialized in teaching foreign languages, and in the afternoons, I did my homework or played tennis. One day (it was autumn) I was home cleaning up a closet, when, amid a pile of assorted discarded stuff, I came upon a shoe box, with the words MOVIE STARS written in large letters on the lid. I remembered that my parents had ordered me to throw this box out, and that I had hidden it carefully so nobody would find it.

Curious, I lifted the lid, took out the many little packages inside, and loosened the elastic bands in which each was wrapped. I got so fascinated looking once more at all the made-up faces, that I was startled when, a couple of hours later, someone tapped me on the shoulder to ask me to come to tea. I was sitting on the floor, surrounded by little stacks of newspaper and magazine clippings.

Later, in straightening my room, I kept the movie-star box aside. That evening, I continued my examination and found something that impressed me so that I couldn't get it out of my mind.

This was an envelope filled with pictures of a family of movie actors, in which three daughters were stars. I came across the address of the girls, whose name was Lane. Then and there, I took a piece of paper and a pen and started writing a letter to the youngest of the sisters—Priscilla Lane.

Secretly, I mailed the letter, which was in English. In it I told Priscilla that I would love to have a photo of her, and also of both her sisters, and asked her to be good enough to answer me, as I was keenly interested in the family.

I waited more than two months and, though I didn't want to admit it to myself, I had lost hope of ever getting an answer to my letter. There was nothing surprising in this, for I realized that if the Lane girls answered the notes of all their admirers and sent photographs to them, all of their time would have to be devoted to their correspondence. But just then my Father one morning handed me a letter addressed to "Miss Anne Franklin."

I hastily opened and read it. My family were very curious and, after I had told them of my letter, I read Priscilla's aloud. She wrote that she would not send photos before she knew something more about me, but that she would be more inclined to do so if I would write her, in more detail, about myself and my family.

Truthfully, I wrote Priscilla that I was more interested in

her personal life than in her film career. I wanted to know, among other things, if she went out much in the evening; if Rosemary had to work as much and as hard as she, etc., etc. Much later she asked me to call her by her nickname of "Pat." Priscilla seemed so pleased with my letters that she answered each one faithfully.

As the correspondence was, naturally, conducted in English, my parents couldn't object, as it obviously provided good practice for me. In her letters, Priscilla told me that she spent most of her days at the studio and gave me an idea of how she divided her time. She corrected my mistakes and mailed my letters back to me, on condition that I would return them again to her. Meanwhile she had sent me a big collection of photos.

Priscilla, who was twenty, was neither engaged nor married, which didn't disturb me in the least. I was immensely proud of my friend, the movie star.

So passed the winter. In late spring a letter came from the Lanes, in which Priscilla asked me if I would like to fly to the United States and spend two of the summer months as their guest. I jumped for joy, but I hadn't reckoned with the objections of my parents. I couldn't accept the invitation; it was impossible for me to travel alone to America; I didn't have enough clothes; I couldn't stay away that long, and all the other worried notions that occur to loving fathers and mothers on such occasions. But I had made up my mind to go to America, and go I must.

I reported all of the parental objections to Priscilla, and she answered each one to my satisfaction. First of all, I wouldn't have to travel alone. Priscilla's companion, who was visiting relatives of hers in The Hague, would take me with her to the States. As for my return trip to Holland, Priscilla would think of a chaperone when the time came.

My parents still objected: Neither I nor they really knew the Lane family, they said, and it was more than likely that I would feel entirely out of place in their home. They made me cross; it almost seemed as though they begrudged me this unusual opportunity. I pleaded that it would be almost an insult to decline such a cordial invitation. After they had received a charming and reassuring letter from Mrs. Lane, they finally decided the matter in my favor. I worked hard in the months of May and June, and when Priscilla wrote that her companion would arrive in Amsterdam on July 18, preparations for my voyage were completed.

On the eighteenth, Father and I went to the station to meet the lady. Priscilla had sent me her photograph, and I recognized her at once among the many detraining passengers. Miss Halwood was a small woman with graying blonde hair, who talked much and rapidly. She looked like a sweet person.

Father, who had once been in America and spoke good English, conversed with Miss Halwood, and I ventured a remark now and then. It had been arranged that she would stay with us for a week. That week fairly flew by, and scarcely a day had passed before Miss Halwood and I were friends.

On July 25, I was so excited that I couldn't swallow a single bite of my breakfast. But Miss Halwood, an experienced traveler, gave no sign of agitation. The entire family saw us off at Schiphol Airport, and finally, finally, my trip to America had begun.

We arrived in the neighborhood of Hollywood on the evening of the fifth day. Priscilla and her sister Rosemary, her senior by one year, met us. As I was somewhat tired from the trip, we drove to a hotel near the airport. After breakfast the next morning, we stepped again into the car, which was driven by Rosemary.

In slightly more than three hours, we reached the Lane house, where I was cordially received.

Mrs. Lane showed me to my room, which was really a charming small apartment with a balcony. This, then, was to be my home for the next two months.

It was not difficult to feel at ease in the hospitable Lane home. Much work and much fun were the daily routine; the three famous young stars, by the way, helped their mother more than I, an ordinary teen-ager, ever did. I soon got used to speaking English. Priscilla was free during the first two weeks of my stay and showed me much of the beautiful surroundings. Nearly every day we went to the beach, and I gradually became acquainted with people of whom I had heard or read. One of Priscilla's intimate friends was Madge Bellamy, who often went along with us on our sight-seeing jaunts.

Nobody would have judged Priscilla to be older than myself; she treated me as a girl of her own age. When her free fortnight was up, she had to go back to the Warner Brothers studio and—oh, joy!—I was allowed to go with her. I visited her in her dressing room and saw Priscilla making tests.

She finished early that first day and showed me around the studio. "Anne," she said after a while, "I just got a wonderful idea. Tomorrow morning, you go to the office where pretty girls apply for jobs and ask the man in charge if there is anything you could do. Just in fun, of course."

"Yes, I'd like that," I said. Next day, I really did go to that office. It was a terribly busy place; the girls stood queued up in the hall. I joined the line and in half an hour I was inside the office. But that didn't mean that it was my turn; there were still many girls ahead of me. Again I waited, this time about two hours. A bell rang—this was for me!—and bravely I stepped into the inner office, where a middle-aged man was seated behind a desk. He greeted me in a standoffish manner. Asking my name and address, he seemed surprised that I was a guest of the Lanes. Finished with those questions, he took another good look at me and asked, "I suppose that you want to be a film star?"

"Yes, sir, if I have the talent."

He pushed a button, and in walked a smartly dressed girl, who asked me, with a gesture rather than in words, to follow her. She opened a door, and the sharp light in the room made me blink my eyes. A young man behind an intricate apparatus gave me a friendlier greeting than the one I'd had before and told me to sit on a high stool. He took several pictures, then rang for the girl, and I was led back to the older man. He promised to send me word whether or not I should return to the studio.

Encouraged, I found my way back to the Lane house. A week later I received a note from Mr. Harwick (Priscilla had told me his name). He wrote that the photos had come out very well, and asked me to come to his office at three o'clock the next afternoon.

Now, armed with an invitation, I was admitted at once. Mr. Harwick asked me if I would pose for a manufacturer of tennis rackets. The job was for just one week, but after I had been told what I would be paid, I gladly consented. Mr. Harwick called the tennis man, whom I met that same afternoon.

Next day I made my appearance at a photo studio, where I was to go every day for a week. I had to change clothes in minutes; I had to stand, sit, and smile continuously; walk up and down, change clothes again, look pretty, and put on fresh make-up. At night I was so exhausted that I had to drag myself to bed. On the third day it hurt me to smile, but I felt that I must keep faith with my manufacturer.

When I came home on the evening of the fourth day, I must have looked so ill that Mrs. Lane forbade me to return to the job. She herself called the man, and got him to excuse me.

I was deeply grateful. Undisturbed, I hugely enjoyed the rest of my unforgettable vacation. As for dreams of movie stardom, I was cured. I had had a close look at the way celebrities live.

My First Article

February 22, 1944

Imagine that the subject of my first article knew that he was going to be used as "material"—wouldn't he turn red and ask, "Why me? What's so interesting about me?" Let me put the cards on the table: Peter is my subject, and now I'll tell how that occurred to me.

I wanted to write about somebody, and as I already had described most of the other people in the house, I thought of Peter. The boy always keeps himself in the background and, like Margot, never causes dissention.

If, toward evening, you knock on the door of his room and hear him call a soft "Come in!" you may be sure that, on opening the door, you'll find him looking at you through two of the steps of the ladder to the attic and saying, "So!" in a gentle, inviting tone.

His little room is—what is it really? I think it is a passage to the attic, very narrow, very drafty, but—he has turned it into a room. When he sits at the left of the ladder, there's surely no more than a yard's space between him and the wall. There stand his little table, laden, like ours, with books (a few steps of the ladder also hold some of his possessions) and a chair.

On the other side of the ladder, his bike hangs from the ceiling. Useless at present, it is carefully wrapped in brown paper, but a small chain, dangling from one of the pedals, is still visible. This corner is completed by a lamp with an ultra-modern shade, made from a piece of cardboard covered with strips of paper.

I am still standing in the open door, and now I look in the other direction. Against the wall—that is, opposite Peter and behind the table—stands an old divan, covered with blue flowered stuff; the bedclothes have been hidden (but not quite successfully) behind it. Above the daybed hangs a lamp, the mate of the other one, and similarly decorated. A bit further on, there is a small bookcase filled, from top to bottom, with paper-covered books that could belong only to a boy. A hand mirror is fastened to the wall beside it. Probably because the owner didn't know where else to put it, a small tool chest stands on the floor. (I know from experience that anything in the way of a hammer, a knife, or a screw driver one may need, can be found in its depths.)

Near the bookcase, a shelf, covered with paper that once was white, was originally meant for such things as milk bottles, but has been converted into an annex of the library; it all but groans under the weight of books. The milk bottles have become neighbors of the tool chest, on the floor.

On the third wall hangs a wooden case that may have contained oranges or cherries, but that now serves as a cabinet for such articles as a shaving brush, a safety razor, a roll of plaster, a small bottle of laxative, etc. Beside the cabinet stands the prize exhibit of the Van Daan family's ingenuity—a closet made of cardboard, held together by two or three uprights of some sturdier material. In front of the closet there hangs a really handsome drape, which Peter, after much coaxing, got from his mother. The closet itself is filled with suits, overcoats, socks, shoes, and the like. The stuff massed on top of the closet is so mixed up that I've never been able to recognize one single item.

The floor coverings of Mr. Van Daan, Jr., also are worth seeing. He has one small and two large genuine Persian rugs of such striking colors that everyone who enters the little room remarks on them. These pieces, which at one time must have cost a great deal, lie on a floor so shaky and irregular that one can't walk on it without the utmost caution.

Two of the walls are covered with green jute, and the other two are generously plastered with pictures of more or less beautiful movie stars and advertising posters. Grease and scorch spots should cause no surprise, for it is to be expected that, with so much stuff in a small space, something or other is bound to get dirty in a year and a half. The beamed ceiling, also, is no longer in good condition and, since there are leaks in the roof and Peter's room is in the attic, he has spread some sheets of cardboard to catch the drip. Innumerable water spots and rings show that this protection is far from adequate.

Now, I believe, I've gone all around the room; I have forgotten only the chairs. One of them is an old wooden armchair of Viennese design with perforated seat; number two is a white kitchen chair which Peter appropriated last year. He started to scrape off the paint, probably with the idea of giving it a fresh color, but he didn't have much luck and stopped. And so, half scraped off, part white, part black, and with only one rung (we used the other for a poker), the chair isn't very pretty. But, as has been said, the place is dark, and the poor wreck doesn't attract much attention.

The door to the kitchen steps is festooned with aprons; there are also a few hooks with dustcloths and a brush. After all this, everyone should know each nook and cranny of Peter's room, but not, of course, the inhabitant himself. And now it's the turn of the owner of all these glorious possessions.

There's a sharp difference in Peter's appearance on weekdays and Sundays. Weekdays he wears cover-alls, from which he rarely separates himself, as he objects to having the things washed too often. I can't imagine the reason for this attitude, except that he fears his favorite piece of apparel might wear out that way. At any rate, it just has been laundered, and its color—blue—is once more recognizable. Round his neck Peter wears a blue scarf, which apparently is just as dear to him as the cover-alls. A heavy, brown leather belt and white woolen socks complete his weekday attire. But on Sundays Peter's clothing may be said to undergo a rebirth. Then he wears a handsome suit, a fine pair of shoes, a shirt, a necktie—everything that belongs to a young man's nice wardrobe.

So much for Peter's appearance. As for the man himself, I have changed my opinion radically of late. I used to think him dumb and slow, but nowadays he is neither the one nor the other. Everybody agrees that he has grown into a fine young fellow. I know in my heart that he is honest and generous. He has always been modest and helpful, and I think that he is much more sensitive than people give him credit for. He has one preference that I shall never forget—the cats. Nothing is too much trouble where Mouschi or Moffi are concerned, and I do believe that those two sense that there isn't much love in his life and try to make up for it.

He's not afraid—on the contrary—and not as smart-alecky as other boys of his age. He isn't stupid, either, and has a remarkably good memory. That he is handsome I needn't say, for everyone who sees him knows that. His hair is wonderful—a wealth of fine brown curls. He has gray-blue eyes, and—describing faces has always been my weak point. After the war I'll paste his photo, together with those of the other people who were in hiding with us, in this book by way of illustration. That will save me the trouble of describing them.

Happiness

Before I begin my story, I'll tell quickly what has happened in my life so far.

I have lost my mother (I've really never known her), and my father hasn't much time for me. When my mother died, I was two years old; my father gave me into the care of a charming couple, with whom I remained five years. So I was seven when I was sent to boarding school. I stayed there until I was fourteen; then I was, happily, allowed to join my father. Now he and I live in a pension, and I go to the Lyceum. Nothing out of the ordinary happened to me until—until I met Jacques.

We became acquainted because he moved into our pension with his parents. First we saw each other a few times on the stairway; then, by chance, in the park, and after that we went several times for a walk in the woods.

From the first, Jacques impressed me as a splendid boy, perhaps a little shy and withdrawn, though that may have been the very quality that attracted me. Gradually, we had more dates together, and now we often visit one another in each other's rooms.

I had never had a close acquaintance with a boy before, and I was surprised to find him entirely different from the boys in my class, who were boisterous and boastful.

I began to think about Jacques, after thinking a good deal about myself. I knew that his parents didn't get along together and quarreled often, and I felt that this must disturb him very

much, for a love of peace and quiet was one of his characteristics.

I am alone most of the time and often feel sad and lonely;
it's probably because I miss my Mother and because I've never
had a real friend in whom I could confide. Jacques is in the
same situation; he also had only superficial friends, and it
seemed to me that he, too, needed someone to take into his
confidence. But I couldn't get closer to him and we continued
to talk about unimportant things.

But, one day, he came with an obviously made-up excuse, as
I was sitting on a cushion on the floor, looking at the sky.

"Do I interrupt?" he asked.

"Certainly not," I said, turning toward him. "Sit down beside
me, or don't you believe in dreaming?"

He stood by the window, leaning his forehead against the
pane.

"Oh, yes," he said, "I dream a lot like this. Do you know
what I call it? Taking a look at the history of the world."

"That's a fine way of putting it; I must remember it."

"Yes," he said, with the peculiar smile that always confused
me a little, because I never knew exactly what it meant.

We talked again of trivial things, and after a while he left.

The next time he called on me, I happened to sit in the same
spot, and he once more took up his place by the window. That
day, the weather was magnificent; the sky was a deep blue (we
were up so high that we couldn't see the houses, at least not I,
from my spot on the floor); dewdrops clung to the bare branches
of the chestnut tree in front of the house, and the sun turned
each drop into a sparkling diamond as the branches slowly
moved. Seagulls and other birds flew, chattering, past our
window.

I don't know why it was, but neither of us could utter a word.
Here we were, in the same room, not far from each other, but
we scarcely saw one another any more. We looked only at the
sky, and talked to ourselves. I say "we," for I am sure that he
felt as I did, and that he was making no more effort to break
the silence than I.

Fifteen minutes—then he spoke. He said: "When you let
beauty and peace sink into you, dissension and strife begin to
look like sheer insanity. Everything that people make a fuss

about, becomes unimportant. And yet, I don't always feel this way."

He looked shyly at me, perhaps afraid that I might not understand him. I was delighted that he expected me to answer, that I finally had found a sympathetic person to whom I could tell my thoughts.

"Do you know what I always think?" I said. "That it is silly to fight with people about whom you feel indifferent. To differ with people for whom you care, is another story. You are fond of them, and it hurts you more than it angers you when they provoke you."

"Do you really think so, too? But you don't quarrel much, do you?"

"No, but enough to know what it is like. The worst of it is that most people go alone through this world."

"What do you mean by that?" Jacques now was looking straight at me, but I decided to persist; perhaps I might be able to help him.

"I mean that most people, married or single, stand inwardly alone. They have no one with whom they can talk about all of their feelings and thoughts; and that is what I miss the most."

All Jacques said was, "It is the same with me."

We took another look at the sky. Then he said, "People who, as you put it, have no one to talk to, miss much, very much. And it is just that realization which so often depresses me."

"No, I don't agree. Nobody can help feeling depressed now and then, but there's no point in anticipating that you're going to be sad.

"You see, what you look for when you are depressed is happiness. No matter how much you miss someone to whom you could express your feelings, happiness, once you have found it and keep it in your heart, can never be lost."

"How did you find it?"

I got up. "Come along," I said, and I went ahead of him, up the stairs, to the attic. There was a storage space with a window. The house was unusually tall, and when we looked out of the window, we saw a great stretch of sky.

"Look," I said. "If you want to find happiness within yourself, you have to go outside on a day with much sun and a lovely blue sky. Or you could stand at a window such as this, and look at our city under the brilliant blue. Sooner or later, you will find it.

"Let me tell you what happened to me. I was in boarding school, which I never liked. The older I got, the more I disliked it. One free afternoon, I went alone for a walk on the moor. I sat down and dreamed for a while.

"When I looked up again, I realized that it was a glorious day. Until then, I had been so wrapped up in my own gloomy thoughts that I had paid no attention to it.

"From the moment that I saw and felt the beauty all around me, that little nagging inner voice stopped reminding me of my worries. I could no longer feel or think of anything but that this was beauty and this was truth.

"I sat there for about half an hour, and when I got up and walked back to that hateful school, I was no longer depressed. Everything impressed me as good and beautiful, the way it really was.

"Later I understood that, on that afternoon, I had for the first time found happiness within myself. I also realized that, no matter what the circumstances, happiness is always there."

"And did it change you?" he asked.

"Yes, it did. I was content. Not always, mind you; I still grumbled from time to time, but I never was downright miserable again. I had learned that most sadness comes from self-pity, but that happiness comes from joy."

When I had finished, he was still looking out of the window and seemed lost in thought. Suddenly he turned and looked at me.

"I haven't found happiness yet," he said, "but I have found something else—someone who understands me."

I knew what he meant. From then on, I was no longer alone.

ESSAYS

Give

March 26, 1944

I wonder if any of the people sitting in warm, comfortable homes have any idea what it must be like to be a beggar? Have any of those "good, dear people" ever asked themselves about the lives of poor people or children around them? All right, everyone gives a beggar a few coppers now and then. But it is usually pushed hurriedly into his hands, and the door is closed with a bang. And what is more, the generous donor usually shudders at having to touch such a dirty hand. *Is it true, or in't it?* And then people are surprised that beggars become so rude. Wouldn't anyone, who was treated more like a beast than a human being?

It is bad, very bad indeed, that in a country which claims to have good social laws and a high standard of culture people should treat each other in this way. Most of the well-to-do people regard a beggar as someone to be despised, dirty and uncared for, rude and uncivilized. But have any of them ever asked themselves how these poor wretches have become like this? Just compare your own children with these poor children. Whatever is the difference really? Your children are clean and tidy, the others dirty and uncared for. Is that all? Yes, that's really the only difference. But if a poor beggar's child were to receive good clothes and learn nice manners, then there wouldn't be any difference at all.

We are all born alike, they were helpless and innocent too. Everyone breathes the same air, a great many people believe in the same God! And yet, yet the difference can be so immeasurably great, because so many people have never realized where the difference really lies. Because if they had realized it, they would have discovered that there really wasn't any difference at all. Everyone is born the same, everyone has to die, and nothing remains of their worldly glory. Riches, power, and fame last only for a few years! Why do people cling so desperately to these transitory things? Why can't people who have more than they need for themselves give that surplus to their fellow citizens? Why should some people have such a hard time during their few years on this earth? But above all, let the gifts be given kindly and not just flung in their faces; everyone has the right to a friendly word! Why should one be nicer to a rich woman than to a poor one? Has anyone sorted out the difference in character between the two? The true greatness of a person does not lie in riches or power, but in character and goodness. Everyone is human, everyone has his faults and shortcomings, but everyone is born with a great deal that is good in him. And if one were to begin by encouraging the good, instead of smothering it, by giving poor people the feeling that they are human beings too, one would not even need money or possessions to do this.

Everything begins with the little things. For instance, don't only stand up in a tram for the rich mothers, no, remember the poor ones too. Say you are sorry if you step on a poor person's toes as you would for someone rich. People will always follow a good example; be the one to set the good example, then it won't be long before others follow. More and more people will become friendly and generous, until finally poor people will not be looked down upon any more.

Oh, if only we were that far already, that our country and then Europe and finally the whole world would realize that people were really kindly disposed toward one another, that they are all equal and everything else is just transitory!

How lovely to think that no one need wait a moment, we can start now, start slowly changing the world! How lovely that everyone, great and small, can make their contribution toward introducing justice straight away! Just as with so many things, most people seek justice in quite another quarter, they grumble because they receive so little of it themselves. Open your eyes, first make sure that you are always fair yourself! Give of yourself, give as much as you can! And you can always, always give something, even if it is only kindness! If everyone were to do this and not be as mean with a kindly word, then there would be much more justice and love in the world. Give and you shall receive, much more than you would have ever thought possible. Give, give again and again, don't lose courage, keep it up and go on giving! No one has ever become poor from giving! If you do this, then in a few generations no one will need to pity the beggar children any more, because they will not exist!

There is plenty of room for everyone in the world, enough money, riches, and beauty for all to share! God has made enough for everyone! Let us all begin then by sharing it fairly.

Why?

The little word "why" has been a very strong thing with me ever since I was a tiny little girl and couldn't even speak properly. It is a well-known fact that little children ask questions about everything because they are unfamiliar with everything. This was very much the case with me, but even when I grew older I couldn't wait to ask all kinds of questions, whether they could be answered or not. This is not so terrible in itself and I must say that my parents tried to answer every one of my questions very patiently, until . . . I began even badgering strangers, and *they* generally can't stand "children's endless questions." I must admit that this can be very tiresome, but I console myself with the idea that there is a saying that "you must ask in order to know," which couldn't be completely true, otherwise I'd be a professor by now.

When I grew older, I realized that it is not possible to ask every kind of question to everyone and that there are many "why's" that cannot be answered. I then followed from that that I tried to help myself by starting to think out these questions on my own. So I came to the important discovery that questions which one mustn't ask can be solved by oneself. Therefore, the little word "why" taught me not only to ask but to think.

Now as to the second part of the word "why." How would it be if everyone who did anything asked himself first, "Why?" I think they would then become more honest and much, much better people. For the best way to become honest and good is to keep examining oneself without stopping. I can imagine that the last thing people like to do is to confess to themselves their faults and their bad side (which everybody has). This is the case with children as well as grownups—in that respect I don't see any difference. Most people think parents should try to educate their children and see to it themselves that their characters develop as well as possible. This is certainly untrue. Children ought to educate themselves from their earliest youth and must try to show real character by themselves. Many will think this is crazy, but it isn't. Even a very small child is a little personality and has a conscience and should be brought up by being treated in this way, so that it will feel that its own conscience is punishing it in the harshest way possible. When children reach the age of fourteen or fifteen, every punishment is ridiculous. Such a child knows very well that no one, not even its own parents, can get anywhere with punishments and spankings. By arguing reasonably and by showing the child the mistakes it is making, one would get much better results than by strong punishments.

But here, I don't want to sound pedantic, but only to say that in the life of every child and every man, the little word "why" plays a big part, and rightly so. The saying, "You must ask in order to know," is true in so far as it leads to thinking about things, and by thinking nobody can ever get worse but will only get better.